# A NEWSWORTHY NATURALIST:
# THE LIFE OF WILLIAM YARRELL

*Portrait of William Yarrell as a young man by Maxim Gucci, printed by Paul Gucci after Eden Upton Eddis. By permission of the National Portrait Gallery, D36233.*

# A NEWSWORTHY NATURALIST: THE LIFE OF WILLIAM YARRELL

Christine E. Jackson

Published in association with the British Ornithologists' Club

First published in the United Kingdom in 2021 by John Beaufoy Publishing,
11 Blenheim Court, 316 Woodstock Road, Oxford OX2 7NS, England
www.johnbeaufoy.com

10 9 8 7 6 5 4 3 2 1



ISBN 978-1-913679-04-0

Designed by Gulmohur
Edited by Robert Prŷs-Jones
Project management by Rosemary Wilkinson

Printed and bound in Malaysia by Times Offset (M) Sdn. Bhd.

Title page captions: Yarrell's Pied Wagtail (top); Yarrell's Blenny (bottom)

Christine E. Jackson F.L.S. Author of:
*British Names of Birds,* 1968, H. F. & G. Witherby
*Bird Illustrations: Some Artists in Early Lithography,* 1975, H. F. & G. Witherby
*Collecting Bird Stamps,* 1977, H. F. & G. Witherby
*Wood Engravings of Birds,* 1978, H. F. & G. Witherby With a chapter on Yarrell
*Bird Etchings: The Illustrators and Their Books, 1655–1855,* 1985, Cornell University Press
*Prideaux John Selby: A Gentleman Naturalist,* 1992, Spredden Press
*Great Bird Paintings: The Old Masters,* 1993, Antique Collectors' Club
*Bird Paintings: The Eighteenth Century,* 1994, Antique Collectors' Club
*Sarah Stone: Natural Curiosities from the New Worlds,* 1998, Natural History Museum & Merrell Holberton
*Dictionary of Bird Artists of the World,* 1999, Antique Collectors' Club
*Sir William Jardine: A Life in Natural History,* 2001 (co-author with P. Davis), Leicester University Press/Continuum
*Peacock,* 2006, Reaktion Books Ltd
*Fish in Art,* 2010, Reaktion Books Ltd
*John James LaForest Audubon: an English Perspective,* 2012, privately published
*Menageries in Britain 1100–2000,* 2014, Ray Society

# CONTENTS

# OFFICES HELD BY WILLIAM YARRELL IN THE THREE MAIN NATURAL HISTORY SOCIETIES:

**Zoological Society**
Founder Member 1826
Secretary 1826, 1836–38
Treasurer 1849–56
Vice-President 1839–44, 1845–51

**Linnean Society**
Fellow 1825–56
Treasurer 1849–56
One of its Vice Presidents

**Entomological Society**
Founder Member 1833
Treasurer 1834–52

Notes:

Fish and Fishes: The noun 'fish' is both singular and plural. When plural it is used to indicate two or more of the same species. The plural noun 'fishes' is used for a group of mixed fish species.

# LIST OF ILLUSTRATIONS

The illustrations are wood engravings from *HBB* = *A History of British Birds* and *HBF* = *A History of British Fishes,* with some photographs. Following the reference to the two books is their location in the books and original size, height by width, in centimetres.

Yarrell's Wood engravings in *HBF* and *HBB* were greatly admired when first published, and subsequently enjoyed by owners of the following editions. A selection of the wood engravings in 12 plates is randomly placed within the chapters for the reader to rediscover and enjoy.

The engravings are reproduced from the first edition of *HBB* 1837–43 and the second edition of *HBF* 1841. Yarrell's spelling has been maintained.

Frontispiece: Portrait of William Yarrell as a young man by Maxim Gauci, printed by Paul Gauci after Eden Upton Eddis. National Portrait Gallery D36233.

Title page: Yarrell's Pied Wagtail and Yarrell's Blenny.

**Chapter 1 Family and Early Life**

**Chapter 2 The Story of Jones and Yarrell**



**Chapter 3 Laying down the foundations – 1820s**

p.58 The Dusky Perch of Couch and Cuvier shown in a detailed wood engraving in *HBF,* 1841,1: 14 (4 x 8 cm).

p.63 'The Common Crossbill' *HBB,* 1843, 2: 14 (11 x 9 cm), present throughout the year in Britain with temporary migrations of Continental birds, sometimes in great flocks as in the 1830s.

p.65 A method of catching Eels in the days when they were present in huge numbers. 'The Eelbuck' was placed on the Thames with the open end of each wicker basket 'opposed to the stream to entice the eel within'. Yarrell fished the Thames and would be familiar with these. *HBF,* 1841, 2:386 ((5 x 9 cm).

p.67 Plate 5 Sea Birds

a Laughing Gull *HBB* 3: 439 (7 x 8.8 cm)
b Laughing Gull colony disturbed by dog *HBB* 3: 443 (6.5 x 9 cm)
c Kittiwake *HBB* 3: 444 (8.5 x 8.5 cm)
d Common Terns *HBB* 3: 396 (7.5 x 8.7 cm)
e Black Guillemot *HBB* 3: 355 (8.5 x 8.5 cm)

p.75 Hooded Crow, *HBB* 1841, 2: 83 (7.5 x 8.5 cm).

p.76 The egg of the Royston Crow painted by Mary Anne Meyer from Yarrell's egg collection. The Hooded Crow was so abundant around the small town of Royston in Hertfordshire that it was given this name there. The local newspaper was named *The Royston Crow* when founded by John Warren in 1855. It is now a weekly paper. Yarrell's measurements were: Length 1" 10 lines; Breadth 1" 3 lines. (see p.167) i.e. one and ten-twelfths of an inch high by one and a quarter inches width. (l. 4.9 x b. 3.2 cm).

p.77 Portrait in oils of William Yarrell, 1839, by Margaret-Sarah Carpenter, A.R.A. (1793–1872). Paid for by 40 Fellows of the Linnean Society. By courtesy of the Linnean Society.

**Chapter 5 Consolidating – 1840s**

p.80 An 1842 1st class railway carriage which would have been used by Sir William Jardine and Lord Derby to travel up to London. *Illustrated London News,* 22 May 1847: 328.

p.80 A flatbed railway conveyance for gentlemen's carriages in which they could travel in comfort.

p.81 A fine wood engraving of the Opah or King Fish originally placed in the genus *Zeus* by Linnaeus, not often captured in European waters. *HBF,* 1841,

*Illustrations of the Eggs of British Birds,* 1831–38, courtesy of W. G. Hale.

p.111 The painting of the egg of a Little stint, inscribed in Yarrell's handwriting, 'Little Stint Brit. Birds. v.2. p.643', with a signature 'W Yarrell' on the reverse. This egg illustration was not included in the entry for the bird in the editions of *HBB.* Courtesy of D. Clugston.

p.113 Plate 8 Perching Birds

a Wheatear *HBB* 1: 253 (10 x 8.5 cm)
b Wryneck *HBB* 2: 151 (7.5 x 7 cm)
c Kingfisher *HBB* 2: 206 (7.5 x 8 cm)
d Snow Bunting *HBB* 1: 425 (7 x 7 cm)
e Stonechat *HBB* 1: 245 (5.8 x 7.5 cm)

p.116 Yarrell's Pied Wagtail, named for him by John Gould, *Motacilla alba yarrellii, HBB,* 1843, 1: 362 (5 x 9 cm).

p.117 *Crax yarrellii* Red-knobbed Curassow Jardine and Selby *Illustrations of Ornithology,* 1836, vol IV, Plate 6.

p.117 *Eulidia yarrellii,* John Gould's *Monograph of the Trochilidae,* Hummingbirds, plate 152.

p.118 Yarrell's Blenny – 'At the superior anterior margin of the eye on each side is a small fimbriated [i.e. fringed] appendage, which is connected with that on the opposite side of the head by a fold of skin forming a transverse union.' Yarrell's precise description. *HBF,* 1841, 1: 263 (2 x 7.5 cm).

p.119 Yarrell's curious choice of tail-piece for his own Blenny *HBF,* 1841, 1: 268 (5 x 3.5 cm). The fish is not a Blenny.

**Chapter 7 Lifestyle and interests**

p.126 Plate 9 Songbirds

a Meadow Pipit *HBB* 1: 389 (5.5 x 7 cm)
b Missel Thrush *HBB* 1: 179 (8.3 x 7.5 cm)
c Skylark *HBB* 1: 409 (7 x 9 cm)
d Willow Warbler *HBB* 1: 302 (7 x. 7.5 cm)
e Redwing *HBB* 1: 198 (6.5 x 7.4 cm)
f Wren *HBB* 2: 162 (5 x 6.3 cm)

p.135 Starling *HBB* 2: 44, one of the best depictions of the plumage of the Starling in any bird book. Signed THOMPSON DEL ET SC (delineat et sculpsit, drawn and engraved).

rare British Bird and but few instances are recorded of its capture.'

p.162 Vignette of rabbits and puffins disputing ownership of a burrow. *HBB,* 1843, 3: 365 (6.7 x 6 cm).

p.164 Original design for an engraving by one of the Thompsons of a Golden Eagle for *HBB,* 1843, 1: 7 (11 x 9 cm), by courtesy of Professor W. G. Hale.

p.165 The Snowy Owl suffered from unfortunate positioning of the glass eyes. *HBB,* 1843, 1: 134 (10 x 9 cm).

p.166 Vignette of nest and eggs of a Hawfinch, *HBB,* 1843,1: 489 (6.5 x 8.5 cm).

p.167 Guillemot's egg, *HBB,* 1843, 3: 529 (5 x 8.6 cm). This coloured plate is only present at the end of vol. 3 in some copies.

p.174 Lithograph made of portrait by Thomas Henry Maguire in 1849 when Yarrell was Vice-President of the Museum, for inclusion in the *Portraits of the Honourable Members of the Ipswich Museum.* 1852.

**Chapter 9 Societies**

p.178 A medallion, diameter 41.5 cm, with a portrait of William Yarrell by Neville Northey Burnard (1818–1878), a Cornish sculptor, presented to the Linnean Society by his publisher, John Van Voorst, in December 1859. Courtesy of the Linnean Society.

p.181 The Gardens of the Zoological Society, Regent's Park, 1829 from 'Zoological Keepsake'. (Henry Scherren *The Zoological Society of London: a sketch of its foundation and development,* 1905. plate 3 (16.5 x 24 cm).

p.185 Plate 12 Birds for St James's Park

- a Tufted Duck *HBB* 3: 251 (5.75 x 8.5 cm)
- b Pintail Duck *HBB* 3: 158 (6.5 x 8.5 cm)
- c Egyptian Goose *HBB* 3: 83 (8.5 x 9.5 cm)
- d Bernicle Goose *HBB* 3: 72 (7 x 9 cm)

p.190 Fancy pigeons at cottage door. *HBB,* 1843, 2: 264 (6.5 x 8.5 cm).

# ACKNOWLEDGEMENTS

I received prompt and generous responses to my requests from librarians and archivists when ascertaining where the contents of Yarrell's library, museum specimens and correspondence are now conserved. These include:

Linnean Society, the retired librarian Lynda Brooks and Dr Isabelle Charmantier now Head of Collections, were always most helpful. Bob McGowan, Senior Curator, Birds, Department of Natural Sciences, National Museum of Scotland, Edinburgh. Society of Antiquaries of London, Alice Dowhy, User Service Librarian. AnnaLee Pauls, Reference Assistant, Firestone Library Department of Rare Books and Special Collections, Princeton University, New Jersey, who arranged for me to receive the copies of the Yarrell letters held in the library. Ann Sylph and Sarah Broadhurst, Library, Zoological Society of London, helped with references and sourced texts for me.

Dr R. M. Peck, Senior Fellow of the Academy of Natural Sciences of Drexel University, Philadelphia, Pennsylvania, took an interest in Yarrell and encouraged the writing of his biography.

Jonathan Oates, Ealing, Local History, Ealing Central Library kindly gave me access to all that he has researched of Great Ealing School.

James Maclaine, Senior Curator, Fish Section, Department of Life Sciences, The Natural History Museum, London. Yarrell's Blennies whose 1844 specimen had no date but 1841 specimen was from Polperro and collected by Couch. The photograph was taken by Harry Taylor.

Renae Satterley, Librarian, Middle Temple, then Barnaby Bryan, Assistant Archivist, Middle Temple, London sent the most useful details of Robert Jones' activities at Middle Temple Lane when the foundations of the firm of Jones & Yarrell were laid in 1734.

Susan Isaac, Information Services Manager, Royal College of Surgeons, 35-43 Lincoln's Inn Fields, London WC2A 3PE kindly sent me the pages of the sale of Yarrell's effects, December 1856. This is a rare J. C. Stevens catalogue of one of his sales that I was particularly pleased to see.

Valerie McAtear, Librarian, The Royal Entomological Society, St Albans, searched the archive records and informed me that the society does not have any material relating to William Yarrell despite his having been their Treasurer from 1834 to 1852.

Leslie K. Overstreet, Curator of Natural History Rare Books, Smithsonian Libraries, kindly provided the evidence I needed for the genus name *Yarrella* from an American source.

I received the most helpful and kindly assistance from Matthew Williams, the Curator and his assistant, Robert Randall when I visited the Bath Royal Literary and Scientific Institution in Queen Square, Bath, to read the letters from William Yarrell to the Rev. Leonard Jenyns. Roger Vaughan (died 2015) had transcribed all of Jenyns' letters enabling me to read them more easily. The catalogue of the sale of Yarrell's library is also in BRLSI and Matt Williams kindly photocopied it. He and Rob also sent me the book to which they had largely contributed, edited by Ian Wallace, *Leonard Jenyns, Darwin's lifelong Friend,* published by the Bath Royal Literary and Scientific Institution in 2005, that supplied many small details which I was delighted to be able to add to my manuscript.

Among my personal correspondents, I am particularly indebted to:

Prof. William Hale who was a constant source of information about the eggs Yarrell illustrated. He generously allowed use of his photographs of related Yarrell items and of the preparatory images for some of the engravings, including watercolours by Mary Anne Meyer from Yarrell's eggs and a copy of the Prospectus for *HBB.* His encouragement and support throughout the process of publishing is gratefully acknowledged. He kindly read the original manuscript, as did Dr Peter Holt of Muri, Switzerland and both provided encouragement and support for the project throughout the long process of getting the book to the printers.

Ann Datta several times proved to be a good friend who never fails to respond when asked for any help for which I am deeply indebted and grateful.

Errol Fuller brought up to date the information on Yarrell's eggs that he detailed in his standard work on the *Great Auk,* 1999.

My nephew, David R. Smith, negotiated sites on the internet trawling for Yarrell information and found several leads for me to follow that provided some of the more obscure references. He found the birth of Francis Yarrell, William's father that had eluded all previous searchers.

I thank Richard Fattorini, Senior Director, Senior Specialist, Printed Books, Manuscripts and Topographical Photographs, Sotheby's, for his generous sharing of knowledge about the sales of Yarrell's own copies of his book, *A History of British Birds* that had once been in his father, Hugh Fattorini's extensive ornithological library in Skipton Castle.

David Clugston generously shared his information about five of Yarrell's egg paintings in his possession and I was delighted to receive copies of them, two of which have been reproduced here.

Without the generous help and expertise of my Apple computer specialist and consultant this manuscript with its illustrations would never have been finished. I owe a great deal to Gill Holman who is very skilful. Also a grateful acknowledgement is due to Nick Rutter of NICOM, Haverhill, whose computer expertise is formidable.

Robert Prŷs-Jones of BOC read the MS and helped to avoid slips and errors for which I thank him. He recently drew my attention to an article published in 2009 by the Rev. Tom Gladwin in the *Transactions of the Herts, Nat. Hist. Soc.*; 'William Yarrell (1784–1856) ichthyologist, ornithologist and friend of Charles Darwin and others' with the opinion: 'Yarrell...is probably the most important British naturalist not to have been the subject of a detailed biography.' Robert also investigated the records of Yarrell's specimens recorded in the Natural History Museum archives, some of which are still present at Tring Museum. I appreciate his attention to detail and these additional facts.

Christopher Storey, the Chairman of BOC has been a sympathetic and judicious aid during the final stages of getting the book completed for which I am very grateful.

Rosemary Wilkinson of John Beaufoy Publishing took the manuscript through the publishing process with exemplary speed, accuracy and sensitivity, for which I am pleased to have an opportunity to thank her.

Lastly, to my husband, Andrew, who has patiently followed the progress of this biography and helped in numerous ways, I have been indebted over many years. Andrew supplied the title for this biography, which pleased me greatly.

# INTRODUCTION

Who was William Yarrell? This question would not have been asked in the 19th century. A contributor to the magazine, *The Cottage Garden*, stated in January 1856 that the name Yarrell 'is a household word to zoologists'. The reason was two-fold. Firstly, he was known as a London bookseller and newsagent whose activities were recorded in newspapers across the British Isles. Secondly, he was recognized as a great naturalist having written the two standard works of the century on fishes and birds, also some 80+ articles detailing new discoveries about birds and fishes, and the presence of species in the British Isles.

He was born and lived within three adjoining streets in the parish of St James's, Westminster, London, between Piccadilly and St James's Park. He went to Great Ealing School, then (the 1790s) regarded as a school equal to Eton under Dr Nicholas. His life centred around people, first in his family and friends, later, when all immediate members of his family had died, with his many friends both in and beyond London. His bookshop and newsagency was the core of a wider acquaintance and the Royal Warrant gave him access when supplying newspapers to the staff of the court at Buckingham Palace with members of the Houses of Parliament.

Despite this, he was not exclusively a townee. As a child, and in his younger years, he frequently went to the countryside in Hertfordshire where his grandparents on his mother's side had a farm, Claypits Farm, at Bayford near the county town of Hertford. There he explored the fields, woods and streams, learning to fish, shoot, and collect birds' eggs and insects. As a young man he took his fishing and shooting skills to London, where there were still fields and woods and the Thames within easy distance. His shooting skills were amazing and displayed in shooting competitions. He became expert in the knowledge of contemporary guns and early flintlocks, forming a friendship with the gunshop owner John Manton of Bond Street.

In 1803 when he was aged 19, he entered into partnership with his cousin Edward Jones in a bookselling and newsagency business that had been founded in 1760 by Robert Jones. Successive members of the Jones family had been joined by William Yarrell's grandfather and father as partners in a firm known as Jones and Yarrell. The business was in St James's parish, Westminster, first in Duke Street and then on the corner of Bury Street adjoining 6 Little Ryder Street that became home to Yarrell. The firm expanded and is still in existence today.

There were three main activities that took up nearly all of William Yarrell's time: his business as a partner and owner of the newspaper agency and bookseller; his contributions to natural history as the author of the standard works of the 19th century on both fishes and birds; his membership from the 1820s of The Linnean, Zoological and Entomological societies, and other London societies. He was sometime Secretary, Treasurer and Vice-President of the first two of those societies for many years. As an office holder he knew all the major London naturalists of the day.

He first came to prominence when he distinguished between the Whooper Swan and a similar species that he named Bewick's Swan. This was in 1830 and was a landmark in his career. To have discovered a species new to Great Britain when he was only 36 years of age was a notable achievement. He published over 80 articles in scientific periodicals and went on to write *A History of British Fishes* and *A History of British Birds*, published in the 1830s and 1840s. Both books became the authority on the subjects and reference works for the remainder of the century.

The respect in which he was held earned him assistance from experts in both fields. His books had been ground-breaking by including an account of the first time species were added to the British fauna in literature. His business was known to newspaper proprietors across the country, and each new part and volume of his books was noted in their pages prompting further letters reporting on species. This is how his name became 'a household word'. His correspondence was vast and his contacts all over the British Isles ensured a steady supply of notes and specimens concerning the presence of species in locations from the Orkneys east down to Kent, west down to the tip of Cornwall and all along the south coast.

Yarrell enjoyed good health, which allowed him to travel across the country in pursuit of information about fish and bird species and to visit his numerous natural historian friends. Edward Lear, John Gould and Sir William Jardine, with his publisher Van Voorst, entomologists and botanists, were not the only friends he had. John Constable sent him a drawing for his fish book. Sir Robert Peel sought him out at a soirée to tell him how much he appreciated his books and sent him a large fish from the river Tame. The Bishop of Norwich, the 13th Earl of Derby, Marshall Hall, the physiologist, were among eminent men of the day whom he counted as his friends. Lastly, he became both friend and mentor to Charles Darwin and was influential in directing his early studies following his return from the *Beagle* voyage. He was pivotal in Darwin's decision to publish the zoology of the *Beagle*.

He was a genial host enjoying parties and hosting dinners for his many friends. His good dinners and fine wines were matched with tableware of silver and china decorated with flowers and birds. His mahogany furniture and picture frames of maple, along with his other possessions itemized in the sale of his effects in 1856 show him to be a man who appreciated quality and had the means to indulge it.

The four main sources from which this biography is written include the story of Jones and Yarrell, newsagents and booksellers. The history of the firm has been written by the author. Yarrell's copious correspondence also has been transcribed or abstracted by the author. From his naturalist correspondents he derived a great deal of information, then in turn gave support to them. Records of his membership of several societies, once again providing him with contacts and useful sources of information, indicated his unstinting loyalty and service. The first of two sales catalogues, of his excellent library, provides insights into his intellectual pursuits and wide interests, while the second sale of his personal effects offers clues as to more immediate personal activities. Lastly, there were over 7,000 references to Yarrell personally and his two books in newspapers that were collected under the name 'Yarrell' by the National Newspaper Archives.

A picture emerges of a businessman, author, sportsman, friend, genial host and sociable member of the leading natural history societies of the day. To sustain these activities Yarrell had used his library for self-education with a lively, highly intelligent involvement across many fields. He had an insatiable curiosity and was not content with merely listing and classifying species but used his anatomical skills to discover the reasons behind species' differences and functions leading to their distinctive ways of life.

Yarrell's obituaries, and there were over 40 in newspapers alone, all suggested a person who was both 'good and kind'. We know he habitually dropped everything he was doing to concentrate on any query that a friend brought to him. That concentration was a character trait that enabled him to compartmentalise his life to deal effectively with his diverse interests. He is remembered today as a great naturalist, not so much as a very successful newsagent and bookseller, but the success of the two went hand in hand during his lifetime.

Chapter 1

# FAMILY AND EARLY LIFE

William Yarrell (1784–1856) was small in stature, but robust and solid in physique like a sturdy yeoman. He was a genial and warm-hearted man who loved children, and easily both made and kept friends. He was kindly and charitable, being liberal almost to a degree, and despite having a warm temper could keep it in control. He enjoyed excellent health until he was 70, when he had a slight stroke, but recovered sufficiently to continue actively in his natural history pursuits. It is for his remarkable contribution to natural history, particularly his knowledge of British fishes and birds, that he was honoured by his colleagues during his lifetime and is respected today.

William was the son of Francis Yerrall/Yarrell (1749–1794) and the grandson of Francis Yerrall (1727–1786). One biographer stated that his small farmer family on his mother's side, the Blanes of Bayford, Hertfordshire, were remarkable for 'nothing but a tartness of temper, a trait perhaps inherited by the grandson'. His father, a gentleman, was said to be proud. William Yarrell's friend and publisher, John Van Voorst, was the first to write an account of his life. He stated that William 'never knew his father's native place exactly, though he used to think that he came from Bedfordshire'.[1] He was correct, and this provided the clue in order to build a family history by using

## YERRALL/YARRELL FAMILY TREE

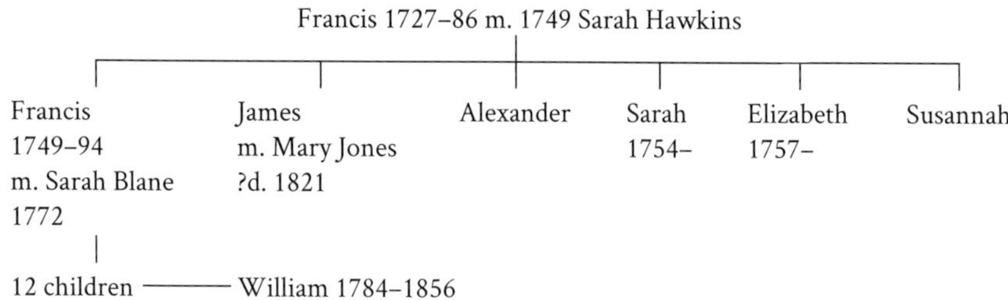


Francis Yerrall, grandfather of William
Bap. 10 March 1727, son of James and Sarah nee Stoughton, at Eversholt, Bedfordshire.
Married 11 December 1749 Sarah Hawkins, St Mary's Hitchin, Hertfordshire.
She was born 1719?, died 12 December 1800.
Buried 8 January 1786 St James's, Westminster, London.

Francis Yerrall/Yarrell, father of William
Born 10 Feb., Bap 29 March 1749, Francis Yeral Hawkins, son of Sarah Hawkins, St Mary's Hitchin.
Francis Yerrall married Sarah Blane of Bayford, Herts at Bermondsey, Surrey 26 June 1772.
He changed the name to Yarrell c. 1775.
Buried 2 April 1794, St Mary's Churchyard Bayford.

the parish registers in the Record Offices of Bedfordshire and neighbouring Hertfordshire. The Bedfordshire members of the family spelled their name Yerrall.

Sometime around 1760, Francis Snr was invited by his cousin William Jones to join with him in establishing a bookselling and newspaper business in Duke Street, London, situated between Piccadilly and St James's Park in Westminster. This firm is still in existence as Jones and Yarrell, and its history is outlined in Chapter 2. Francis took his family to London, where they would live a very different life from that in rural Bedfordshire. Francis stated in his will, written in March 1778, that he was then living in St James's parish, and he appeared in a Poll Book for this parish in 1780, qualifying to vote by being in possession of property/land worth twenty or more shillings.

Despite living in London, Francis Snr retained property back in Bedfordshire. In his will, proved on 20 January 1786, he left his cottage and barns with three acres of land, then occupied by a tenant, in Mills End in the parish of Eversholt, near Woburn, to his wife Sarah. After her decease it was to be sold and the proceeds distributed between his children. He also left £100 in the New Joint Stock of the South Sea Annuities that he had purchased on 17 September 1768. He was a man of modest but adequate means, who had been given an opportunity to make a richer life in London, where he had prospered.

Francis Snr's eldest son, also named Francis, would have gone with the family to London in the 1760s. He married Sarah Blane (1749–1812), daughter of the farmer George Blane of Claypits Farm in Bayford, Hertfordshire,[2] at St Mary Magdalene Parish Church, Bermondsey, Surrey, on 26 June 1772.[3] Banns were necessary because the couple were not originally of the parish, although they were both recorded as 'of this parish' in 1772. At this time Francis Jnr would probably have been working alongside his father in the business and capable of taking charge in the Duke Street shop when his father died in 1786. Part of Bermondsey bordered the Thames, with several 'stairs' or landing places where he could have boarded boats ferrying passengers either east to the City or west to St James's. At that time, travelling round London was most easily achieved by employing the watermen on the river Thames.

Francis Jnr and Sarah took their first two children, Sarah in 1773 and Francis in 1775, back to Bayford for their baptisms. After that most of their

The children of Francis Yerrall/Yarrell 1749–1794
and Sarah Blane 1748–1812, married 1772.
They were all buried at Bayford.

| | |
|---|---|
| 1773 Sarah bap Bayford 1 August | buried 4 January 1790 aged 17, from London |
| 1775 Francis bap Bayford | died 15 April 1782 |
| 1780 Harriot Frances bap 12 November | buried 12 Feb 1796 aged 16 |
| 1783 Sophia bap 7 March | buried Jany 14 1790 aged 7 from London |
| **1784 William born 3 June** | **buried 8 September 1856 aged 72** |
| 1785 Sophia bap 17 November | buried 1790 Jany 14 aged 4 |
| 1787 George bap 23 January | buried 22 April 1787 |
| 1788 Caroline born 22 September | died 30 May 1839 |
| 1789 Jane born 30 Oct, bap 22 Nov | died ante 1794 |
| 1790 James | buried 14 Feby 1790 "0 months" |
| 1791 Francis | buried 2 April 1794 aged 3 |
| 1793 James bap 7 August | buried 15 Sep 1795 |

children, including William, were baptized in St James's Parish Church, in Piccadilly, Westminster, where the business was situated. Some time around 1775, Francis transposed the letters 'e' and 'a' in his surname so that his children baptized post-1776 were Yarrells. Several of William Yarrell's obituaries, and some subsequent authors, state that he was the ninth child of Francis and Sarah, but the evidence taken directly from the parish registers points to his being the fifth child.

William was born 3 June 1784 in Duke Street, London, in the parish of St James's, Westminster and baptized at St James's Church, Piccadilly on 27 June 1784. His home continued to be in that parish for the whole of his life, first at Duke Street, then Great Ryder Street, lastly at number 6 Little Ryder Street.

Although William's parents lived in London, they often returned to Hertfordshire to visit his maternal grandparents, George and Hannah

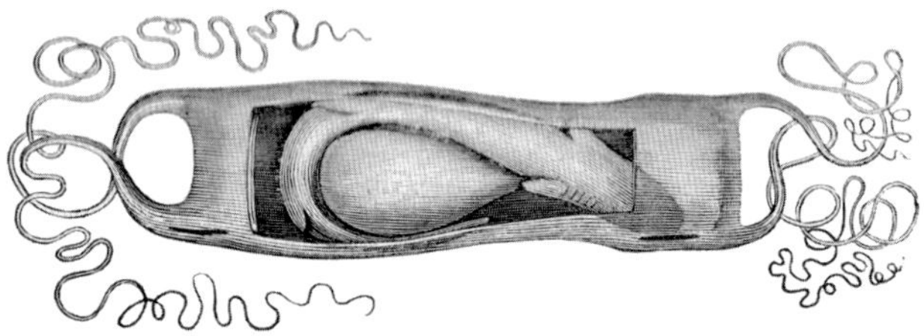

*Mermaid's purse, the horny egg case of the Small Spotted Dogfish or Shark, with one side removed to show the young fish within* (A History of British Fishes, 1841, 2: 488). *The oblong case has tendrils to catch in seaweed and prevent it being washed away to deep water.*

Blane, at their Claypits farm, so William would have grown up enjoying the countryside, learning to shoot, collect eggs and to fish. There appears to have been no shortage of money. His mother enjoyed frequent excursions to the coast, travelling in the *Margate Hoy* stage-coach, where her children could have all the fun of paddling, investigating the pools and building sand castles, among the other delights of the seaside. William also picked up shells and seaweeds that he and his sister afterwards laid out on paper. Perhaps they also found a mermaid's purse, deposited near the shore.

The family's close links to Bayford meant that each member of the Yerrall/Yarrell family was returned there after death to be buried in the churchyard. William's grave bears the inscription, 'He was the survivor of 12 brothers and sisters, who, with their father and mother are all placed close to this spot.'

William was sent to Great Ealing School in St Mary's Road, Great Ealing, when it was at its peak of excellence under the Reverend Dr David Nicholas (not Nicholson as given in most obituaries of Yarrell), and was reportedly a quiet and studious boy. In its heyday in the early 19th century, the school was as famous as Eton or Harrow, and was even considered by some to be the best private school in England. Dr David Nicholas, headmaster from 1791 until 1829, had been educated at Wadham College, Oxford, where he had graduated as a classical scholar, and he appointed graduates to be masters in his school. The boys, both boarders and day boys, mostly aged 10–18, were taught Latin

*Great Ealing School with the tower of St Mary's church behind.*

and to read texts from the Roman and Greek classics, as well as mathematics. In the 1790s, William Yarrell, his cousin Edward Jones, and two other life-long friends of both, Edward Bird and Edward Goldsmith, would have been among the 100+ pupils. Edward Jones, who would later marry Edward Bird's sister, Grace, was to become William's future business partner in the firm of Jones & Yarrell booksellers and newsagents that their fathers had established in Duke Street.[4]

William's parents would probably have taken him to see the lions in the

Tower menagerie and Exeter 'Change among other London entertainments. St James's Park would have been a happy playground very close to home. Just watching the horses and carriages of the nobility in neighbouring streets would have been an entertainment in itself. William may also have been taken to the theatre – his love of theatre as an adult suggests that his first experience of it occurred while he was young. However, when he was ten, a family tragedy cast a shadow over his life.

At home in Great Ryder Street early in 1794 William's father, realizing he was nearing his end, made his will on 8 March before dying on 25 March, having made sure of providing for his son William's good education. He was described in the will as 'Francis Yarrell, gent. of Great Ryder Street', and left '£2000 vested in government annuities funds', bringing in an annuity of £100 per annum, to be used in bringing up his four surviving dependant children until they were aged 21. The number of children may have been a drain on the family finances, but the legacies were substantial. There could have been more if the little rhyme engraved on Francis's tombstone in Bayford Churchyard can be so interpreted:

Riches had wings and fled away
We are but vanity and a lump of clay
Francis Yarrell d. 25 March 1794.

Sarah was bequeathed their home in Great Ryder Street to take care of the four surviving young children, but two soon died, James in 1795 and Harriot in 1796. Caroline and William were the only two surviving when their mother died in 1812. It is incredible that each child's death had entailed a trip from Great Ryder Street in St James's parish, London, out to Bayford in Hertfordshire for burial. There must have been something seriously wrong with the household for all those deaths -- 10 children who did not reach their majority (then when aged 21). How did William escape? Was he away at Great Ealing School as a boarder during the long period of sickness in the family? Exceptionally, he was hardly ever ill throughout his long life.

William may have planned a career in banking. On 17 November 1802, when he was 18 years old, he entered the banking house of Herries, Farquhar & Co as a clerk, but a little before 30 July 1803 he was presented with a proposition that needed careful consideration. Edward Jones, his friend,

a

b

c

d

e

a. A couple and their dog
b. Boy birds' nesting
c. Man with gun
d. Two men and a boy fishing
e. Boy looking out to sea

PLATE 1 FAMILY AND EARLY LIFE

cousin and old schoolmate, had taken possession of the family newsagency and bookselling business in St James's, Westminster. At that time Edward was 19 years old, and there had not been a Yarrell in the firm since the death of William's father in 1794. Edward may have worked in the business for a short while before 1802, but he was young to take on the full responsibility. He needed a partner, and one with some banking training would be invaluable. Knowing that William was a steady, sensible young man, he invited him to join the business. William was persuaded, and he left Herries, Farquhar & Co. to join Yarrell and Jones, newsvendors, to which he was to devote the next 52 years of his working life. The two young well-educated men would make a success of the business and it provided a good living for them both.

William was not as wealthy as Edward and would probably always be the junior partner. Edward and William were both of the 'gentleman' class by virtue of each of their fathers having been so; a 'gentleman' being defined as a man of good birth and character, well-to-do, of no occupation and therefore generally including every man above the rank of yeoman. By moving into the business they would be associated with trade, and that was not a wise move in early 19th century British society. However, there appears to have been a subtle difference between a tradesman and the owner of a business. Edward Jones, who had an estate in Hampshire, always kept a low profile where the business was concerned, withdrawing to live elsewhere in London and purchasing a second estate in Essex when he could, leaving William Yarrell to live in the house next door to the business. Over the next 50 years, Yarrell's standing in society was governed less by his ownership of a flourishing business than by his outstanding achievements in natural history.

Those who came to know William personally over the following years valued him both as a friend and a great naturalist, accepted in the major natural history societies as a colleague and an equal among leading naturalists of the day. His knowledge and expertise were given due regard by his social superiors interested in natural history, but there is nevertheless one instance when the rigid code of social delineation acted against him. Before he was very widely known, his name was put forward for membership of the most prestigious of all scientific societies, the Royal Society. His certificate was signed but then suspended because a member expressed some objection to his being elected and, learning of this, William requested that his certificate be withdrawn. Many years later, his membership was again suggested, 'with the full concurrence of the Council but this time he declined the honour solely on the ground of advancing age'.[5]

William may well have debated whether to marry about this time. However, because he would have been the sole earner/supporter of a family unless he married into money, he would have needed to try to assess his prospects in the firm and his likely earnings before he could take on the responsibility of a wife and children. He was fond of children, and it is recorded that both he and his future friend, the author John Gould, would give specimens to

*Boy with eggs in his hat (*History of British Birds, 1843, 1: 93*). Did Yarrell's placing the Great Auk's egg in his hat remind him of his early egg collecting as a boy?*

boys interested in natural history to help the formation of their own private museums. William nevertheless did not marry, but he certainly thoroughly enjoyed all the advantages of his bachelor existence for the rest of his life.

St James's parish, where William spent his life, was elite and interesting. His home was always just a few minutes' walk from St James's Park. There were some splendid houses in the area, where at least three dukes visited. Yarrell's own house itself must have been pleasant and clean otherwise the fastidious Sir William Jardine, who was obsessive about anywhere he resided being 'clean', would never have stayed there. The close proximity of St James's Theatre in King Street, built 1835, producing burlettas and operas ('The Beggar's Opera' was popular) would have delighted Yarrell, although he had previously frequented the Adelphi Theatre in Piccadilly.

William's love of angling was indulged in the streams around London and he joined other friends to fish. In London he was tutored by an old sportsman called Adams, who taught him to fish in the Thames by Putney Bridge and other local streams. Adams also accompanied him out shooting, which led to William's acquaintance and then friendship with the Bond Street gunsmiths, Joseph and George Manton. William bought a double-barrelled gun from the Mantons and consulted them about any new form of breech or lock in a fowling piece. His 'double gun by John Manton' was a prized possession throughout his life and after his death was especially noted on the title page of Steven's sale catalogue of his effects.[6]

Through Manton, William also befriended Shoobridge, a Bond Street hatter. They joined in shooting competitions, Shoobridge engaging in betting with heavy stakes, whereas Yarrell never wagered beyond shooting for a gun, a pointer or a sporting picture. They became rivals, but William was eventually deemed the slightly better shot, and he was widely acknowledged and remembered as an excellent marksman. His shooting success in matches held near London became legendary. 'He would bring down a dozen brace of sparrows from the trap, with his double-barrelled Manton, running.'[7] Other sources recorded 'two brace', which sounds more likely. Through Shoobridge, William became a member of the eccentric Old Hats Club.

William visited Paris 'not many years after the peace of 1815', where he bought his Great Auk's egg (see p.111). According to Alfred Newton, William told him that 'In a little curiosity shop of mean appearance, he saw a number of eggs hanging on a string. He recognized one of them ... as *Alca impennis*, and was told that they were one franc apiece, except the large one, which from its size was worth two francs. He paid the money and walked away with the egg in his hat.'[8]

Wishing to broaden his education, in 1817 William used his spare time to study chemistry, and then systematic zoology and anatomy, as a member of the Royal Institution. Natural history studies soon took over and chemistry was largely abandoned, but at his death there were three chemistry books in his library dating from this period (1814–21) and he experienced a renewed interest in the subject in 1842 in relation to agriculture. His increasing interest in the zoological science of natural history is also reflected in his broader choice of books, as seen in the sale of his library on his death (see Chapter 7).

William had acquired many skills and learned a good deal about natural history during his early years, attributes that were to shape his future as a naturalist. While a boy, he had gathered a great deal of practical knowledge of species in the field, becoming familiar with their habitats and habits. In his youth, he had learned more from bird collectors and sportsmen in Hertfordshire and held many specimens in his hands. During this time, he had been forming valuable collections of fishes, birds and birds' eggs, as well as studying and making notes on their habits. In his early twenties, he had spent more time earning his living and helping his cousin to develop a prosperous business than on natural history. However, from the lectures at the Royal Institution he came to appreciate the importance of anatomical study and making careful records, with drawings, of his discoveries. He was also spending part of his salary on books to complement his natural history studies. By 1820 William, now 36 years old, was growing sufficiently knowledgeable and confident to begin to write up any new facts he had learned for potential publication. He was ready to embark on a second career as a naturalist.

*One of the many vignettes in* A History of British Birds (1843, 3: 19). *A Dunlin chick soon after hatching. This was a print that Yarrell was aware had accidentally got among the text of the Little Crake – and there it remains, one of the most delightful of all the vignettes.*

Chapter 2

# THE STORY OF JONES AND YARRELL

The story of the firm of Jones and Yarrell, which still exists today, began in 1734 with Robert Jones, an employee in the law courts. He was not a lawyer, but probably a clerk to one in the Chambers of Middle Temple in the East End of London. He obtained a lease on small premises in Middle Temple Lane and opened a shop. The Rental Books for Middle Temple from 1749 to 1770 show that three more chambers, with three flights of access stairs to them, were rented by Robert over this period to accommodate an expanding business. The rental in total for these amounted to £22 per annum.[1]

Robert was referred to as a 'stationer', which from about 1625 had been used for a trader, chiefly a bookseller, who had a 'station' or 'shop' as distinguished from an itinerant vendor. By 1706 the term included a tradesman who sold writing materials. The scope of Jones' business, originally a bookseller, diversified into supplying newspapers: the *London Gazette* had been a favourite with the public since its foundation in 1665, and there was also *The Daily Universal Register* that became *The Times* in 1785. There is a curious practice with newspapers at that date of which most people today are unaware. We are familiar with an old book with its edges left uncut, but early issues of newspapers also had their edges left untrimmed. A newspaper reader needed to own a short, sharp-pointed, paper knife to deal with every newspaper. The newsvendor may have taken advantage of this to sell the knives to his customers.

Robert Jones did not live in the City but in the parish of St James's, Westminster, in Jermyn Street that runs parallel to Piccadilly. In 1760, following up the success of his venture in Middle Temple Lane, he decided to open a shop in fashionable St James's and asked a relative, William Jones, to manage it. Robert died in 1766 and his son Richard succeeded him in the Middle Temple Lane shop, but the St James's business remained a separate entity from that time on for the next hundred years or so.

William Jones was joined soon after by his cousin Francis Yerrall Snr, the grandfather of William Yarrell, and the two ran a branch at 14 Duke Street, St James's, that sold newspapers as well as books. The shop was in a select district, surrounded by houses of the nobility, clubs, and exclusive shops such as Fortnum and Mason, established long previously in 1707. Yerrall and Jones prospered and by 1790 supplied West End Clubs such as White's (founded in 1693) and Boodles (founded in 1782), both in St James's Street, and later they added the Athenaeum when it was founded in 1824. Francis Yerrall Jnr succeeded his father when he died in 1786.

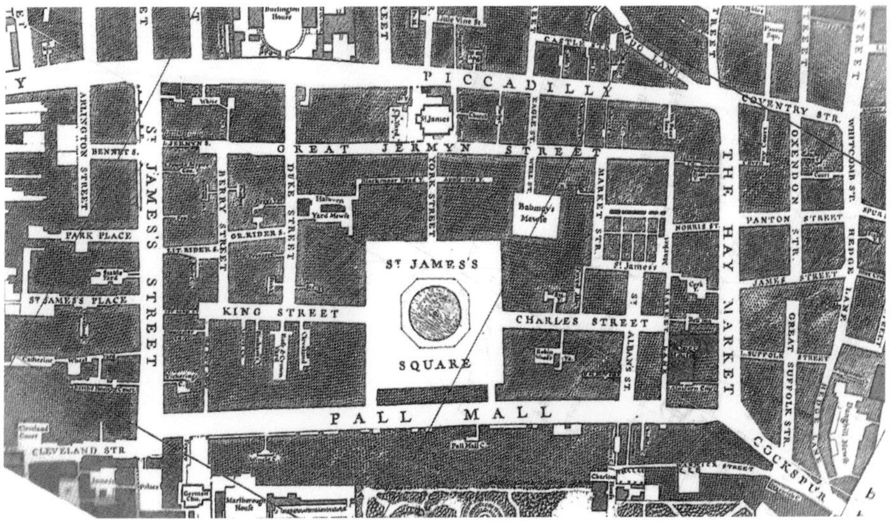


*Map of area south of Piccadilly in St James's Parish, Westminster, showing Duke Street, Little and Great Ryder Street, where successive homes of William Yarrell were situated. Copy of John Roque's map from his Survey of London mid 18th century engraved by George Vertue c.1739 survey, published circa 1746/7.*

William Jones's son Edward Snr (1749–1808) married Martha Blane of Bayford (see below), whose sister Sarah married Francis Yarrell Jnr in 1772 (Chapter 1). This meant that Edward Jones Jnr, who was in business with William Yarrell from 1803, was his cousin. The fact that Edward Jones Snr and Francis Yarrell Jnr married two sisters led to the remarkable situation that their families were all buried in the churchyard at Bayford, the small Hertfordshire village where the Blane's Claypits Farm was situated. The girls must have been so attached to their Hertfordshire village that they wanted to be buried there, the result being that the Jones railed chest tomb and the dozen or so railed Yarrell graves were just feet apart in a remote village churchyard. This established the burial place of all the Yarrells and Joneses from the 18th century until both lines of these families became extinct, Jones in 1850 and Yarrell in 1856.

---

JONES FAMILY TREE

| | In the business |
|---|---|
| **Robert died 1766** | **1734–60** |
| **William born c.1720**, married Susanna Shelley<br>2 Nov 1743 St Mary Magdalene, Old Fish Street<br>d. 27 June 1802 St James's (?) | **1760–1802(?)** |
| **Edward b. 9 April 1749** St Botolph without Aldgate. Married Martha Blane (31 March 1751-14 Sep 1820)<br>d. 28 October 1808, aged 59 | **In the business?** |
| Edward born 3 Aug 1783 Chelsea Hospital, son of Edward & Martha, married Sophia Pallett, (b. 26 Feb 1786 St Katherine Cree Church, Leadenhall, d. 9 July 1834, aged 49) daughter of Thos & Mary, d. 30 Dec 1820 at St Pancras Old Church. m. (2) Grace Bird 1837<br>d. 18 Nov 1850 aged 68 | **1803–50** |

---

There is no documentary evidence that Edward Jones Snr was ever active in the firm, except perhaps financially. If we can infer anything from what we know of him, it is that he was a gentleman of means, who bought an expensive house in a newly developed fashionable area at 17 Brompton Crescent, Kensington. His son, Edward Jnr, who had been educated at Great Ealing School with William Yarrell, one year his junior, took over the business in 1802/3 on the St James's site. Edward Snr left legacies of £365 in his will and houses and an estate to his wife, Martha, and then after her death it was left to their son Edward Jnr.

The firm was not entered in the London directories until 1801, when it was named as 'Yarrell & Jones newsmen 14 Duke Street'. *The London Book Trades* directory had briefly entered the business in 1784–5 as 'Yarrell, Francis, stationer and newspaper agent, Duke Street', but there was no further entry until from 1801–1806 it named Yarrell and Jones at 14 Duke Street. Why had William Jones and then Edward Jones Jnr been willing to allow the name Yarrell to take precedence when it was they who had both invited a Yarrell to join the firm? Was it because the entries in the directories were under the heading 'Traders' and this was anathema to the wealthy gentlemen Joneses? The Yarrells were probably on site and managing the shop, while the Joneses were living elsewhere.

Edward Jones Jnr invited William Yarrell to join the firm in 1803, when Edward was aged 20 and may already have had a year's experience working in the Yarrell and Jones business. William had been in banking for nine months and could assess his future prospects as a banker. He had no patronage and as his career advanced he would almost certainly lose out to men of higher social status, but it was a profession of some standing. For both Edward and William, however, there was the compelling consideration that they should keep alive the firm that had sustained their fathers and grandfathers. Their fathers left either substantial estates or sums of money when they died. If William and Edward could expand the firm and make it prosper, their own fortunes would be assured. For William there was the additional family loyalty towards his cousin Edward, who needed him. For Edward the same family commitments applied and William was a friend as well as a cousin. The decision was made, William resigned from the bank in July 1803 and in August 1803 joined the firm as a partner in what was then Yarrell and Jones newsagents.

The two young men must have worked hard to build up the clientele and,

YERRALLS/YARRELLS IN THE BUSINESS

| | |
|---|---|
| Francis (1727–1786) | In the business 1760–1786 |
| Francis (1749–1794) | In the business pre-1786–1794 |
| From March 1794 to August 1803 | There was no Yarrell in the business |
| William (1784–1856) | In the business 1803–1853 |

as well as the bookselling business, expand into being newsagents and then into an advertising agency. In 1808, only five years after they formed the partnership, they moved into property on the corner of Little Ryder Street and Bury Street. This was the year in which Edward's father died, though his son was not left an immediate legacy. It was also the year in which the firm was re-named 'Jones and Yarrell', and Edward and William advertised it in the London directories under that name in the section 'Traders'.[2] The young Edward Jones was the proud owner of the firm's legacy and established his seniority by this change of name. At first Edward Jones lived in Little Ryder

*The corner of Bury Street where the business of Jones and Yarrell was situated and the house on the left, number 6, in Little Ryder Street where Yarrell lived. Drawn from a photograph of 1878 in the Crown Estate Office, this would have been as Jones and Yarrell knew it.*

*Trade card of Jones & Yarrell with the Royal Warrant granted by George IV in 1828 and renewed by William IV and Queen Victoria. It advertised 'Reviews, Magazines & Periodical Publications. Book-Binding in all is Branches. Visiting and Invitation cards, neatly Engraved.'*

Street but soon left, allowing William Yarrell to move in and continue to live there until his death. The house was commodious and needed to be to house Yarrell's museum and library. His two servants also required accommodation as did his sister Caroline, who lived there until her death in 1839.

The firm became an advertising agent, with advertisements in newspapers all around Britain naming Jones and Yarrell in London as contacts, and was familiar to readers across the country. When Yarrell began to publish his books in the 1830s, it was soon realized that the 'Yarrell' of 'Jones and Yarrell' was William Yarrell. Newspapers notified their readers when parts of his *A History of British Fishes* (at 2/6d) and then of *A History of British Birds* were issued, followed by reviews for the completed first and second volumes, and when they could finally be bought as completed works. These advertisements and short articles about the books accounted for hundreds of notices of his books nationwide. Not only were sales of the books enhanced, but the important flow of information to Yarrell from fishermen and bird watchers about species in their localities increased immeasurably. The firm also had a book-binding service, which catered for purchasers of the books published in unbound parts that were then bound to the owners' specifications to fit into their private libraries.

In 1828, when the business had flourished and become eminently respectable, Jones and Yarrell were granted a royal warrant and appointed 'bookseller and newsmen to his majesty and the royal family' by George IV (reigned 1820–30); this was then renewed in William IV and Victoria's reigns.

The royal warrant was noted in the London Trades Directory up to 1855 for Jones & Yarrell, booksellers and newsmen. Royal warrants had been granted to tradesmen who reached a high standard of goods and services since the 15th century and were highly prized. A warrant permitted the holder to supply his goods to members of the royal family and the court.

On a personal level, from odd references in his correspondence it is evident that Yarrell supplied his close friends, including the naturalists and authors John Gould and T. C. Eyton, with their newspapers.[3] He also obliged by obtaining foreign natural history books for his friends, and when his friend Leonard Jenyns urgently needed some Yarrell let him have them at trade price.[4] Yarrell was a keen book collector himself and amassed a splendid library of natural history books that assisted him in his studies and provided the references in his own books. The Jones and Yarrell bookselling department allowed him to source those by both English and European authors.

Each Monday Yarrell went to the east end of London on business and would have visited his publisher friends, John Van Voorst, and Thomas Norton Longman at his Paternoster Row business established in 1804. On 17 August 1835 Yarrell told his colleague Jenyns of a long-established routine. 'Monday being my day for visiting the city I called this morning at Messrs Longmans on the subject of your book.' Yarrell was dealing with the business end of Jenyns' publishing of his *A Manual of British Vertebrate Animals* and arranged for prospectuses to be printed and distributed. Van Voorst was also involved in publicity and the allotting of £5 for free copies for reviews, etc. Yarrell found it valuable inside knowledge when he came to publish his own two books in the mid-1830s. Obtaining foreign titles necessitated a visit to the Baillière shop in Regent Street where Hyppolyte, co-operating with his brother Jean-Baptiste in Paris, specialized in medical texts and published texts on chemistry, physics and natural history, particularly translations from French and German authors. Yarrell obtained European natural history books both for himself and his naturalist friends. Bookselling was still the foundation of the business, with news-vending and advertising taking increasingly important roles that were likely to have been Edward Jones' responsibility.

Edward Jones did not marry until 30 December 1820, three months after the death of his mother, when he inherited his father's estate and houses. His wife was Sophia Pallett, whom he married at St Pancras Old Church, north London. Sophia may not have been robust for she died on 9 July 1834, and

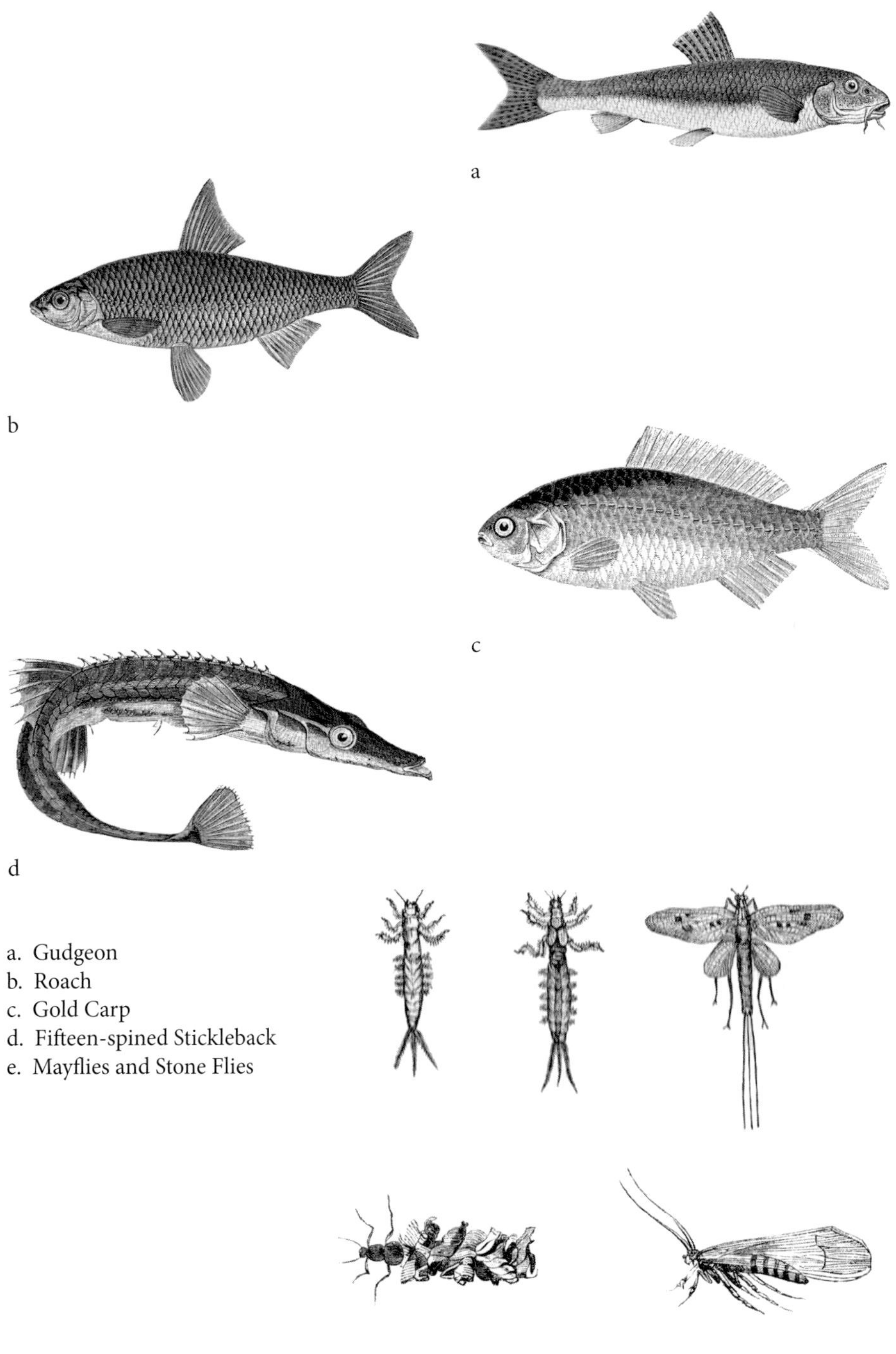


e

PLATE 2 FRESHWATER FISHES

Edward had inscribed on the Bayford tomb that he had lost a much loved wife. At some date prior to 1831, Edward Jones purchased Birchanger Place, in the village of Birchanger, Essex, which would have been a retreat in the countryside for Sophia. Besides the house there were a yard, outbuildings and a garden, amounting to 450 acres. William Yarrell spent Christmas at Birchanger in 1831.

The 1830s were busy times for them both, but more particularly for William Yarrell. By then he had already published many articles in scientific journals, had a considerable collection of specimens of birds and fishes, and was producing his ground-breaking books *A History of British Fishes* and *A History of British Birds,* published by his close friend Van Voorst in parts. In 1837 Edward married again and chose Grace, the sister of his school friend Edward Bird, as his second wife. That same year both William and Edward decided they did not wish to be tied to the business every day and arranged to work alternate months on and off. The newsagency part of the business demanded daily attendance, with deliveries to the court and also to the Houses of Parliament.

Edward Jones had made his will in 1840, but did not die until 18 November 1850 and was buried at Bayford. He left all his 'messuages, farms, land, tenements and other hereditaments in Birchanger and at Pilley, Warborne and Boldre in the County of Southampton and City of Westminster to his wife Grace Jones and my two friends Edward Bird of Brixton, Surrey, and William Yarrell in trust'. He also bequeathed all 'his household goods, furniture, plate, linen, pictures, china, jewels, trinkets, dressing and writing desks with all contents, books, wardrobes, wine in my cellars in London and the country, horses, harness, carriages to my wife Grace for her own use and benefit'. £5000 was to be invested, and if Grace were to die before him, all was to be shared by Edward Bird and William Yarrell of Ryder Street, St James's. £500 was left to invest in 3% Consolidated Bank for the benefit of the people of Bayford. He made a generous gift, which he asked Edward Bird and William Yarrell to accept: 'one pipe in the wood of the best port wine that could be secured for carrying out the terms of his will'. A pipe contained about 105 gallons. This raises visions of convivial evenings that had been shared by the three friends over many years before, sipping the best port wine available.

On the vestry wall of the church a charitable bequest by Edward Jones is

*The Jones tomb, just feet away from the Yarrell graves, has inscriptions for the two Edward Jones partners in Jones and Yarrell. Their two inscriptions are on the short sides:*

*'Edward Jones of Brompton Crescent in the County of Middlesex who departed this life Oct 28 1808 aged 59 years. Martha Jones his widow died September 14 1820 aged 69.'*

*'Sacred to the memory of Edward Jones Esq of Birchanger Place Obiit 18th November 1850 Aetat 68 and Sophia Jones the Beloved wife of Edward Jones of Birchanger Place, Essex, died July 9th 1834 aged 49.'*

recorded. Edward Jones had no children and that branch of his family died with him. When William Yarrell died a bachelor in 1856 the same situation obtained, as he was the last of his immediate family, so the two men who did so much to put the firm on a sound footing left no immediate successors.

A notice of the death of a 'respected and trustworthy assistant and clerk of Messrs Jones & Yarrell newspaper agents, Bury Street', James Lindus (1755–1849), had appeared in a newspaper when he had died on 27 August 1849 in Museum Street, St James's, in his 94th year. Experienced and dependable, Lindus would have been the mainstay of the shop when Yarrell and Edward Jones were not there, although he may have retired several years before his death. Two men named May and Williams were assistants in the shop in the late 1840s and early 1850s, but they were to prove entirely different characters.

When Edward Jones died in 1850 it was a devastating blow for Yarrell. It came at a time just when he least wanted to be left alone with running what was now a much bigger, busier enterprise than when they had taken it on.

It is likely that Edward had always been the senior partner in the firm and probably did much of the administration. Now Yarrell had to cope with every aspect and be on site all the time unless willing to leave his two assistants in charge. *The London Post Office Directory* Trades Section of 1852 recorded business as usual for the past 50 years, but in 1853 there was a change. The firm became known as Jones Yarrell and Clifford. After spending 50 years building the business of Jones & Yarrell, Yarrell may have been pleased to hand over to his cousins, Charles and Joseph Clifford, but they lost the royal warrant, which was humiliating. The two assistants, May and Williams, had set up a rival business at 42 Bury Street.

In the *Post Office London Directories* of 1855 and 1856 a stark, unhappy story lies behind the cryptic entries under the 'Commercial' and 'Street' lists. Everything appearing in the 1855 edition had been set afoot in 1854, in time for publication the following year. In the 1855 directory 34 Bury Street, the former site of the Jones and Yarrell shop, was now let to Samuel Scott, a tailor, and at 6 Little Ryder Street, the ground floor of William's house was now the site of 'Jones Yarrell & Clifford bookseller & newsagent', but there was no royal warrant and no statement 'newsagent to Her Majesty and the Royal Family'. That accolade was now attached to 'May, Frederick, news agent to Her Majesty & the Royal Family' at 42 Bury Street, St James's.

At some time during 1854, Frederick May, Yarrell's 'bookseller's clerk' of the 1851 census, had resigned and left Yarrell's employ. May had been busy arranging a lease of number 42 Bury Street, just a few doors away from number 34, fitting the premises out to become a newsagents and making contacts with agencies and suppliers. He also applied for a royal warrant. In 1856 his entry in the London Directory read 'May, Frederick, British and Foreign newsagent to Her Majesty and the Royal Family at 42 Bury Street.' May was already aspiring to big business by going for foreign agencies, and he was taking a great deal of business from Jones Yarrell and Clifford. In addition he had obtained a royal warrant which was extraordinary for a new business. Had May been telling Yarrell's customers that the firm was moving down the road to number 42 and also informed the Royal Warrant office similarly?

Fortunately, the damage done to Jones Yarrell and Clifford was not terminal. Joseph Clifford, who, although a surgeon (MRCS) by profession, had taken over the business from William Yarrell, had the oversight of his elder brother

William, who was the owner/manager of a similar, very successful business on an Inner Temple site in the East End of London. By the time Joseph died in 1872 much of the damage done by May and Williams had been repaired.

There was an even happier series of events lying in the future for the firm. Jones and Yarrell, as they had become again on Clifford's death, bought out the business of Frederick May in 1956 and the royal warrant was again granted to it in 1960. The firm became royal warrant holder by appointment to the Queen, the Duke of Edinburgh and the Prince of Wales. Jones and Yarrell joined the Menzies group in 1970, so the name lives on and they still provide news deliveries to major corporations and government ministries across London and other major cities, and to individual addresses. This continues a long-standing tradition, since Yarrell several times told his friend Jenyns that he could not leave London 'while Parliament is sitting' but would be free by a given date, presumably when the house rose. The Commons and Lords needed the latest news from home and abroad as soon as it was published. Today the company delivers four times a day as standard practice and oversees deliveries to government, continuing a priority established by Jones and Yarrell when Edward and William were in charge.

*Sundown* (A History of British Birds, 1843, 3: 63).

## Chapter 3

# THE 1820S: LAYING THE FOUNDATIONS

Yarrell was aged 40 before he wrote his first periodical article that was published in 1825 in the *Zoological Journal,* entitled 'Notices of the occurrence of some rare British birds observed during the years 1823, '24, and '25'. His recording of birds in different parts of the country, with particular attention to rarities, had been in progress for several years and was to be a continuing study over many more years.

A second deep interest lay in his anatomical studies of birds. In the winter of 1823–24, he had prepared and preserved the trachea and part of the bones of a young wild (i.e. not Mute) swan, shot in this country, that possessed peculiarities he had never observed in the bones of a Whooper Swan of any age. This induced him to believe that he could eventually prove it belonged to a different species. He had insufficient evidence to publish as yet and had to wait for several further autumn swan migrations to Britain, hoping to obtain more specimens from Leadenhall Market. There the matter rested for another six years.

In Yarrell's library there were several editions of Thomas Bewick's *A History of British Birds,* including a first edition of 1797. By 1825 Yarrell had become aware that Bewick was preparing a sixth edition and began to correspond with him and send scarce birds with notes on their distribution and habits to figure in this.

His own museum contained a series of British birds and their eggs, and he now cultivated the society of scientific men among whom he made the acquaintance of Sir William Jardine of Jardine Hall near Lockerby, Dumfriesshire, and Prideaux John Selby of Twizell House, near Belford, Northumberland. The circle widened to include John Gould, Thomas Bell (dental surgeon at Guy's Hospital), Nicholas Aylward Vigors (the first secretary of the Zoological Society) and Dr George Thackeray (the Provost of King's College, Cambridge from 1814–1850), a great lover of birds who had a fine collection of British bird species and an excellent library of rare books. Thackeray introduced Yarrell to the Reverend Leonard Jenyns, Vicar of Swaffham Bulbeck, Cambridgeshire (from 1823–49), a naturalist and author with whom Yarrell would cooperate closely and exchange copious notes and specimens.

Besides Jenyns, who had graduated from St John's College, Cambridge in 1822, his friend John Stevens Henslow, a St John's graduate who also became a clergyman and professor of botany at Cambridge, was also acquainted with Yarrell. Henslow's pupil, Charles Darwin (who graduated in 1831) was enthused with a passion for natural history by him, and in turn became the third Cambridge graduate to form a close friendship with Yarrell that lasted a lifetime. That these friendships were formed in the mid-1820s between Yarrell, a non-graduate who nevertheless became an established authority, and men who were all to become eminent is an indicator of Yarrell's personal qualities, not only as a naturalist.

On 1 November 1825 Yarrell was admitted as a Fellow of the Linnean Society, having earlier, in April, published his first paper in the second volume of the *Zoological Journal,* of which he soon afterwards became one of the editors. Yarrell was an active life-long member of the Linnean Society, taking part in its meetings and later as a member of the council and Vice President and Treasurer from 1849–56. He was a keen member of the Zoological Club of the Linnean Society, which provided opportunities to meet fellow naturalists of all ages at its regular dinners and excursions. On 1 February 1825 it had been proposed at the Club to form a Zoological Society with a library and a museum, which attracted 151 subscribers including Yarrell when it began in 1826.

As early as 1825 Yarrell had already collected a considerable number of British birds and their eggs, and bought others. He continued in later years to increase his collection. His earliest correspondence with Jardine was about birds' eggs. Jardine sent him a box with a Merlin's egg that got crushed in the post. Yarrell already had Merlin eggs, but he sent Jardine the first 12 birds named on Jardine's desiderata list. Yarrell wanted drawings of eggs that he had not obtained yet, but wrote that there were only 18–20 species that he needed to complete his records of the eggs of British birds. Three years later Jardine sent him a Red-breasted Merganser's egg and said he was happy to exchange eggs with him.[1] In 1830 Yarrell hoped to visit Cambridge and take for the Cambridge Philosophical Society's collections one or more of every British bird's egg that he possessed, beyond a pair. Yarrell visited Cambridge to meet friends there and exchange specimens. In 1831 he purchased out of the Sowerby collection many different card trays of various species and had 30–40 in series, of several different kinds. This is one of the few references to Yarrell's purchases of specimens. He knew that all the current books still contained errors about several species' eggs, because he could describe them from the eggs themselves and he did this subsequently for a book proposed by Jenyns.

*The egg of the Collared Pratincole with detailed markings skillfully engraved.* A History of British Birds, 1843, 3: 5.

*Yarrell's painting of a Pratincole's egg with the inscription 'sent by W Yarrell to W M Tuke', that is William Murray Tuke. By courtesy of D. Clugston.*

The collecting of eggs provides evidence that Yarrell was not entirely a closet naturalist but continued to spend many hours making observations of birds in the field. He reported a major discovery in the *Zoological Journal* under the title 'On the small horny appendage to the upper mandible in very young chicks'. The article had been written on 17 October 1825 and published in 1826. This appendage of hard material at the tip of the bill, now called the 'egg tooth', is used by the chick to first crack the shell and then remove fragments from it until there is a hole sufficiently large to permit the chick to escape from the shell. Yarrell had watched ducks and hens hatching in this way and his close observation meant he was the first to describe this small ornithological miracle.

Yarrell's attendance at the Royal Institution in 1817 to learn anatomy was now put to good use. He dissected birds and fishes to preserve examples of their skeletons. By 1825 Yarrell had such a good collection of birds that he had made a series of dissections of water birds and presented a collection of the tracheae to the Royal College of Surgeons. His anatomical studies had revealed the modifications of the trachea in ducks, geese and swans, and in 1827 he published the first of a series of papers on these structures and their associated muscles (see Periodical Publications, p.169). At the Royal College of Surgeons he was given access to the country's most extraordinary collection of anatomical specimens, the Hunterian Museum.

In the sale of Yarrell's effects in December 1856 there were files and folders of his anatomical drawings. Besides tracheae, there were sketches of the bones of birds, a few of them used in his *A History of British Birds* as vignettes. Charles Darwin read the first volume of the second edition and commented to Eyton that Yarrell had 'done a good deal in the bone line in Brit. Birds - he showed me a lot of breast bones the other day'[2], thus proving that Yarrell had retained the bones that he had dissected himself and subsequently drawn.

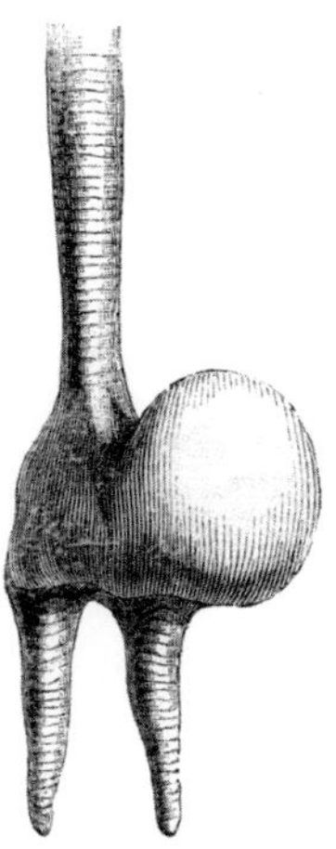

*The tube of the windpipe in the adult male Widgeon, about six inches in length. (Volume 3: 195). The vignette for most of the ducks in* A History of British Birds, 1843, *was a diagram of the trachea, or windpipe, drawn by Yarrell from his own dissection.*

Several authors have stated that Yarrell stopped shooting in the 1820s, but two letters dated 1834 clearly refute this suggestion. Several naturalists, including Yarrell, had been in Scotland attending a British Association for the Advancement of Science (BAAS) conference in Edinburgh and on their way home to London stayed with P. J. Selby at Twizell House, five miles from Bamburgh. Selby's friend, Sir William Jardine, knew of this and wrote to Selby 'Your party on Wednesday would doubtless be a pleasant one. What did you do and see? Did Mr Yarrel [*sic*] shoot a grouse. I regret being absent & should have enjoyed seeing him bag a little.' Replying, Selby told Sir William that 'Yarrell had a turn upon the moor but the grouse were wild & he did not succeed in getting a shot at them. He floored the partridges, however, right & left.' Yarrell's reputation as a first-class marksman had spread way beyond London.[3]

Yarrell was a very fit and healthy man throughout his life. He lived between Piccadilly and Pall Mall, in the parish of St James's, Westminster, and there is no doubt that he did a great deal of walking around London. He may have hired conveyances but it is more likely that he walked every Monday, his day to do business in the City, to visit the publishers Van Voorst and Longman in Paternoster Row, near St Paul's Cathedral. When attending the meetings of the Linnean Society he went to Soho Square, a 20 minutes' walk away. He was a frequent attender at the dinners of the Zoological Club of the Linnean Society from 1825–29. The British Museum in Great Russell Street was another short walk to inspect its collection of natural history specimens. He could also have used the ferries on the Thames and horse-drawn buses. Omnibuses designed by Shillibeer became part of London public transport from 1829. Yarrell may not have needed these in the 1830s, but as his life became busier and he became older there would have been times when he was glad to use them.

The London-based societies soon became a big part of Yarrell's life. His fellow members invariably found Yarrell quickly grasped any situation and then employed his efficient business habits, combined with a plain method of stating facts. He had a straightforward simplicity of character. These qualities were in evidence throughout his association with the societies until the end of his life. There were mutual benefits for Yarrell, who made acquaintance with so many naturalists with similar interests.

In 1826 Yarrell became a founder member of the Zoological Society and took an active part in its proceedings both as naturalist and man of business. The progress of the Zoological Society was monitored by Yarrell for his

a. Woodcock
b. Common Snipe
c. Red-legged Partridge
d. Black Grouse

PLATE 3 GAME BIRDS

friends in his letters. Initially the museum was a most important part of the Zoological Society, housed at 33 Bruton Street in 1826, a few minutes' walk away across Piccadilly and up Bond Street. Yarrell was always conversant with the contents of the museum. The administration offices and library later moved to Leicester Square where the meetings were held.

Yarrell reported in 1828 to Sir William Jardine, a fellow member: 'Progress of Zool Soc beyond all precedent. From 1 Dec 1827–29 Nov 1828, 575 new members were admitted, previous number 685 (visitors to the Gardens 130,000) Eleven thousand (12600 written over) visitors to the Museum. Receipts in the same period £10,000 of which £4000 was taken as exhibition money in six months. Live Quadrupeds 130. Birds 300. The museum in Bruton Street contains about 600 Mammalia, 4,000 Birds, Rich in Reptiles particularly Serpents. - 1000 Fish, 30,000 insects, etc. We had an excellent assembly of about 130 naturalists to commemorate the anniversary of the Birth of Ray - for a list of the Stewards see the Morning Post of the 24th or Morning Herald of 25th ult. for the proceedings of the day, read the newspaper I have the pleasure to transmit to you by this day's post.'[4] There are few references to his newsagency business in his correspondence, but reminders such as this crop up when he supplied newspapers, but more particularly books, to his fellow naturalists.

In 1827 the appointment at the Zoological Society of a curator and taxidermist brought another ornithologist to London who would become a close colleague and friend for Yarrell, namely John Gould, a gardener's son. Like Yarrell, John Gould had to make his way in the world and gain the respect of all classes. His pivotal appointment as Curator and Preserver of the museum at the Zoological Society brought him into contact with men of different ranks, and he would soon find a congenial fellow naturalist in Yarrell. Both of them made useful contacts and gathered materials that enabled them to begin book publishing in the 1830s. By mid-life each had earned a place in the scientific world and gained universal respect.

By 1827 Yarrell was now fully active in societies and was contributing many articles to scientific journals (see Periodicals, p.168). In February he began to contribute a series of important papers to the Linnean Society's *Transactions, Proceedings and Journal.* To these he added *Transactions and Proceedings of the Zoological Society*; reports of the BAAS; the *Zoological Journal*; *Annals & Magazine of Natural History, Philosophical Magazine*; *Entomological*

*Magazine*; and *Zoologist*. Yarrell exhibited preserved specimens to illustrate his lectures and papers read at the society meetings. Over the ensuing 30 years it all constituted an extraordinary amount of original research in some 80 articles. He added yet another society membership when he was elected to the Council of the Medico-Botanical Society in 1827 (see Societies, p.180).

Yarrell used all his spare time to visit natural history museums and towns on the south coast to gauge the availability of fish specimens caught there, as well as fishing in the Thames for freshwater species with Adams, his old fisherman friend. Returning to Hertfordshire he visited Royston, where he knew Joseph Trigg, a local sportsman, and John Newman, the taxidermist. He also went to Cambridge where his friend John Stevens Henslow was Professor of Botany with a pupil, later to become another friend and collaborator, Charles Darwin. In Cambridge from 1828 there was a fine natural history museum at the Cambridge Philosophical Society, the first in the city.

As a bachelor Yarrell was most comfortable among the all-male members of the various societies and enjoyed the camaraderie of the meetings. His correspondents were all male. His sister, Caroline, lived with him for several years and was the subject of solicitous enquiries from his friends who came to know her from visiting Ryder Street for dinners. She is the only female mentioned in Yarrell's letters apart from Mrs Lee, author of a book on fishes, his solicitous references to Mrs Jenyns, the wife of his friend the Reverend Leonard Jenyns, and to the wives of Dr Johnston and Audubon.

In September 1828, Yarrell had a famous visitor when Bewick went to see him while in London. Bewick was then 74 and had undertaken this journey against his will and better judgment in order to sell off his 'great remaining stock of Birds & Quads.' Bewick subsequently reminisced 'I called upon Mr Leadbitter Bird preserver &c to the British Museum - & then upon Mr Yarrell from them I met with a most kind reception & offers to do everything in their power to serve me in my ornithological or on my intendi[n]g fishy publication - I never in my life was so gratified at seeing any thing, as I was with Yarrell's Museum - he has left nothing untouched that could assist him in probing ornithological knowledge to the bottom - he invited me most pressingly and kindly to dine with him, chiefly for the purpose of my meeting with Mr Vigors there - but I dclined [*sic*] I had made up my mind as I thought, not to dine with anyone for fear of being Buzzed to death in London.'[5] Yarrell overcame Bewick's apprehension by his kindliness and gave the old engraver a most enjoyable time among his museum collection of birds and fishes. Bewick died in the November following this visit.

Bewick's influence on Yarrell was profound and long lasting. Yarrell would construct his own bird book in imitation of Bewick's *A History of British Birds,* adopting the same title. He followed the layout of the sections for each species, with an engraved portrait of the species followed by a synonymy then description, ending with a small engraved 'tailpiece' as Bewick called it or 'vignette' as Yarrell preferred. The long preparation gathering the information

*'The representation of the Cream Coloured Courser was the last bird engraved by Bewick. A proof of it was sent to Yarrell by George Atkinson of Newcastle' and copied for this illustration in Yarrell's* A History of British Birds, 1843, 2; 376.

occupied Yarrell for many years in the 1820s and early 1830s. His great love of wood engravings was also inspired by Bewick and was a life-long interest for Yarrell, who collected books with wood engravings and cut out examples. A large collection of these in his library suggests he might have contemplated writing a book on woodcuts and wood engravings.

In 1829 Yarrell finally fitted together the pieces of the puzzle about wild swans and his suspected new species and wrote up the evidence. On 29 November he attended the evening meeting of the Zoological Club of the Linnean Society and took a sternum and trachea of a swan to illustrate his lecture. The text was published in the *Transactions of the Linnean Society* (1830), where Yarrell described the differences between the Whooper Swan and the other very similar swan that he had himself first identified as a British bird in 1824. To the new species he gave the name *Cygnus bewickii*, 'Thus devoting it to the memory of one whose beautiful and animated delineations of subjects in natural history entitle him to this tribute.' Yarrell had long admired Bewick and treasured Bewick's book on British birds. The publication of his discovery, adding a new bird to science and the British avifauna, brought Yarrell to the notice of the naturalist establishment. The name Bewick's Swan was adopted by all naturalists and remains its name today. At the time of its publication, the article proved a career landmark for Yarrell. The reason for the two swans appearing on the memorial tablet to William Yarrell in St James's Church (see p.109) indicated that to his friends his discovery of Bewick's Swan, new to science, was his greatest achievement.

Yarrell passed on a pleasant comment from the American George Ord about Bewick's book, of which he said 'Alexander Wilson was so enthusiastic in his admiration and praise of Thomas Bewick that he almost always carried one of the volumes under his arm, or in his pocket – this was told me by Mr Ord, Wilson's intimate friend and biographer.'[6]

Yarrell was very hospitable and an invitation to dinner meant an excellent meal with both first-class wines and good company. At this time those privileged to meet at Yarrell's dinner table included Thomas Bell, who later shared the publisher Van Voorst for his books on *A History of Quadrupeds* (1837) and *A History of Reptiles* (1839); Edward Turner Bennett, the author of a book about the inhabitants of London zoo, *The Gardens and Menageries of the Zoological Society* (1830–31), about which Yarrell also knew a great deal, and another on *The Tower Menagerie* (1829); James Ebenezer Bicheno, a staunch supporter of the Linnean Society, elected to the Royal Society in 1827, who left London to live in Glamorgan in 1832; Marshall Hall, a physician and physiologist who practised in London from 1826–37; and Nicholas Aylward Vigors, Secretary of the Zoological Society from 1826–32. All of these gentlemen were early colleagues of Yarrell before he himself became famous.

Jenyns has left us a convivial picture of this bachelor's delightful dinner parties, the organisation of which was probably assisted by his sister until 1839, along with his two maidservants. 'Yarrell was particular about his dinners and cookery, and had everything very nicely served up. He was an excellent carver, and his knowledge of comparative anatomy told him where exactly to plant his knife in dissecting for the table, fish, game or any small joint that required nicety in helping. His wines were always first rate. After dinner, if pressed, he would sing a song. He was always fond of the theatre and he would often pick up and get quite by heart some humorous song of the day he heard upon the stage that he took a fancy to. I remember one evening when he and I went together to a large evening party at Gould's, the ornithologist, he suddenly, at the request of a friend standing by, struck out in a stentorian voice –"I'm *afloat*! I'm *afloat*!" – the first words of an amusing sailor's song, which immediately brought to a stand the whole party engaged in conversation at the time. All ears were turned in breathless silence to Yarrell, who threw so much life and spirit into his subject as to elicit loud bursts of applause when it came to a close.'[7] Yarrell may have learnt the tune quickly, but the words were too swiftly sung so he wrote down the first, third, fifth, etc. lines on the first occasion he went to the theatre and on a second visit he wrote down the second, fourth and sixth, etc., lines. In his library, there were at least 26 volumes of catches and glees, ballads, and a treatise on the art of music, besides loose sheets of music by various composers.

Yarrell went on several trips with Jenyns to the south coast to see what fish novelties they could get, visiting Hastings and then Eastbourne, and going to meet returning fishermen in order to have the pick of their nets and secure fishes that would often have been thrown away as unsaleable in the market. Several times they went out with the fishermen in their boats. While at Eastbourne they ventured to sea when it was overcast and ran into a squally and rough sea, wind and heavy rain. Jenyns and Yarrell took refuge in the bottom of the boat beneath a dirty, smelly tarpaulin. Jenyns suffered uncomfortable feelings of seasickness but Yarrell 'who stood it well rather chaffed at my being so bad a sailor. After a while however, the tables were turned. The storm over and the sky clear, we crept from our hiding place, and not feeling disposed to renew our fishing, we came to the shore and walked home to our hotel. By the time of our arrival there, I felt quite well again, but it was Yarrell who began to complain of qualms he had not felt before ... he had to lie down upon the sofa for half an hour or so before we could get to work. Our usual plan of proceeding was immediately on getting home, and while the fish to be examined were still fresh in their colours, to have them on our table and forthwith describe or take notes as required. Afterwards we often had them for dinner, curious to try the flavour of several kinds not usually esteemed fit for the table. Some of these we thought very fair eating;

others rather indifferent; two or three of such as we never wished to put in our mouths again.'[8]

At the end of 1829 the Zoological Club of the Linnean Society came to an end and the means to meet informally, while not as urgent as when he had been a newcomer on the scene, was probably regretted by Yarrell. At the last meeting before the club closed, held on 29 November 1829, Nicholas Aylward Vigors, the President of the Zoology Club, spoke of Yarrell's researches into the comparative anatomy and physiology of animals that had 'already secured for him the highest rank in science ... Within the year of my presidency he has given us a continued series of erudite observations on the osteology and internal structure of the animals which have died in the menagerie of the Zoological Society.' Vigors further drew attention to Yarrell exhibiting at the last meeting specimens of the trachea of a new swan that, as outlined above, he intended describing at the next meeting of the Linnean Society, and a footnote indicates that he had indeed subsequently read this paper and named *Cygnus bewickii*.[9]

Vigors' appreciation of Yarrell's qualities as a naturalist so early in his career was remarkable. Events in the following decade were to provide proof that Vigors' belief in his capabilities were well-founded.

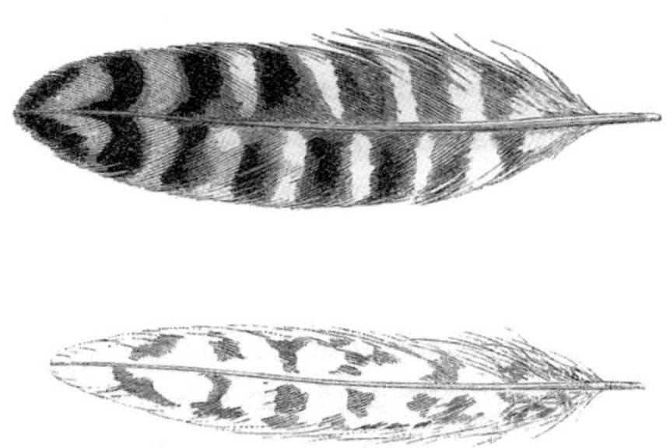

*Feathers from the axillary plume and middle of the tail of the Wood Sandpiper.* A History of British Birds, *1843: 2: 538.*

## Chapter 4

# THE 1830S: THE DECADE OF ACHIEVEMENT

The 1830s was a most remarkable decade in the story of natural history, zoology in particular, in Britain. The seeds had been sewn in 1826 with the formation of the Zoological Society of London, followed by other societies of which Yarrell became a member and served on several of their committees and as Secretary or Treasurer. Interest in natural history increased with a great flood of new periodical titles and books on natural history being published. Yarrell was to add two titles to the new books and 55 periodical articles. In this decade alone the new periodical titles that commenced and to which Yarrell contributed were: *Transactions and Proceedings of the Zoological Society* (began as *Proceedings of the Committee of Science and Correspondence of the Zoological Society of London* in 1830); BAAS *Annual Reports* 1833–; *Entomological Magazine* 1832–; *Proceedings of the Linnean Society* 1838- and Jardine's *Magazine of Zoology and Botany* in 1836. The decade also saw epic voyages by two of Yarrell's friends, Charles Darwin on the *Beagle* from 1831–36 and John Gould sailed to Australia in May 1838. Yarrell played a small part in assisting his friends both before and after their time abroad. Residing in London he was at the heart of the burgeoning interest in natural history and did much to promote it.

Yarrell's library reflected his varying degree of interest throughout the decade in first fishes then birds, with most books acquired on these subjects, but other fauna were included and there were about 100 natural history books altogether – a number double that for all other subjects. His eclectic taste covered both language and literature, art and architecture, travel, history, sport and coins, with a few medical and religious books.

In 1830 when thanking Leonard Jenyns for a present of fishes, Yarrell invited him to stay at his house. For the rest of his life a close friendship formed in these early years continued unbroken, with mutual support for their writings, exchange of news, specimens and information, and joint holidays on the coast several years in succession. They visited Weymouth in 1832, where Yarrell told Jenyns his 'principal place of resort must be the fish market and also Sherrill's shop the fishmonger close to the market'. Taking the coach, Yarrell went to Aldeburgh on the Suffolk coast to join Jenyns in August 1833. Yarrell also instructed Jenyns to 'Bring your Memoranda and catalogue of fish. I will do the same, and we shall have amusement for the evening as during the day.'[1] Yarrell stayed with Jenyns at his Swaffham Bulbeck Vicarage near Cambridge when he went to Cambridge for a meeting or to visit the museum of the Cambridge Philosophical Society.

These trips to the coast to arrange for unusual specimens to be sent to him, and several others undertaken by Yarrell alone, meant time out from the business. While visiting the expanding towns of Bournemouth, Brixham, Hastings, Eastbourne, Devonport, Weymouth and Poole, did Yarrell also do some business? As small villages developed into towns in the 1830s, they acquired circulating, subscription libraries that provided newspapers for their clients. Yarrell could have done a brisk business as a London newsagent and bookseller supplying new publications. This could also justify his absences to his partner Edward Jones.

From 1831 until his death Yarrell served the Zoological Society in various capacities, including temporarily as Secretary from 1836–38. This opened up a whole new world of animal species for him that, as a Fellow, he could go and visit when he wished. In 1833 Yarrell became a founder member of the Entomological Society and served as its treasurer from 1834–1852. The annual meetings of the British Association for the Advancement of Science (BAAS) afforded an opportunity to meet many of the most eminent scientists in parallel disciplines. When it was held in Edinburgh in 1834, he joined friends of P. J. Selby who had attended to stay at Twizell House near Belford for a few days to enjoy the fishing and shooting with their host. Jenyns wrote, 'On the return journey from Edinburgh we spent a few very pleasant days with Selby at his hospitable mansion Twizell House, Northumberland.' (Jenyns, *Reminiscences*). Selby returned the visit to Yarrell in 1835 and reported to Jardine on Yarrell's busy life in London, in contact with all the naturalists and societies in the capital. It was in sharp contrast with Selby's experience as a naturalist isolated in the country many miles from London.[2]

Yarrell's health was always good, but he had a scare in 1831 when he had inflammation of both eyes for three weeks in August, which was sufficiently alarming for him to seek medical advice and was told to read and write as little as possible. This was one of the very few physical setbacks he experienced. His sister Caroline, who lived with him, was less fortunate and beginning to show symptoms of the cancer that eventually caused her death at the end of May 1839. Her health fluctuated and occasionally threatened to curtail his own activities. It was only because Caroline's health had improved slightly that he was able to take a two weeks' break in September 1834 taking in the BAAS meeting in Edinburgh.

In September 1831 Charles Darwin informed his Cambridge tutor, the Professor of Botany, the Reverend J. S. Henslow, that he was busy getting advice and information from Yarrell, who had already played a part in the preparations for his role in the voyage of the *Beagle*. Who better could Darwin consult than one of the best shots in London, who was also extremely knowledgeable about pistols, guns and fowling pieces in particular? However, Yarrell, though badgering the dealers for lower prices for Darwin, failed to find pistols below £60 a pair and Darwin refused to pay this. Yarrell bought quality goods, but a student not yet earning anything could not afford top quality firearms. Darwin, later in the day, went with Captain Robert Fitzroy around the London gunsmiths and got his pistols for £40, to his delight. Yarrell helped him in the purchase of other equipment to get the best deals and taught him how to successfully prepare specimens for long term preservation in jars of spirits, using bladders with foil and varnish.[3] Two months later, Yarrell had a visit from Darwin who was about to embark. He was apprehensive of this dangerous voyage his young friend was about to embark upon. Yarrell wrote to Jenyns: 'On Saturday last I shook hands with him for the last time here. He was to start for Plymouth the following morning, Sunday the 23rd and expects to sail early in November.' With contrary winds Darwin did not set sail until the 27th December 1831.[4]

There was great excitement in London when 'the Charing Cross Whale' was exhibited in 1831. It had been found dead, floating in the North Sea between Belgium and England, in November 1827 by a crew of fishermen. They had hailed two other boats to help them move the enormous mass (190 tons, 173 tonnes) and tow the whale into Ostend harbour. After being stripped of its 40,000 pounds of oil and 170,000 pounds of rotten flesh that was buried in the sand, it was eventually taken to London as a reportedly 95 foot long by 18 foot wide skeleton. Yarrell, of course, had to go to see the whale and to measure it for himself. He found it displayed inside a tent on a site on the northern side of Trafalgar Square where the National Gallery is situated today. He conveyed the result to Jenyns on 17 April 1832, 'To ascertain its real length I first measured the outside of the building, on two different occasions, and found it to be 36 yards and 2 feet long – say 110 feet – I made a third visit – but that was to the inside, and found that the extreme point of the jaw was 11 feet 6 inches short of one end of the building, and the tail twelve feet short of the other – together 23ft 6 – leaving 86 feet 6 inches – as the real length of the skeleton – I can make out only 60 vertebrae – they say 62. I find them thus, cervical 7, Dorsal 14, Lumbar 14, Caudal 25. They have also now assumed a specific name – Musculus - I send you one of their present printed bills.' The whale was displayed in a tent propped on iron supports and could be entered via its rib cage for the cost of two shillings. Visitors could then listen to a 24-piece orchestra while sitting on 'cosily placed tables and chairs'. The visitors were given free copies of natural history publications to read.[5]

*The Charing Cross Whale exhibited in 1831–32 in London. The steps led up to the rib cage of the whale where chairs were placed for visitors.* Balaenoptera musculus *is the Blue Whale.*

Yarrell maintained close relationships with several people in Hertfordshire long after he became engaged in business in London. In 1833 he went to Royston for two or three days and visited to Mr Baker at Melbourn, who had just set up a specimen of Temminck's Sandpiper and the Arctic Tern, both killed by himself at 'Foulmire moor' (now the RSPB's Foulmere Reserve). He went shooting with a friend, Thomas Wortham, on manors in Hertfordshire that they rented. Numerous fishing expeditions with Frederick Nash of Bishop's Stortford in Hertfordshire strengthened Yarrell's ties to the county. It was in Hertfordshire that he did much of his early field work, collecting eggs and shooting birds, but he revealed that he also collected small mammals. He told Jenyns 'I fear that the difference you speak of in the weasels, is only sexual, during the years I have been a sportsman I have by myself or dogs, killed several I had almost written many, but never saw a large female or a small male – yet it is singular that neither Pennant or Fleming should have noticed the great difference in size – which is certainly equal to a fourth, if not to a third.' This is an instance of Yarrell's careful observation and records, made many years before adding to scientific knowledge, this time of mammals.

When Lord Derby, a keen ornithologist (whose estate, Knowsley Hall in Lancashire, housed a very large menagerie), recommenced egg collecting he contacted Yarrell who sent him some of his duplicates, including Jackdaw and Moorhen eggs. Yarrell also promised to send the instrument he used for emptying eggs by a single aperture for Lord Derby to keep and use. That was on 7 June 1832, and ten days later Yarrell sent 8 Guillemot eggs, a Razorbill egg and others. He added: 'Your Lordship appears to have succeeded completely in expelling the contents by a small, neat and circular aperture.'[6]

There are three letters in 1833 to Lord Derby, then President of the Linnean Society. Yarrell thanked His Lordship for a basket with '2 Irish hares and fish &c' and said that they ate one hare at a Linnean Society dinner. 'The other hare with an English one alongside was exhibited at the meeting and they decided they were 2 different species.' Yarrell followed this up in August, asking if he should call the Irish hare *stanleyanus*.[7] In this letter he also declined the offer of becoming Vice-President of the Zoological Society at great length. Lord Derby sent Yarrell a *Numidia cristata* (a guineafowl) and the bird skeleton had arrived on the 'day before and Leadbeater was going to preserve it and to prepare that part of the skeleton which your L.[=Lordship] will find in the 15th vol of Linn Trans p. 379 tab. 09 – this figure taken from bone in College of Surgeons'. The Leadbeater family were well respected animal dealers and conservers based in London.

There was a new society for Yarrell to join in 1833 and in November he reported to Jenyns 'The first meeting of the Entomological Society went off admirably – about 80 have joined, Mr Kirby, Mr Spence, his 2 sons and a son in law were there – the latter all joined the society.'[8] William Kirby (1759–1850) was venerated as the 'founder of Entomology' in this country, and was one of the last remaining original founders of the Linnean Society in 1788. He was a friend of William Spence of Hull, author of an *Introduction to Entomology*, (1815–26, 4 vols). With three other founders, F. W. Hope and his friend J. O. Westwood, and James Francis Stephens, Yarrell immediately became acquainted with yet another group of respected naturalists. He quickly joined them on the committee in the following year and served as their treasurer from 1834 to 1852.

We know what took place at one of the Entomological Society meetings to which Yarrell took Sir William Jardine in 1842, from a mischievous letter Jardine wrote to his wife shortly after. 'At the Entomological, and met many old acquaintances, Hope with his prominent eye and run-about-manner introduced the Marquis de Brême, a six feet some inch French-man, open, good-humoured countenance bearing out the indication of his manners, which are frank without being French, moustaches, and altogether an inconvenient figure for what James Wilson would call "pucking beetles"... Entomological a thriving society ... and it is interesting to a new member, Naturalist though he may be, to sit in a corner and see the members assemble before business, the rampant big Frenchman alluded to, the dandy man everything as neat and clean as can be, a staid quaker, some body rather rotund in a buttoned great coat and spectacles, 'Pickwick' himself and office-bearer &c &c all pulling out boxes of this size and that, various large trunks, sundry small neat things, some bound with pink paper some with blue, one or two glossed on the top not to open on any account. Then comes the opening of the closed ones, some one has something very rare, cover only is exhibited at once, another doles a long preface to an old member he has got something never seen, never heard of before, and at last pulls out his treasure, the old stager sees the corner displayed and "O! quite common, quite common, I had a hundred last week." Allows the incipient Ent. to pocket his disappointment with his box, both of which are put up as soon as possible. Mr Hope again advances to the table with the greatest confidence, and in a loud voice holding the box in one hand and the lid scarcely off in the other, "Gents, I have an insect of greatest rarity now to exhibit to the Soc." while Mr J. O. Westwood Secretary, takes the opportunity of a side peep, (and being only two days returned from Paris) whispers to his neighbours "quite common over the waters and have brought plenty with me." These two are not in company, but so it is, one to beat the other as if they were producing Bantams at the club, instead of working for the real advancement of their pursuit or anxious to communicate to each other what each knew. A remarkable coccus from the spindle-tree *Euonymus europaea* in one of the London squares was exhibited, but private cross-questioning could not elicit whether it was considered peculiar to Euonymus, and indeed little seemed to be known except that it was there.'[9]

The Marquis de Brême was a member of the Entomological Society of France in 1838 and its President in 1844. He was also a member of the London Entomological Society. The *coccus* was a great plague on the trees of Jardine's friend Selby in Northumberland, hence his great interest and follow up on this insect that had been found in Lincoln's Inn Fields. Jardine, who was not a committee man by choice, must have wondered how Yarrell could tolerate so many committee meetings that he obviously willingly attended.

'Pickwick himself' meant Yarrell. Charles Dickens, whom Jardine read and admired, commenced publication of *The Pickwick Papers* in 20 monthly parts in April 1836, with a complete volume in 1837. Mr Samuel Pickwick was chairman of the fictional Pickwick Club that he had founded with members, including one called Sam Weller, to report their journeys, adventures and observations of characters and manners. Situation humour, with idiosyncrasies of personality, are the bases of the ensuing stories. Yarrell very occasionally shared Jardine's sense of humour, but there was no Dickens in his library and nobody has suggested that Yarrell had a keen sense of humour. He would probably not have relished being likened to Mr Pickwick had he known of Jardine's nickname for him.

Yarrell employed Gould, the taxidermist, to mount some of his birds. 'You may put up for my own collection males of the following species, Sylvia tithys – Blue-breasted warbler – Hedge sparrow – Stone-chat and Grasshopper warbler – in separate cages of 6½ inches wide – the same high – 3½ deep outside measure and without ornament.'[10] Two years later, in 1833, Yarrell asked him for further cases of birds to be set up for him for his museum. He asked for an 'arctic tern to be put in a case replacing the tern now in it. Also a Montagu's harrier set up in a case 15 ins wide by 17 ins high to match my other harrier cases. The merlin already at your house may be put into any size case that will best suit it.' Yarrell added 'I should like to have them back again, with the wood wrens you have of mine as soon as you conveniently can, with any other bird of mine now in your possession.'[11] It was well known among his friends that once a specimen got among other skins in Gould's possession he forgot its original owner.

In April 1833 Yarrell was waiting for P. J. Selby to complete his *Illustrations of British Ornithology*, needing another part because: 'At present I have occasion for it now and then, helping Mr Gould with the letter press of his 6th number of "Birds of Europe", as soon as that is at press you shall have the use of it, if you are ready for it, and the volume not then published.'[12] They were all – that is Gould, Selby, Jenyns, Jardine - keeping an eye on one another's bird publications so that they did not miss a new addition to the British fauna. The amount of cooperation is commendable, even to accepting help from a fellow author, as here Gould is happy to have Yarrell's input.

Yarrell and Jenyns were checking and discussing each other's manuscripts. Yarrell had Jenyns' MS of the Mammalia in June 1832 and reported that he had gone over it carefully and made occasional memoranda and queries in pencil which he hoped Jenyns would not think were intended as being critical. This is just one example of the correspondence with Jenyns through the years 1830–35, when Jenyns' *Manual of British Vertebrate Animals* was published, revealing a constant flow of queries that were being answered by Yarrell. He would have encouraged Jenyns to acknowledge the importance of anatomy and even ordered two small scalpels for him in 1831. One can trace Jenyns' progress through the mammals and fishes (though not the reptiles and amphibians) sections of his work from their letters.

The resulting book by Jenyns, having no illustrations, short entries for each species with a short synonymy, and fewer anatomical details than one would have expected from the lengthy correspondence with Yarrell, was published in 1835. There was acknowledgement to Yarrell for his contributions, also to the Cambridge Philosophical Society for Jenyns' use of their extensive collection of British animals. There was no reference to the Charing Cross whale among the Cetacea, but among numerous drawings in an envelope marked 'Drawings of Cetacea Etc' are 21 pen and ink drawings, probably one by Yarrell (in Jenyns

Archives, Bath Royal Literary and Scientific Institution). An engraving of the Charing Cross whale, identified as a *Balaenoptera*, Fleming, is in Jenyns' collection.

By 1834, after lengthy exchanges with Jenyns about fishes, Yarrell realised he had far more information in the form of specimens and drawings, including those that he had made himself at the British Museum or got Charles Curtis to draw for him, so that he could write a book himself entirely on British fishes. Already, he had published nine periodical articles on fishes between 1828 and 1834, including the important discovery of the oviparous method of 'Reproduction of the Eel' in 1833 and three new species of English fishes in 1828. He told Lord Derby he was assisting the Reverend Robert Lowe with an article on fish and fishing in 1838 and had sent a drawing and description of two new fishes which he hoped to exhibit at the next meeting of the Linnean Society. He habitually took specimens to the meetings, when he gave a clear and graphic description of the species.[13]

The work on collecting fishes, contacting fishermen and training them to supply him with any unfamiliar species; articles in journals on fishes; and correspondence with naturalist friends, had all been sifted, organised and written up to the point where Yarrell had begun work on putting the first part of a book together. He wrote to Jenyns in August 1834 saying 'I have begun work in earnest upon my history of British Fishes in imitation or rather the plan of Bewick's British Birds. The engravers go on very well with the woodcuts. I shall have a long string of the proofs to show you when you come to London...I have written the prospectus.'[14] There had been no seeking advice or approval just a bald statement of intent from an experienced writer in full knowledge of his own capacities and mastery of facts. By August 1835 the prospectus had been printed and issued.[15] For details of the story of *A History of British Fishes* see pp.140–156.

Having gathered known facts about each species Yarrell found he had to attempt to reconcile the differing views of his expert, sometimes eminent, contributors. He was very knowledgeable himself and he had a wider view than most of his contributors, having gathered data from all over the country while they were only familiar with small areas round their homes. Although their correspondence and specimens were a positive additional benefit to his work, there was a downside to this. What was he to do when their accompanying comments contradicted his own findings? He could safely evade including information from a correspondent who was merely reporting on one area, but when a close friend was also a respected naturalist and expert fisherman with a large collection of his own, and on top of that, a baronet of the realm, what then? Yarrell shared his worries over this dilemma with his close friend Jenyns. The problem had arisen over the young of trout. He did not believe that the *Herling* was distinct from the *Trutta*, neither did Jenyns, but the problem was 'my specimens were supplied to me by Sir William Jardine – as he has published his notion that they are distinct, it puts me at issue with him (in print) on the subject of characters. I had rather that his name as supporting me with specimens should be omitted, if you have no objection. My M.S. of S[almo] trutta is at the Printers.'[16] In his *A History of British Fishes* Yarrell described the Salmon Trout as *Salmo trutta*, stated his specimens of the Phinock or Herling exactly resembled the young of the Salmon Trout on its first return from salt water, then tactfully made reference to Jardine's beautiful book on the Salmon, without further comment. Everyone at that date was having trouble distinguishing both adults and young of Salmon and Trout. Today we have Salmon *Salmo salar* and Trout *Salmo trutta*. Yarrell ended up with a Salmon *Salmo salar*, a Grey Trout *Salmo eriox*, a Common Trout *Salmo fario* and a Salmon Trout *Salmo trutta* – and they were just the adult fishes. The names of immature fishes of this family proliferated.

Salmo trutta, *Linnaeus, the Salmon Trout in* A History of British Fishes, 1841, 2: 77, *introduced by Yarrell as 'of the migrating species in this country, the next in value to the Salmon. It is most abundant in the rivers of Scotland, and its flesh is excellent.'*

Yarrell tackled problems that other authors preferred to ignore; for example, in the introduction to his fish book, he discussed the evidence for the senses of fishes – touch, hearing, taste and smell (Introduction xvi–xix). He also received several fishes for which he could find no description or synonymy and gave them a name, though some were subsequently corrected when it was found another naturalist had forestalled him.

After Yarrell completed the second edition of his *A History of British Fishes* in 1841, he virtually had no competition in this field until 20 years later, when Jonathan Couch's *A History of the Fishes of the British Isles* was published in 1860–65 with 252 coloured plates. Despite this, in British newspapers Yarrell was being quoted as the authority well into the 20th century whenever readers raised questions about fishes.

When compiling the text for both of his books, before he even wrote a profile for each species he needed to record the physical description; known localities for distribution with reference to the people sending specimens and information; each reference in books and journals with a record of which author, title, volume, page, but not dates of publication; a drawing made for the wood engraver and notes of where there had already been an illustration published. There was a vast amount of time and careful organisation required for all these aspects, but he also had lists sent to him of fishes and birds by county or smaller districts that correspondents lent to him, and they had to be thanked, with some comments made by Yarrell in letters posted daily.

From 1834 to 1843 was a period of intense activity for Yarrell while he concentrated on getting his two great works published that quickly followed one another. His correspondence increased vastly at the same time, with notes about fishes and then birds being sent to him not just by friends and other naturalists but complete strangers. Yarrell was assiduous in dealing with the letters, the queries they raised, and appreciation of new information received. It was time consuming and wearisome. There is just one hint in all the extant correspondence that Yarrell was weary of the burden of so much writing and information pouring in. He told Jardine in December 1836 that some 'fishes had arrived from Agassiz, delayed by Customs and one third went to B[ritish] M[useum]', another third was for him and he was now adding a third for Jardine as he 'is too tired to cope with fish in spirits'. Yarrell added that he 'had no chubb and had asked Gould, who is a zealous angler, to get one'.[17] Yarrell had been aged 50 when he began work on publishing *A History of British Fishes* in 1834/5 and was nearly 60 when he finished his *A History of British Birds.* When his work for several societies was added to his production of articles with discoveries and experiments prompted by his anatomical studies of specimens for his books, the workload was immense, not to mention his Jones and Yarrell business responsibilities.

Despite the effort in publishing his books, Yarrell also had 55 articles

a. Cleaning boat
b. Two men river fishing
c. Gentleman and lady fishing
d. Boy and girl fishing
e. Polperro harbour, home of Dr Jonathan Couch
f. Flying fish fantasy

PLATE 4 FISH VIGNETTES

published in journals in the 1830s. Many were notes of species added to the British fauna, but there were also longer articles with original anatomical details. They included species new to science as well as the British fauna, e.g. 'On two species of Mammalia new to Britain, one of them (*Sorex remifer*) new to science.'[18] Between 1828 and 1853 he notified journals of seven new species and four articles with species new to Britain, and they were of mammals as well as fishes and birds. Such startling new discoveries were slipped in among short suggestions on the preservation of Crustacea, the growth of Salmon in fresh water, the change of plumage of Pheasants, organs of voice in a new species of wild swan, and many more. In handling so many specimens for his fish and bird books, Yarrell was coming across anomalies and curiosities that not only aroused his interest but impelled him to find the reasons for them.

One deviation from birds and fishes occurred following the invasion of a sawfly that killed turnip plants in six counties in 1834. This was an important staple crop in the countryside. Yarrell pointed out that applied entomology had important economic influences and suggested some methods of insect control.[19]

The highlight of the year 1834 for many naturalists was the BAAS meeting in Edinburgh in September. During the meeting, the botanist Dr Robert Graham asked Yarrell and Jenyns to dine with him at his house in Great King Street along with Dr Robert Kaye Greville. Yarrell would have been pleased to get to know two more northern naturalists. After the BAAS meeting, Yarrell joined Gould and Jenyns to visit P. J. Selby at Twizell House. This coincided with the anniversary of the Berwickshire Naturalists' Club, that had been founded by Dr George Johnston, and Selby gave a grand dinner party at a late hour on 17 September for the members plus his BAAS guests Yarrell and Jenyns. Selby gave the Presidential address and reported to Jardine afterwards that Jenyns & Yarrell had been much pleased with their visit, the former delighted with the Dean and Burns, so different from anything they had in Cambridgeshire. 'Dean' is a Northumbrian name for a ravine, not to be found in flat Cambridgeshire.

Selby was slightly ahead of his naturalist friends in that he had been publishing his *Illustrations of British Ornithology in their full natural size* since 1819 and was to finish it in this year. He had drawn most of the birds himself and then proceeded to etch them, having learnt to etch from his brother-in-law who had been to Newcastle to learn how to etch from Bewick. At the time

Selby was issuing his book, his brother-in-law, a jovial captain in the navy, Robert Mitford, who rose to become an admiral, stayed at Twizell House frequently. At this early stage in his career, he was a great help to Selby in etching 16 clearly signed plates for him.

The ability to draw was a great asset for any naturalist. Selby and Jardine were very good draughtsmen, and Yarrell could draw detailed studies of any species and then employed wood engravers to create illustrations from his own drawings for his books. Gould could do rough sketches and plan the composition of each plate, then his wife Elizabeth made the drawings and paintings from which she lithographed the stones for Hullmandel to print from. Jenyns did not illustrate his book about British vertebrates and, though a meticulous collector and organiser of facts, he confessed, 'My own utter inability to draw was a far greater disadvantage to me as a Naturalist, than not being a shot.' It is noteworthy that Darwin, in his autobiography, laments the same deficiency in himself, saying how the possession of this art would have assisted him in his natural history investigations.[20]

Both Jardine and Selby could also etch, but none of Selby's other (Jardine was absent) guests to the Twizell House party could, so seeing the process of etching would have been a novel experience for them if Selby had demonstrated it. Yarrell would have seen how much work etchers put into their illustrations. It was far too expensive to have plates engraved on copper or lithographed onto stones by professionals, so the alternative chosen by nearly all of the natural history authors was to etch their own plates. They then faced the need to get the plates printed and hand-coloured. The colouring was a large part of the cost of producing the plates. (When costing their plates in *Illustrations of Ornithology*, Jardine told Selby 'The expense of colouring is the only thing I am the least afraid of.'[21]) There was a small additional cost where a significant number of different colour washes had to be applied. The paper of the illustrations became cockled and rippled and had to be hot-pressed to flatten it. Yarrell acquired first-hand experience of this when in 1837 he mediated between Henslow in Cambridge and the excellent colourist Gabriel Bayfield in London, who had sent in a bill for 25/- per hundred plates for colouring and hot pressing four sets of 250 plates. If, in the unlikely event Yarrell had not known the cost of coloured, separate, plates before, he was aware of it now.

By choosing the use of uncoloured wood engravings, Yarrell avoided the most costly part of the operation for authors using coloured illustrations –

the cost of colouring. A further advantage was that the wood engraving was printed down on the page with the text – and not on separate plates often on a different grade of paper. Many of Yarrell's wood engravings are exquisite, some of the best in any natural history book, because he could afford to employ the best wood engravers in London, the Thompsons (see p.161).

However, Yarrell compounded his own problems over research by making his books histories of his species. That meant a great array of classical texts on his shelves. Some of these he listed in his synonyms, others he mentioned in the text. With the birds, he added another complication when he peppered his text with known localities in European countries. This involved buying foreign bird books and periodicals. As a bookseller himself, he knew how to source these and each Monday, his day to do business in town, he would have called on Baillière (see p.18) to find out what was being published abroad. We know he purchased copies of *Annales des Sciences Naturelles* for Jenyns and he would probably have scanned them to find out the latest news of activities in Europe, as this journal was not in his library in 1856.

Yarrell provided the names of authors and their titles but a criticism that can be levelled at him quite legitimately is that he did not give a date of his sources for synonyms, though he provided dates for some recent publications in his text. Nor did he provide a bibliography.

As he published each title in parts over several years, having new information being sent to him weekly, if not daily, keeping the text up to date was a problem. He issued single sheets of updates for his buyers to insert before their parts were bound up. He also attempted to keep pace by issuing supplements in between editions.

Despite the immense wealth of detail for many fishes not before known or admitted as British, the 'species' that attracted most attention in the newspapers for the next 80 or more years was the whitebait. Before 1890 there were 40+ such queries printed in newspapers asking what was whitebait? Yarrell was the accepted authority on British fishes so it was upsetting that he had, reluctantly one suspects, decided that whitebait was a distinct species. These little unspotted, unmarked, white fishes, 2–6 in long, shoaled in vast numbers in the Thames between the end of March and September, at which time feasts of the floured and fried fry were enjoyed by the Lord Mayor, Cabinet Ministers, Royal Society members and other eminences at annual dinners. Yarrell proved that the fish could not be Shad, because those spawned later, but they resembled the young of the *Clupea* clan – Herrings, and among them some little Sprats occasionally swam. Yarrell tried to keep some whitebait long enough to grow into adult fishes and so reveal what they were, but that failed when they all died. So, fatefully, he named them *Clupea alba* and set off a long debate about whether they were a separate species or the young of some, as yet unproven, other species. Today, people still enjoy eating delicious whitebait, but ichthyologists know they are the young fry of various species of Herring, Sprat, etc. So, however famous is an author, however revered for his monumental work and achievements, it is a failure for which he may best be recorded.

*Whitebait, caught in considerable quantities in the Thames by a particular mode of fishing with an unlawful net,* A History of British Fishes, 1841, 2: 202 and 2: 207. *'The mesh of the bag-end of the net was very small. The boat was moored in the tide-way, where the water was 20–30 feet deep, and the net on a wooden frame was attached to the side of the boat.'*

When under pressure while issuing both the fish and bird books, Yarrell wrote an uncharacteristically irritable letter to Jenyns about a Neville Wood who, he said, 'has served me just as he had served you – sent me 2 or 3 unpaid letters and a number of the Analyst which cost me 3.6d carriage, which I could have bought for 1/1d – got me see into an opinion on his nomenclature and then wanted me to write and give him for his work an account of the anatomy of the British birds. He is one of the greatest bores I ever knew, and has written to Mudie, Leadbeater – Gould - Pierce [*sic* = Prince] Gould's Clerk –

asking for their opinions on Systems, value of Genera, modes of preservation etc. with a promise to put all their opinions in his forthcoming ornithological work. I know nothing of him except by his letters, but as he is very fond of long communications – and you are now quite at leisure – you can bestow upon him as much of your time and as many of your opinions on systematic arrangement, value of genera – and rules for nomenclature, as you now think him entitled to.' There was a short follow up to this exasperated outburst on 20 November 1836. 'Your friend Neville Wood is, I hear, only 18 years old, the coolest [sic] hand of his age I should think you ever knew. When referring to his own novel nomenclature he calls it that of the modern systematists.'[22] Gould was asked, as a favour by John Natterer of Vienna on 1 Jan 1837, to purchase 'Neville Wood Esqre the ornithologist's text book'.[23] Gould remarked to Jardine 'The English nomenclature of our birds will certainly admit of reformation but then it should only be done by very skillful [sic] hand, and not as it has been done by Neville Wood!!!' Wood, who lived at Campsall Hall, near Doncaster in 1837, hoped for a paper from Gould for his short-lived periodical *The Naturalist* (published 1837–39).[24] Gould was trying to sell parts of one of his books to Wood who thanked him for several parts, which he used, then duly returned them and asked for parts 13-16 to be sent.[25]

Yarrell wanted to see some drawings of British Eels by Mrs Lee so he called on her in August 1835.[26] She was an accomplished fish artist who worked from newly caught specimens to preserve the skin colours in her paintings. She used watercolours, silver and gold foil. She cultivated fishermen with whom she could make acquaintance and got them to catch fresh specimens for her to draw on the spot. Dr George Johnston wrote to Yarrell 'Last week I had a very pleasant comely and accomplished friend of yours – Mrs Lee, who came here to make a drawing of the Bull Trout. I was fortunate to procure her a very fine specimen in the most perfect condition. Of her figure I may remark that there is something about the head that does not please me what it is I cannot distinctly say – but otherwise it is very correct. I got Mrs Lee to do me a drawing of our Parr also, because whenever I saw her Parr I at once declared it was not Parr at all, & I am still of that opinion. On comparison with ours hers is an inelegant trout-like fish & I verily believe is no more than some odd looking trout generated in your filthy Thames. Ours is a genteel active finely proportioned creature, as different from the trout as a lady of fashion from a country lass. Please do look at it.'[27]

Mrs Lee, born Sarah Wallis, married Edward Bowditch (1790–1824) whom she assisted with *An introduction to the Ornithology of Cuvier for the use of Students and Travellers,* published in Paris. She married, secondly, Robert Lee, in 1826. Mrs Lee wrote the biography of Cuvier the year after he died (issued in 1833). When Jenyns wanted to know about specimens in European museums, Yarrell suggested he contact Mrs Lee, who could tell him about the Paris Museum where Cuvier worked. Yarrell owned a copy of Cuvier's prospectus for his *Histoire Naturelle des Poissons,* in which on page 20 he mentioned how many species and specimens he had and that there were 6,000 specimens in the King's collection from which he was doing his research and expected more by the time he published.

The Vendace was proving troublesome. Jardine had found it in a loch at Lochmaben and was convinced it was a new species. He persuaded Yarrell to give it the name *Coregonus Willughbii* (HBF 1841, 2: 146). 'I have adopted your suggestions of calling the Vendace Cor. Willughbii.'[28] It is now known that this species (*Coregonus albula*) is widely distributed in northern Europe and the English Lake District, but at the time Jardine and Yarrell were writing it was thought to be unique, not just in British waters, but anywhere.

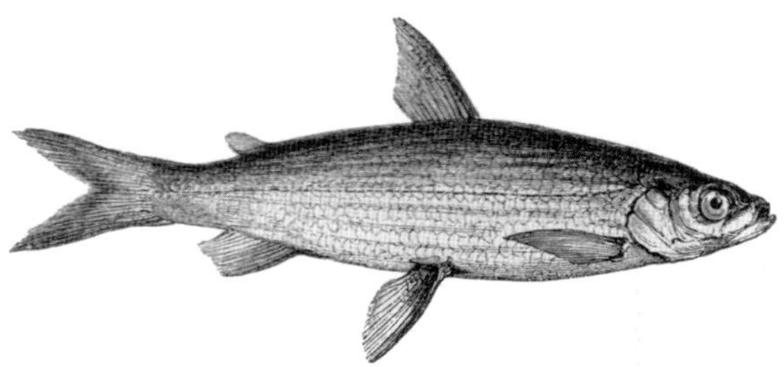

*The Vendace* Coregonus Willughbii, *Jardine, Illustrations of Scottish Salmon, pl. 6. Yarrell's* A History of British Fishes, 1841, 2: 146.

In September or October 1835 Yarrell wrote Jardine a detailed account of another muddle – this time over naming *Cygnus bewickii.* He stated 'The name originated with me, no one has, or can deny it; the anonymous writer of the article in Taylor's Philosophical Journal for August admits it – Mr Selby admits it – I have in my answer quoted his own words – Mr Hutton of Newcastle has written to me to say that he was the writer of the anonymous articles and acknowledged he had written it under a wrong impression – in addition to this I have now a copy of the Newcastle Transactions in which Mr Wingate's remarks are recorded without a name and I find by the represented figure of their own specimen that it is only a very young bird & I feel myself justified in believing that without the full foolscap sheet of materials I supplied them with they could not have made out their subject – how then, may I not fairly ask, can this be called the Bewickii of Wingate? But to turn to a more agreeable subject for I hate controversy.'[29]

So here was the background information about the counter claims that Wingate had discovered and named the bird. What did Yarrell do about this when he published the account of *Cygnus bewickii* in his *A History of British Birds*? He accounted for the specimens that he had collected and the fact that he had 'preserved and prepared the trachea and part of the bones of a young Wild swan shot in this country, which possessing peculiarities I had never observed in the bones of the hooper at any age, induced me to believe it would prove to belong to a distinct species'. That was in 1824–5 and he waited for more specimens and his dissections of those to exhibit at the Linnean Society meeting on 24 November 1829, 'where I proposed to call it Bewick's Swan as a distinct new species. Mr Richard Wingate, of Newcastle, had obtained specimens, and observing the difference between them and the hooper, read a notice upon the subject, at the Natural History Society at Newcastle, and as he was one of the oldest as well as one of the warmest friends of Thomas Bewick, immediately adopted the name I had proposed. It is gratifying to observe that Mr Temminck, who is acquainted with the merits of Bewick's works, has set the example on the Continent and adopted this name also.' Having given

*'Head of Hooper Swan' and 'Head of Bewick's Swan' showing the main external difference between the two swans.* A History of British Birds 1843, 3: 101 and 104.

Wingate due recognition, and '*Cygnus bewickii* Yarrell' was accepted as the correct name. It is now *Cygnus columbianus.*

Nomenclature presented problems for these 19th century authors that we can hardly begin to comprehend today. Jardine suffered the same time-consuming efforts to find all the synonyms for each species as did other ornithologists. He told Selby he had to spend days hunting through his library to find all the names already recorded for each species. He tried to solve the problem by collecting coloured drawings and plates and putting them in scientific order by genera and species. It meant purchasing the parts of books as issued, taking them apart for the plates, then buying them again when the complete books were published. The basic requirement for an authorised list just for British birds was not resolved until 1883 with the publication by the British Ornithologists' Union of the first edition of a checklist of the Birds of Great Britain and Ireland. The ichthyologists are still waiting, relying on textbooks of British fishes.

Jardine had not been alone in attempting to put together a complete pictorial record of all the known birds. William Swainson was repeatedly asking other authors for copies of their plates and Eyton also had a collection. Gould attempted it by asking an artist, Newton, to make drawings for him. One unfortunate casualty of these collections was when Audubon's plates were included. Being too large for the usually folio or quarto format of the albums, Audubon's double elephant folio plates were cut down to the size of the album. Yarrell also had collections of plates, but by using uncoloured wood engravings he did not need to constantly rely on coloured plates. He relied on texts and the plates in his library to provide the evidence for his classification.

Jenyns' *A Manual of British Vertebrate Animals* was published in 1835. The nomenclature in this book could have acted as the template for names of British species, but, for some reason, it did not. A note has been made in this text of the extensive communications and collaboration between Yarrell and Jenyns before his manual was printed. In the Preface the author acknowledged his friends' help, writing: 'To Mr Yarrell in particular, he begs publicly to return his sincere thanks for the able help which he had experienced at his hands, and such as alone has enabled him to complete the work upon the plan first contemplated. This help has been especially felt upon the subject of the British fishes. Had it not been for the very liberal manner in which that gentleman offered him the almost unlimited use of his manuscripts and rich collections, the author has no hesitation in saying that he could never have extended the manual to that department or presumed to enter upon a field to which he was previously almost an entire stranger. Assistance, however has been not the less afforded him in other Classes. Mr Yarrell's well-known practical acquaintance with our British Birds has enabled the author to detail more at length the change of plumage to which some species are liable, and to correct a few errors into which previous writers have fallen on this subject. The same gentleman kindly volunteered an accurate description, accompanied by measurements, of the egg of every species, of which his extensive collection afforded specimens; thus enhancing the utility of the work by the addition, which, but for the circumstance, the author would have been unable to supply. He begs that it may be distinctly understood that this portion of it is from the pen of Mr Yarrell.' It was generous of Jenyns to spell out the extent of Yarrell's assistance, but it was also well deserved.

One of Yarrell's major contributions to science was when he proved how the related pipefishes and seahorses breed. At a meeting of the Zoological Society Yarrell exhibited a dissected specimen of the male Greater Pipe-fish

*Seahorse of the* Hippocampus *genus, the males of which Yarrell found carrying fertilized eggs in an abdominal pouch.* A History of British Fishes, 1841, 2: 452.

*Syngnathus acus* containing in its pouch the ova from the female. This was reported in the *Morning Post* on 26 November 1835, whose editor at this time took a close interest in the meetings of the Zoological Society and reported

Yarrell's discourses, among other naturalists' papers. It is interesting to see how often Gould read a paper when Yarrell was in the chair at these meetings.

In 1836 Yarrell completed his *A History of British Fishes* - notable in that it was the earliest of a series establishing a format used several times by Van Voorst, his publisher. From July 1837 to May 1839 his *A History of British Birds* was issued in 36 bi-monthly parts. This proved to be another great success, much valued and admired owing to its accuracy of information and the charm and fidelity of the wood engravings. It proved to be an important landmark in British ornithology by being the first scientific textbook on British birds of deep scholarship, and from 1837 until 1899, in successive editions, it was the greatest standard reference British bird book.

Yarrell's *A History of British Birds* was welcomed in the press and now enjoyed favourable references in even more newspapers than his fish book. Birds were the favourites and the response to his new work brought in many more records of sightings and localities, habits such as nesting and details of eggs, with the times of year when the birds were seen.

There was further evidence of the generous sharing of information from bird watchers and ornithologists. Private compilations of catalogues of birds seen in individual English counties were sent to Yarrell from Norfolk and Suffolk, Oxfordshire, Orkney and Shetland, Devonshire, Lancashire, Leicester and the Midland Counties, Lincolnshire and Cumberland. When Yarrell told Sir William Jardine that he was concerned that he knew little of the birds of Scotland, Jardine promptly sent him his own list of the birds he knew had been sighted in the whole of Scotland.

There is a long list of people (at least 130) who sent Yarrell information about birds, besides information he collected from books and magazines. Jenyns, in his *Reminiscences of Yarrell,* expressed the view that much of Yarrell's 'knowledge of birds was obtained from public and private collections, where they might be seen, either in the living state, as at the above gardens, or preserved as at the British or other museums. He was well acquainted with birds in the hand, and thoroughly understood their variations of plumage according to age and season. But living so much in town, he was under a disadvantage in respect of getting well acquainted with the habits of our British species...' Jenyns overlooked Yarrell's formative years spent in the Hertfordshire countryside, with subsequent frequent visits there and to Cambridgeshire and Essex for at least 30 years after he was in business in a London residence from 1803. At all times, Yarrell received news and notes from agents who collected skins and taxidermists who kept an eye open for unusual species. His old Hertfordshire associates kept in touch with him, especially Joseph Trigg, who shot a Rock Thrush sitting in an ash tree at Therfield and took it to John Newman of Royston to be stuffed. Joseph Clarke of Saffron Walden continued to send Yarrell fishes and birds long after Yarrell was no longer able to visit the countryside frequently. From all the correspondence, Yarrell spent months sifting the evidence of appearances and locations of birds, and sorting the multiplicity of local names, habitats, diets and nesting routines.

Yarrell lost one of his oldest and closest friends when Edward Turner Bennett died in 1836. They had been members together of the Linnean and Zoological Societies (*q.v.*). To Jenyns, Yarrell said he had consulted Bennett, who was the best London authority he knew, about Cuvier's *Serranus gigas*, the

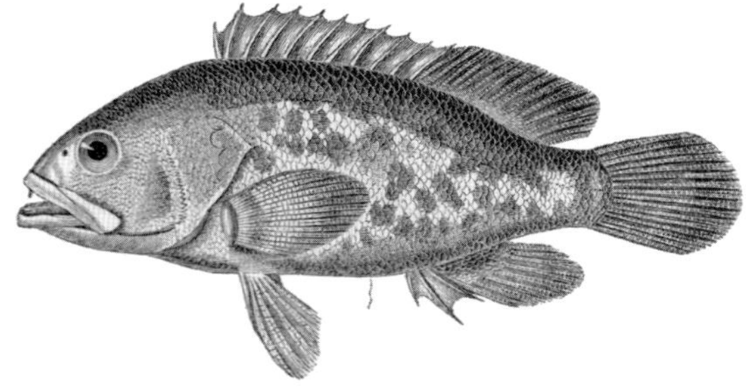

*The Dusky Perch of Couch and Cuvier shown in a detailed wood engraving in* A History of British Fishes, 1841, 1: 14.

Dusky Serranus, a specimen having been drawn and engraved from Cuvier's figure of his 'Dusky Perch' (which last name is the one used today). It still is a rare fish in northern European waters. Yarrell reluctantly took on Bennett's duties as secretary of the Zoological Society for the next two years when he already had more than enough to do.

Sir William Jardine, Selby and Dr Johnston were editing a new *Magazine of Zoology and Botany* in 1836 and Jardine had a happy thought – he sent Yarrell 'two ichthyological plates which we have had In the Magazine, as you may wish to put them in your collection of figures and authorities of Brit. Species. I shall keep impressions for you as we go on for it is more than probable that an Ichthyol. Paper will be with each No.'[30] Jardine had previously asked Yarrell to contribute articles to another new periodical, the *Edinburgh Geographical*

*Journal*, only to receive the half-serious reply from Yarrell who said he 'knew not how to answer'. He was happy to comply 'but what will one or two of our Southern Editors say or think of me?'[31]

Edward Jesse was an occasional correspondent and had a kind, if ungrammatical, thought for Yarrell in a letter of 20 September 1836, in which he wrote: 'I am going out with the prawn fishers to try if I cannot add a new fish to your supplement. Pray take care of the Carpio Mexicanus until I see you & I wish you was here to go out with me. I hope your sister is better.'[32] Jesse was a member of the Walton & Cotton Club (*q.v.*), soon to be joined by Yarrell.

On 2 October 1836 Darwin returned home from the *Beagle* voyage and Yarrell soon after took him as a visitor to a Linnean Society meeting. Darwin brought home many specimens, some probably preserved as Yarrell had taught him. They included birds, mammals, fishes and insects, also more easily transported rocks and shells. Darwin needed help to describe and identify each item and now the network of naturalists, that had widened and strengthened while he had been away for five years, came into operation. When he left England in 1831 he would have regarded John Gould merely as the Zoological Society's taxidermist. In the meantime, Gould had not only published a book on the birds of the Himalayan region but was engaged in issuing parts of *The Birds of Europe* (1832–37). Darwin's Cambridge colleague Leonard Jenyns had published his book on British vertebrates (including fishes) in 1835 and Yarrell was near the end of issuing his book about the history of British fishes. Darwin had to catch up with all of these events.

In April 1837 Darwin consulted Jenyns following the urgings from several zoologists to publish an account of the zoology of the *Beagle* specimens. McLeay in particular, but Gould, Bell, Waterhouse, Owen and Hope were all in favour. It would be an enormous undertaking, with several people involved, for Darwin did not want to research all of the specimens and not being able to draw he would need illustrators and engravers or lithographers for the illustrations. Darwin informed Jenyns: 'I mean tomorrow to see Mr Yarrell; if he approves, I shall begin and take more active steps; for I hear he is most prudent and most wise.'[33] The next step, following Yarrell's response, which apparently was favourable, was to choose the men to take on each section: birds, fishes, reptiles, mammals and geology.

T. C. Eyton, a fellow Cambridge University friend from college days, was a correspondent of Darwin and made him aware of John Gould's bird books.

Through the Zoological Society Darwin made contact with Gould and enlisted him to deal with the birds. The resulting third volume of the five for Darwin's *Zoology of the Voyage of H.M.S. Beagle 1832–36* (edited by C. Darwin 1838–41) has illustrations by John and Elizabeth Gould on 50 bird plates, sketched by John and lithographed by her.

The part with the fishes from Darwin's expedition was dealt with by another Cambridge man, the Reverend Leonard Jenyns, well known to Darwin whose place he had taken on the *Beagle* when Jenyns felt he could not desert his parishioners. Jenyns admitted that no-one else had wanted to take on the fishes. There is a curious comment by Yarrell to Jenyns while he was working on the fishes. 'I am a little surprised that you do not have Darwin's fish at your own house; the advantage of having them worked out would surely be worth the trouble or expense of sending them from Cambridge to you and back.'[34] Yarrell may have forgotten that it was only some eight miles for Jenyns to ride his horse to Cambridge. Darwin consulted Yarrell on who to ask to do the drawings of the fishes and told Jenyns 'I do think he [Yarrell] has hit upon the right artist, namely W. Hawkins, who engraved the fish for Richardson's volume.'[35] Hawkins was duly engaged and Darwin informed Jenyns 'Yarrell kindly says he will help me in comparing the accuracy of the pencil outlines of the fish.'[36] Benjamin Waterhouse Hawkins had illustrated the fishes in John Richardson's landmark book *Fauna-Boreali-Americana or the Zoology of the Northern Parts of British America,* 4 volumes, 1829–37, collected during John Franklin's first Arctic expedition. Hawkins illustrated two of Darwin's zoological reports from the *Beagle,* on the fishes and reptiles.

In 1838 evidence of the cooperation between Darwin and Yarrell continued. Yarrell sent Darwin a Zoological Memorandum on the wild cattle at Chillingham Castle. In 1839 Darwin and Yarrell exchanged publications, Yarrell acknowledging a gift: 'Many thanks my dear Sir for your interesting volume [*Journal of Researches*], and in return I beg your acceptance of the 1st volume of the History of British Birds.'[37]

The close friendship between the young naturalist (Darwin was just out of college in 1831) and the highly respected older naturalist, Yarrell, led to Darwin consulting Yarrell from 1831 until Yarrell died in 1856. Evidence is to be found in the frequent mention of Yarrell's name in Darwin's species notebooks, his *Life and Letters* and de Beer's *Darwin's Notebooks.* Most important was Yarrell's focusing of Darwin's attention on domesticated pigeons that ranged in colour, the number of feathers and both shape and size of the bones. These alterations had occurred over the long period men had been breeding domesticated pigeons and were pertinent to Darwin's studies. Urged by Yarrell, Darwin took up pigeon keeping and learned a lot from his pigeons as well as enjoying the hobby of fancy pigeon keeping.

Richard Parnell began to correspond with Yarrell and was to prove a tremendous asset with his notes and records. He brought a youthful enthusiasm and sound education to the study of ichthyology. An early letter informed Yarrell of the 'salar and eriox having teeth along the vomer when small but lose them early', just the sort of close observation much loved by Yarrell.[38] Parnell was noted in the correspondence two years later as being a young physician studying medicine and ichthyology at Edinburgh, where he soon became known to Sir William Jardine with whom he became a copious correspondent. He visited Jardine at Jardine Hall near Lockerbie, who had been quick to value Parnell's ability and had him to stay with him when a Sturgeon was taken in the Bay during his visit. Parnell attended the BAAS in Newcastle in 1838, where he gave Yarrell a Cornish specimen of the rare *Cepola*, Red Bandfish or Red Snakefish.

P. J. Selby had taught Sir William Jardine how to etch in preparation for their joint publication *Illustrations of Ornithology*. They bought sheets of copper and etching ground that were sent to them from London, in order they could etch their own plates before taking them to W. H. Lizars in Edinburgh to be printed. In October 1836 Jardine was completing the manuscript and had etched the figures and written the text for the first number of a second series of their *Illustrations of Ornithology*, which was published the following February. It contained what they thought to be a new bird that Jardine had named *Crax yarrellii*, a Red-knobbed Curassow, for which Edward Lear had made the drawing from a living bird in the London Zoological Gardens. Jardine stated that E. T. Bennett had given the first description of this bird in his *Gardens and Menageries of the Zoological Society*, which had a woodcut of the Curassow and had queried the name of *Crax carunculata*? Jardine said that the bird in the gardens had died soon after the publication of Bennett's description and was dissected by Yarrell, who reported that the trachea exhibited several appearances differing from other known similar species, but mostly resembled *Crax allector* Linn.; while in the external characters the bird approached *Crax globicera* Linn. That is why a new name had been needed and allotted to this bird: *Crax yarrellii.* That is also why Jardine asked Gould, for whom Lear was currently working, 'Can Mr Lear furnish a drawing of Crax Yarrellii, it is a species.'[39] Lear had done four other drawings for this part of six plates, imperial quarto size, that sold for 12/6d, though the backgrounds were not coloured. The book was designed to illustrate both new species and those that had been described but not figured before, taken from living specimens wherever possible. (For an illustration of *Crax yarrellii* see p.117.)

Dr George Johnston was a contributor to Jardine, Selby and Yarrell in their books. He gave Yarrell a ringing endorsement when he heard that he had decided to publish a history of British birds: 'no one cd [could] do it better'. Johnston had sent Yarrell an irregular supply of fishes, including an Eagle Ray, with an occasional text correction. He would contribute far fewer birds. He thanked Yarrell for sending him copies of the *Annales des Sciences Naturelles,* which Jenyns also got from Yarrell, and thought this publication a 'real treat, especially when supplied so punctually' by Yarrell.[40] In 1838 he was appointed Mayor of the Borough of Berwick-upon-Tweed. The same year, however, was also a disappointing one. After just two years Johnston, Jardine and Selby's *Magazine of Zoology and Botany* failed for lack of support. It was taken over by Richard Taylor and survived in his hands.

In 1837 the Reverend Lambert B. Larking, of Ryarsh Vicarage near Maidstone, wrote to say 'Mr Leadbeater had told you I have a very ash-coloured falcon in a state of change' then gave the further news, 'Loxia coccothraustes Grossbeak has been completely naturalized for 3 or 4 years in my neighbourhood in Kent. I have the eggs. Children take their young and I see them in cages.' These were in fact Crossbills *Loxia curvirostra* (Larking was using an incorrect scientific name), and he wrote a long piece about them erupting in some years, starting with a visitation in England in 1593 which had arrived 'when the apples were ripe and villagers used the apples to shy at the birds and found them both good to eat'.[41] Yarrell repeated Larking's account under Common Crossbill in his *A History of British Birds* (2: 16), along with comments from all over the country where the crossbills had been seen in every month. He also noted that Audubon had taken the opportunity to compare the birds that had invaded England with those he knew in America and concluded the Crossbills were identical. Yarrell was constantly referring to, and quoting from, Jardine's edition of Alexander Wilson's *American*

*'The Common Crossbill'* A History of British Birds 1843, 2; 14, *present throughout the year in Britain, according to Yarrell, with temporary migrations of Continental birds, sometimes in great flocks as in the 1830s.*

*Ornithology*, 1832, and Audubon's plates *The Birds of America* and text *Ornithological Biography*, which had increased his awareness of the number of species that were seemingly identical on both sides of the Atlantic.

Another three letters from a complete stranger, William Euing, arrived, saying he had spent the summer near Rothesay on the Isle of Bute, and compared fishes he met with in Yarrell's *A History of British Fishes*. He 'packed the specimen of the small smelt in a small box to your address after receiving the fish, in the way you suggested, replacing it in the bottle of spirits'. He added that he had collected fish specimens for some years but had no guide as to identity until a friend lent him Donovan's work, but now he had *A History of British Fishes* by Yarrell. He sent a list of 51 species he had, plus the 'doubtful kinds' of sea fishes. He gave Yarrell permission to use his name but stressed that it was spelled 'Euing' not 'Ewing'.[42] These odd remarks are typical of so many letters that Yarrell received and to which he had to respond, but it was gratifying to be told fishermen found his book so useful.

Richard Lubbock, when a Vicar in Eccles, kept Yarrell informed of catches of both fishes and birds in Norfolk. Yarrell frequently paid tribute to the copious notes that the Reverend Lubbock sent to him. He also supplied this tidbit about the new Bishop of Norwich: 'We have heard in this diocese but one character of your friend the present Bishop of Norwich, that he is in every respect fitted for the station he is called upon to fill.' Edward Stanley (1779–1849), a long-standing friend of Yarrell, was appointed Bishop of Norwich in 1837 and not long after he was elected 4th President of the Linnean Society. Natural history was one of his pursuits and his *Familiar History of Birds* had been published in 1835 and was in Yarrell's library.[43]

The following December (1837) Lubbock notified Yarrell of his move from his Eccles parish to Larlingford, also in Norfolk. He was hoping to visit London soon and to meet Yarrell and noted that a fisherman said *Anguila mediorostris,* the Snig Eel, is to be found in some localities in Norfolk – he called it the Glazed or Michaelmas Eel. Yarrell devoted pages 399–401 in his fish book to the Snig Eel and said it most resembled the Sharp-nosed Eel that also had numerous 19th-century English and scientific names not used today. Lubbock further regretted that the Great Bustard was so rare in Norfolk that there was not even a specimen in the county museum.[44]

Eels held a certain fascination for Yarrell. On one memorable occasion Jenyns took him to see the stuffed skins of two huge Eels exhibited in a fishmonger's shop in Cambridge. They were each almost '6 feet long and together weighed more than fifty pounds. He gazed at them awhile in astonishment; and then after close inspection pronounced them to be his *Anguilla acutirostris.*'[45] Jenyns called the Sharp-nosed Eel 'his', i.e. Yarrell's, because the scientific name had been bestowed on it by Yarrell, albeit in Jenyns' *Manual of British Vertebrate Animals.*

Yarrell also discussed eels with his friend Marshall Hall, who explained why, during thunder storms, there were 'such enormous captures made in some rivers by the use of gratings, boxes, and eel-pots or baskets, which imprison all that

*A method of catching eels in the days when they were present in huge numbers. 'The Eelbuck' was placed on the Thames with the open end of each wicker basket 'opposed to the stream to entice the eel within'. Yarrell fished the Thames and would be familiar with these.* A History of British Fishes, 1841, 2: 386.

enter'. The Eels, through their skins, were highly sensitive to the atmospheric disturbance during a thunderstorm and sought shelter. In addition, Eels that became frozen in snow and ice could recover, if slowly, when put into warm water. Dr Hall also discovered that Eels have a pulsating sac near the end of their tails and Yarrell included a diagram of this feature in his section on the Sharp-nosed Eel in *A History of British Fishes* (1841, 2: 387).

George Ord, an English emigrant to America, while visiting London was present at a meeting of the Linnean Society in 1830, where he was introduced to Jenyns. There are no comments on what he and Yarrell thought of Ord, but one can imagine their conversation when next they met following Ord's letter in September 1837 to Yarrell, after he had heard about the publication of *A History of British Birds*. He made some extraordinary remarks to guide Yarrell for future parts of the book. 'Surely you will not repeat the fable of the Dipper's walking on the bottom of pools ... With regard to the Cuckoo, pray do not repeat Jenner's tale, unless you are enabled to confirm it after personal observation ... I do maintain, that no bird whatever, the day it is hatched can perform the feat which Jenner declared he saw a young Cuckoo achieve ... the story of the Partridge's running, as soon as hatched, with the egg-shell on its back, is a fable ...'[46] In the section devoted to the Cuckoo (*A History of British Birds* 1843, 2: 182–4) Yarrell quoted extensively from Dr Edward Jenner's paper in the *Transactions of the Royal Society*, 1788, where the close observation of a young Cuckoo's behaviour had been detailed.

In 1838 Ord returned to the attack: 'On the subject of your History of British Birds you say that it is not your intention to mark with reprobation the errors of others.' (Ord had suggested Yarrell did that in his letter of 14 Sep 1837 and Yarrell had evidently refused to comply with this proposal.) 'Why not, if done with decorous language, and in a becoming temper? It is a duty we owe to each other to take notice of mistakes in works of science, where it is to be presumed, our main object is the illustrations of truth...'[47] Ord and Yarrell were like chalk and cheese: one almost courting controversy with everyone; Yarrell detesting controversy.

Another American, Audubon, the French emigrant to America who was in England to get his book on American birds aquatinted, was sounding off about the same time as Ord. Audubon was irritated by anyone writing about birds while he was publishing, even if it were British birds that barely competed with his *American Birds*. One of his diatribes against other authors included Yarrell. He complained to his friend Bachman, 'Yarrell is publishing the British birds quarto size – and about one thousand other niny tiny works are in progress to assist in this mass confusion already scattered over the world.' What 'niny tiny' meant seems known only to Audubon.[48]

William Swainson opened up a correspondence with Yarrell in 1838. He wanted various things from Yarrell, including a specimen of *Cepola rubescens*, the Red Bandfish. Yarrell had given his specimens to Dr Parnell, but expected soon to receive a dried specimen from the Devonshire coast that he promised to send to Swainson.[49]

Yarrell was acquainted with Thomas Bell, who was a dental surgeon at Guy's Hospital and Professor of Zoology at King's College London from 1836–61. Bell was writing a *History of British Quadrupeds and Cetacea* to be published in a volume uniform with Yarrell's *A History of British Fishes* by Van Voorst. Yarrell referred Jenyns to 'the wrapper on the next no. of Mr Bell's Brit. Quads. that he and I intend completing the Brit. Vertebrata as soon as he has finished his present vol. He will do the Reptiles and I am going to try my hand at the Birds.'[50] A frustrated Yarrell, four years later, warned Jenyns, 'It is of little use asking Mr Bell for any specimens. I have never yet received British Quadrupeds. I lent him 12 months ago all my specimens of Lizards and Triton. I asked to have one example of the warty species to send to Thompson when

a

b

c

d

a. Laughing Gull
b. Laughing Gull colony disturbed by dog
c. Kittiwake
d. Common Tern
e. Black Guillemot

e

PLATE 5 SEA BIRDS

I was making up a parcel for him, but I did not get it. His time is very fairly occupied, and he is so good natured, you cannot be angry, though annoyed – he always promises but the things do not come. When you are in London next we must send him a note and go and fetch them.' [51]

Jardine subsequently sent a bottle of fishes to Yarrell with a share for Bell. It contained the largest example of Lesser Weever that Yarrell had ever seen. He suggested that 'M. Nilsson, professor of natural history at Lund, would welcome exchanges probably.'[52] Yarrell had written on *Syngnathi* in reference to remarks of M. B. Fries of Stockholm on that genus in the October number of the Annals ('Remarks on some species of *Syngnathus*' appeared in the *Annals of Natural History* 1839, 3: 81). Yarrell had several foreign correspondents who were professional naturalists, rather than amateurs. In *A History of British Fishes*, under *Syngnathus acus*, the Great Pipe Fish, Yarrell stated that he 'found a statement in reference to the sexes of *S. acus* which has since been confirmed by four Continental naturalists', then he detailed how the male differed from the female physically and held the eggs from the female in his pouch until they hatched.[53]

Yarrell confessed to one of those moments when he missed a golden opportunity. He told Jenyns he was pleased that he had made contact with the naturalist T. C. Heysham of Carlisle who had a particular interest in fishes, but this had raised a query, 'The Carlisle Market must have produced two species of marine trout – for there is no fact of which I am more certain than that the specimens I examined on the day I was there (but the supply was short) had only three teeth on the extreme anterior part of the vomer [there was a drawing of it here] and I have been angry with myself whenever I think of Carlisle for not bringing some away with me – I gossiped with the fish salesman and heard the same opinion that this fish never exceeds a pound and a quarter ... when this fish is twelvemonth older and has added another pound or more to his weight, he does not run up the fresh water at the same period with the young fish of the year and is no longer called, or allowed by them, to be a Whiting.' A tiny point (who else would remember how many teeth there were on a trout vomer?) but one he could not prove without the evidence left behind in Carlisle – a town now blighted by an irritating memory.[54]

In 1839 Yarrell's postbag was heavier than ever before. He was now receiving evidence of new locations of species from all over the country, not just fishes but birds as well. Supplements were needed to describe species newly added to the list of avifauna and fish records in the British Isles.

Thomas Campbell Eyton was a wealthy banker living at Eyton Hall, a handsome stuccoed residence in Eyton-upon-the-wild-moors, a small Shropshire village near Wellington. He used his yacht to investigate the oyster fisheries around the British Isles and was interested in dissecting and describing the anatomy of fishes. He also prepared his own specimens of birds. This led to his *A History of the Rarer British Birds*, published in 1836 with 80 wood engravings by a local wood engraver called John Mark. Eyton, like Yarrell, followed the precedent set by Bewick, using wood engravings of his bird figures and tail-pieces. He also named a number of ducks and described them for the first time in his *Monograph of the Anatidae* of 1838. He was generous, sending boxes of specimens and offered Yarrell his catalogue of where his birds were collected in the British Isles. He was always mindful of the cost of postage and conveyance of parcels and paid for their return to him when sent on loan.

Eyton was one of the Cambridge University group of naturalists including Henslow, Jenyns and Darwin, who were to advance the knowledge of zoology so much in the mid-19th century. He corresponded with all of them and many others mentioned here. He sent Gould boxes of birds with identification labels that Gould spent hours unravelling and correcting, and Yarrell received information on fishes when Eyton had been away on his yacht. His letters were scrawled, breathless, three sentences on a small page, but he was good-hearted and anxious to play a part in the London natural history scene. In 1839 he was writing an account of the 'pink colour of the feet, with remarks on nearly allied species, a hatching of Canada Geese and a new goose that had been described lately by Mr Bartlett at the Zoological Society closely allied to the Bean Goose, is it a species?' He promised to forward the eggs by the first safe conveyance, having already sent Lord Derby a pair 'which highly delighted him'. Next he had some Barnacle Geese laying and asked Yarrell if Hewitson had one to figure in his zoology – and of some Canada Geese too. Eyton also sent a prospectus of his lectures on birds, divided into eight orders, and thanked Yarrell for a Codfish.[55]

In his *A History of British Birds*, 1843, 3: 64, Yarrell recorded that on the 8 January 1839 'Mr Bartlett exhibited several species of Geese in order to illustrate a paper which he communicated to the meeting on the new British species of the genus Anser, for which he proposed the name of phaenicopus ...'. This is the name which Yarrell preferred for the Pink-footed Goose, in terms of its descriptive precision, though he carefully noted in his text that it was now known that the name *brachyrhynchus* Baillon had date preference and 'will be adopted by others'.

William Chapman Hewitson's *British Oology* was being issued over the period 1831 to 1838, published by Van Voorst. Yarrell would have been well aware of this publication, as Van Voorst would have told him about it. Hewitson already knew of the fine collection of eggs owned by Yarrell and had seen them.

Audubon wrote to Yarrell in 1839, just before leaving Edinburgh for the last time before sailing home to America. He had been 'in expectation of meeting with four persons of our acquaintance going to London and to whom I could give charge of the Breast bones of Swans which you kindly lent to me; being disappointed thus far, and fearing that you may be in immediate want of them, I have concluded to send them to you by the Steamer which leaves Leith tomorrow, and hope that you will receive them all in as good condition as when they were placed in my hands'. He reassured Yarrell with the words, 'I think that I can safely say, that if a specific difference exists between any two Birds, the differences are most obvious between the Cygnus bewickii and the hooper.'[56]

Audubon's *The Birds of America* had 435 aquatinted plates when he finished his four volumes. The 433rd plate included a *Spinus yarrellii*, a last-minute tribute to Yarrell. He also included it in his *Synopsis of the Birds of North America* as *Carduelis yarrellii*, the Yellow-faced Siskin (p.115). It comes from N.E. Venezuela and eastern Brazil and retains its tribute to Yarrell to this day.

Audubon told Yarrell, 'The 5th and last volume of my Ornithological Biographies will be out on the 1st of next month, and should I not at that time be ready to return to London, I will take care that Two Copies of it are placed into your hands, one for yourself, the other for my good friend Doctor Richardson, to whom I trust you will have easy means of conveying it. My Dear Wife is now as I conceive quite out of Danger, and sends you her best thanks for your kind enquiries respecting her health. The Rest of my Family are all well. How is your sister? Have you heard lately respecting the state of Health of the Good Earl of Derby? or anything from our young friend Lear?'[56]

When Gould set sail for Australia on 16 May 1838, Yarrell informed Jardine that 'Mr Prince is Gould's head man and he lives now in Gould's house in Broad Street, carrying on the [taxidermy and publishing] business, and sending a packet out to Gould every month.'[57] The packets to Gould have been preserved and are now in the Sydney Mitchell Library, Australia. Prince wrote an abbreviated account of everything he had done, whom he had visited with results of collecting a subscription or selling the next part, or, quite often, finding the person out necessitating another visit. He was literally scurrying all over London and finding it difficult to extract the money for the sale of Gould's books, especially from members of the aristocracy who would get annoyed at being pestered.

Contact with Prince was quickly established after Gould sailed for Australia. Prince not only wrote to Gould and called on Yarrell, but kept Jardine abreast with all that he was doing on Gould's behalf. Concerning Gould's *Report on Caprimulgidae* (Nightjars), Prince reported, 'I have had the plates carefully printed and colored by the original drawings and the part will be ready on Monday next. Mr Yarrell will be so good as to take 2 copies with him to Newcastle, one for yourself and one to be laid before the Meeting this latter copy Mr Gould wishes to present to the Association if they form any Collection of books etc. Mr Yarrell will also bring you Parts 3 & 4 of the Synopsis of the Birds of Australia which I hope will merit your approbation.'[58] Yarrell also took a parcel for Selby. All of the naturalists willingly carried packets to one another to save postage.

In February, March, April and September 1839, Edwin Prince had need to ask Yarrell for advice concerning Gould's affairs. He 'called on Mr Yarrell and asked his advice about Adv[ertising] your books as the time was now come when he recommended it to be done; he considers the best plan would be to insert it in the Sporting Mags, now, subsequently in the Nat hist Mags and then in the Edinb & Quart Rev; these 3 different kinds of publications being the most likely means of bringing it before all the classes of the public'. In September, Prince told Gould he had followed this advice and 'Agreeable to Mr Yarrells suggestion I have inserted the advt in the *Quarterly* but no effect yet'.[59]

In March Prince had a customer who needed tactful but firm handling. A client was wanting 10 per cent off one of Gould's titles and Yarrell said it would be better to let him have it for immediate payment because 'he could go to Longman's, Hatchard's etc and get any book on those terms, it was better to allow him 10 [% off] than a Bookseller 20 and I should be safe in so doing.'[60] Prince, in his monthly round up of news for Gould in Australia mentioned Caroline Yarrell's death, among other things. Occasionally, Yarrell availed himself of Gould's contacts abroad and saved himself postage on parcels. In one of his monthly reports to Gould, Prince noted: 'Some books and breast bones of Swans from Mr Yarrell to be forwarded to Temminck. Miss Yarrell died lately. Mr Yarrell continues to send you his Birds and has just sent the supplement to British Fishes.'[61]

Prince constantly needed to reassure Gould that his absence was not proving detrimental to his publications. 'In no instance have you been forgotten by your friends here - indeed they are frequently making anxious enquiries respecting you: have readily afforded me any assistance I may have required at their hands and several of them Mr Yarrell more particularly have made it a point to inform me of anything that came to their knowledge likely to affect your interest in any way, whether for or against.'[62]

Bonaparte, or the Prince of Musignano, used Gould, among others, to acquire books that he needed. 'The Prince requiring me to purchase several expensive books and the Booksellers not choosing to let me have them without paying the full price I mentioned the subject to Mr Yarrell who advised me to apply for a Ticket. Called on Mr Richardson several times, not finding him wrote a note on the subject and recd a reply desiring me to call after 5 P M: did so and was told the application should be laid before the committee but feared it would not be granted you being merely a publisher of your own works, informed Mr Yarrell of the result, he was very indignant and considered their conduct most unjust; he also very handsomely offered to get the books for me at Trade Price which liberality I of course availed myself of with thanks; indeed, as I think I mentioned in one of my former letters nothing can exceed the kindness of that gentleman, no opportunity of obliging or furthering your interest being forgotten.'[63] Dealing with more mundane affairs Prince reported: 'Paid Mr Yarrell's bill for papers sent to you to end of 1838 £1.11.6d'. At least Prince had free newspapers to read while living in Gould's house in Broad Street.[64]

The death certificate, issued on 30 May 1839, for his sister at 6 Ryder Street stated, 'Caroline Yarrell female 51 years old, spinster, died of 'Canser of the womb. Catherine Finch of 6 Ryder Street present at the death.' Following the death of their mother in 1812, Yarrell had probably taken responsibility for, and care of, Caroline. For several years before 1839 a number of Yarrell's friends had enquired after Caroline's state of health, having met her in Little Ryder Street where she may have acted as hostess and supervised the preparation of his many dinners. Her illness had sometimes curbed his activities so he was freer now, but when he buried Caroline at Bayford, he also had to come to terms with the uncomfortable fact that of all his immediate family of two parents and 12 children, he was now the only one left alive.

News of Gould was exchanged between Jardine and Yarrell among other items. 'Gould is making a large collection in Australia and then in Van Diemen's Land with Sir John Franklin.'[65] This was one item in a long letter from Yarrell covering a wide range of topics with gossip and news and offers of help to sell Jardine's beautiful full-size pictures of Salmon in his book just published. Yarrell had received a packet with two copies or sets of the first six plates of *Salmonidae* and delivered one to the library of the Linnean Society, exhibited the other at a meeting of the Zoological Society and 'shown it to Lord Cole and others of the fish loving or fish catching fraternity whose visits I occasionally have here, and I shall most gladly promote the sale as far as my influence goes, but the class of buyers of books at three guinea parts, is, as you are aware, very limited'. Yarrell mildly complained that Jardine had not commented on the coloured illustration on the growth of Salmon he had sent to him. Agassiz had written and said the first part of 'his Fishes of Central Europe is on the road to this country'. Yarrell wanted to know more about Jardine's intended visit to London.

In April 1839, when writing to Lord Derby, the President of the Zoological Society, Yarrell mentioned (or reminded him of) the approaching anniversary of the Zoological Society. However, Yarrell's correspondence with Lord Derby was not confined to business matters. In May 1839 he sent Lord Derby a list of fishes which throve in fresh water, also a proof of his article on the growth of Salmon in fresh water.[66]

When Jenyns stayed with Yarrell in London, Yarrell planned these visits meticulously. In a letter of 20 January 1839 he said 'I shall hope to see you here at dinner by 5 o'clock on Monday Feby 4th; in the evening we can go to the meeting of the Entomological Society if you like; on Tuesday to the Linnean – on Wednesday there is a dinner, among the Entomologists, given to Doubleday and Foster, on their return from America, which we will either go to, or not, as you please – Thursday is a monthly meeting of the Zoological Soc. in Leicester Square, and devoting a little time each day to our own matters we shall thus get through a zoological week as usual.'[67]

That was Yarrell's idea of a holiday. Jenyns would not mind for he was every bit as well organised and 'In the company of Mr Yarrell I often dined at the Linnean Club, previous to attending the evening meeting of the society.'[68]

When the urgency for collecting specimens was past, in March 1845, Yarrell invited Mrs Jenyns to accompany her husband on his next visit to London. She was the eldest daughter of the Reverend Edward Anthony Daubeny of Eastington in Gloucestershire, whom he married in 1844. She was also the niece of Charles Giles Bridle Daubeney, a Professor, first of Chemistry and then of Botany, in Oxford, so she was accustomed to naturalists and their preoccupations.

The 1830s had seen a remarkable flow of 10 books about British birds. Such a flurry of publishing had never been witnessed before. Selby's *Illustrations of British Ornithology* – just plates and then separate text, came out between 1819 and 1834. The slight volume of R. Sweet's *The British Warblers* saw a 7th edition in 1832, while Thomas Bewick's *A History of British Birds* was also a 7th edition in 1832. R. Mudie's *The Feathered Tribes of the British Isles* in 1834 was followed in 1835 by J. Cotton's *The Resident Songbirds of Great Britain* in 2 volumes. Then, in the middle of this flurry of bird books, came Yarrell's *A History of British Birds* in 3 volumes across 1835–43, at the same time as H. L. Meyer's *Illustrations of British Birds* in 4 volumes with delicate watercolour paintings. There had been a plan to produce Yarrell's and Meyer's books complementing each other, but that fell through. Yarrell was highly organised and delivered his manuscripts on time to Van Voorst. It may have been wishful thinking on the part of Longman, Meyer's publisher, because the Meyers were raising children and still adding to their family so it would be difficult to maintain the schedule of two-monthly parts. A useful by-product of this failed arrangement was Mary Anne Meyer's having had access to Yarrell's egg collection for the egg that was painted for each species in her husband's book. (For details see W.G. Hale, *The Meyers' Illustrations of British Birds*, 2007.)

T. C. Eyton used wood engravings in the manner of Bewick to illustrate his *A History of the Rarer British Birds discovered since the time of Bewick*, issued in 1836. The scholarly but far less attractive *A History of British Birds* by William MacGillivray in 5 volumes began in 1837 but suffered from the competition and he did not complete it until 1852. MacGillivray was never friendly with the other naturalists, remaining isolated in Edinburgh and then Aberdeen. Finally, Sir William Jardine published the small volumes of the Naturalist's Library, including the 4 volumes of *Birds of Great Britain and Ireland* 1839–42. When Yarrell had been notified in 1837 by Jardine that he proposed to write about British birds for the Naturalist's Library, Yarrell's courteous reply was 'I am

*The Hooded Crow,* A History of British Birds, 2: 83.

quite of your opinion that we need not interfere with each other, and I hope we shall find room enough for both. It is my intention to paddle my own canoe along my own way, and if possible, without jostling or even splashing anyone.'[69] In the Sale catalogue of Yarrell's library, there was a lot for all of these books.

How had Yarrell's book on British birds stood up to the competition? A glance at the number of subsequent updates and new editions (see p.157) provides the answer. His was the standard text for the rest of the century. Through Yarrell's contacts with newspapers all over the country, who knew him as a well-known newsagent in London, each new part of one of his books, and every completed volume, was noted in newspapers from the Shetlands down to Cornwall across to the east coast, also in Ireland and Wales. The publicity for his works was enormous – with hundreds of references from 1834 until well into the 20th century. Those in the last century were when readers' enquiries reached editors about fishes and birds, and Yarrell was still being quoted as the authority until mid-century. In British Newspaper Archives, there are 7,390 notifications and articles, published between 1750 and 1999, with the name Yarrell in them. Discounting the small percentage for other people named Yarrell, a property named 'Yarrells', and a larger percentage of references that were to his firm, 'Jones and Yarrell', that still leaves some thousands of entries for him and his books.

*The egg of the Royston Crow painted by Mary Ann Meyer from Yarrell's egg collection (by courtesy of W. G. Hale). The Hooded Crow was so abundant around the small town of Royston in Hertfordshire that it was given this name there. The local newspaper was named* The Royston Crow *when founded by John Warren in 1855. It is now a weekly newspaper.*

*Portrait in oils of William Yarrell, 1839, by Margaret-Sarah Carpenter, A.R.A. (1793–1872). By courtesy of the Linnean Society.*

## Chapter 5
# THE 1840S: CONSOLIDATING

The letters in this decade are diverse in content, covering all the interests of Yarrell and his close friends. The activities of those friends are related with news of their researches and publications. Queries abound, and not just on natural history matters. Gould is still abroad and his affairs continued to give his secretary Prince problems that he needed Yarrell to help solve. Gould had issued strict instructions to Prince that he was not to open any packets or barrels sent from Australia or to let any other naturalist view them, so when some obviously damp barrels arrived early in 1840 Sir William Jardine and Yarrell were both consulted. Prince reported to Gould that 'they have suggested that the barrells should be opened and the contents examined, did so and I regret to say found many of them so much decomposed that I fear they will be useless. Mr Yarrell recommended that the good specimens should be separated from the bad, placed in a Barrell by themselves and the barrell filled up with pure Sprs [=spirits] of Wine, which has been done at the cost of Four gallons of Spirit @ 19/6 per gall.'[1]

Prince further conveyed to Gould the alarming news of Lord Derby's paralytic stroke in February 1840. 'He is a sad cripple the left side being perfectly useless.'[1] Despite this, Prince said his lordship looked remarkably well, and that he had asked after Gould. When he heard the news, Yarrell would have wondered how this was going to affect the Zoological Society, with its President now crippled and less able to travel up to London for meetings. The consequences were that Lord Derby was far less active in the affairs of the society and Yarrell, as a Vice-President, was more often in the chair at meetings. There were mutterings about Lord Derby's inactivity on occasions, but no-one could voice them to him and he remained President until his death in 1851.

When writing to Audubon a year after Lord Derby's stroke, Yarrell reported, 'Earl Derby remains much the same – very well in health, but deprived of use of one side entirely, limbs as well as body – unable to attend to other things, he appears to devote himself almost entirely to Zoology.' He added, 'Lord Derby came to London by the Rail Road last March [i.e. 1840] and Thompson tells me, His Lordship means to come up again this spring.'[2] Travelling on the new railroads was an adventure at this time, and Lord Derby, confined to a wheelchair, was brave to venture on a journey to London from Liverpool. Sir William Jardine recorded his first railway journey when writing to his wife, contrasting it with mail coach travel. In 1842 (while on his way to visit Yarrell) he took the train in Darlington to Euston Station, London, taking 'thirteen and a half hours, first class, for £3-8-0d'. He enjoyed the experience: 'In a most comfortable carriage being the front division of the first class Train (but separated from the engine by Her Majesty's mail-bags and another machine) containing two seats only ... Our luggage being placed over our heads and not touched until the end of the journey. It is the easiest and best conducted mail I have been on, and is quite a change in travelling, the whole character of the people about you different. No 'Sam Wellers', or ostlers or boys or porters who will work only as you pay them, all conducted very smoothly. No servants of any kind paid yet no want of attention. Dined at York, supped at Derby, at both stations extensive establishments and accommodation of all kinds.'[3]

The 'no Sam Wellers' referred to Dickens' *Pickwick Papers*' character, friend of Pickwick. Jardine also commented on the refreshment rooms that had been built at the stations that were 'capable of containing hundreds, the meals all ready, plenty of waiters and pages, and while there is no hurry, there is not a moment's delay; every drink even from small beer to champagne, rooms beautifully lighted at night, and cleanly painted and papered.' Despite the

*An 1842 first class railway carriage that would have been used by Sir William Jardine and Lord Derby to travel up to London.* Illustrated London News, *22 May 1847: 328.*

*In the early years of rail travel, flatbed trailers were provided on which the gentry could place their carriages and travel inside in comfort.*

presence of two huge hotels at Euston, a bed could not be had, so Jardine was 'obliged to content myself with a warm bath and a dressing room'.[3] For Lord Derby, another factor that would have delighted him was that it was far less jolting than in a horse-drawn carriage.

In September 1840 Yarrell passed a fortnight in Lancashire, Cumberland and Dumfriesshire, including four days at Jardine Hall while P. J. Selby was also there. When back home he would have a good deal of correspondence with which to catch up. The flow of correspondence not only provided evidence of new species of birds and fishes but of additional localities. Yarrell had no alternative to adding this new material in 2nd and 3rd editions and supplements to his two titles. He did not complete his *A History of British Birds* until 1843 and was then also issuing a supplement for *A History of British Fishes,* only two years after the 2nd edition appeared. The amount of detail for the birds was immense, not just the physical descriptions, but about where they could be found, variations in numbers present, information when migrants arrived and departed, and their presence in several Continental countries.

T. C. Eyton continued to send Yarrell news and bird specimens, though he expected Yarrell to take great care of them. He sent a hybrid (did not say of what) which Yarrell 'was welcome to figure and an engraver can take it out of its case if Yarrell supervised the operation'. Eyton also said he had been 'working at some birds for Darwin which are very curious'.[4]

Harry Lawrence, of Liverpool, decided to send Yarrell some comments on heronries, Barn Owl, Golden Plover and Long-legged Plover (= Black-winged Stilt), which Yarrell probably did not need. In a second letter two months later, he sent a handbill relating to a fish caught at sea near the mouth of the Dee and Mersey about May or June 1838, which agreed exactly with the description of the Opah in *A History of British Fishes.* This is typical of the letters from men across the country who had found Yarrell's books invaluable as the first source in which they could check species they came across. It was also a pleasure to share with the author the excitement at finding a species they had not known before. It was also typical of fishermen living abroad; in Madeira for example, the Reverend Nathaniel Bell and Reverend Richard

*A fine wood engraving of the Opah or King Fish placed in the genus* Zeus *by Linneaus, not often captured in European waters.* A History of British Fishes, 1841, 1: 194.

Thomas Lowe (who had published *A History of the Fishes of Madeira* in 1838) both wanted to share knowledge of species held in common on that island.

Before 1840, letters were mostly written on one sheet of paper only, folded over with a space on the outside for the address of the recipient. The cost (dependent on weight) was paid by the recipient, not the sender, so everyone tried to limit the bulk and size of the letter, which led to the irritating habit of writing across an already written page at right angles. In 1840 Rowland Hill introduced a universal penny post for the first half ounce, and then introduced postage stamps, bought by the sender. The innovation of envelopes followed. Today, when reading mid-19th century letters there are frequently neat little squares cut out to remove the highly collectable penny black stamps decorated with Queen Victoria's head. Yarrell's correspondents now used envelopes, and when they were retained, postmarked, they help to date the letters when their author forgot to do so. The profile of our monarch, with a statement of the price of the stamp is, to this day, all that is seen on our postage stamps – the only country in the world that is not required to state the name of the country on its stamps. This is in honour of the British invention of the postage stamp, and today's stamps are similar to the first design of Queen Victoria's profile beneath the word POSTAGE and with the words ONE PENNY underneath.

John Edward Gray was appointed Keeper of Zoology at the British Museum in 1840, having been in that department since 1824. He published a thousand papers, some describing new species. He was a useful ally of Yarrell, allowing him, and his visitors, to inspect specimens and exhibits at the museum when they wished. He also had another interest, postage stamps. In 1840, he purchased several penny blacks on the 1st of May when first issued, and he became one of the earliest serious collectors of postage stamps.

John Gould returned from Australia in September 1840, to the immense relief, one suspects, of Edwin Prince his faithful secretary. Gould immediately set about issuing information gathered on the kangaroos and other mammals and published a beautiful ground-breaking book *The Birds of Australia* between 1840 and 1848 with some 600 species. He issued his book on kangaroos in two parts with 30 plates in 1841–2, *A Monograph of the Macropodidae or Family of Kangaroos.* He sent a copy of the first part to Yarrell, who said he would retain it and subscribe.[5] In Yarrell's library (sale catalogue November 1856) there were copies of Gould's books on the birds of Europe, of Australia and of Asia, toucans and trogons as well as *Icones Avium*, and *Century of Birds from the*

*Himalaya Mountains.* Living so close to one another and meeting frequently at the Zoological Society, there was hardly any need for letters between them, which leaves us with little written evidence of their undoubted friendship and cooperation.

Jenyns noted in December 1840 that Yarrell had been with Selby when visiting Jardine at Jardine Hall in September. On his return to London, Jenyns had breakfast and dined several times with Yarrell, where he found him busy with the second edition of *A History of British Fishes* and on *A History of British Birds.* Jenyns wrote many letters to Yarrell (63 are conserved in the BRLSI) and was a useful conduit of Cambridge news.

In the 1841 Census[6] at Little Ryder St (no number) 'William Jarrell (*sic*) 55, Newsvendor, born same county? - Yes' was listed, albeit incorrectly as Jarrell, with two female servants, Mary Wilson and Catherine Goodchild. The misspellings in the transcripts of this census are numerous, the people employed to do the transcription not being adept at reading 19th-century handwriting.

The Reverend Richard Lubbock of Eccles and Larlingford, Thetford in Norfolk, was actively surveying what Yarrell had said about Water Rail eggs being rare and reported that he had 'taken from a Norfolk nest and was sending Yarrell three of them' and in return requested Fieldfare eggs.[7] In November he wrote to thank Yarrell for some Fieldfare and Redwing eggs and recalled when he had seen Yarrrell in the spring he had promised to send him notes and now enclosed them. Those notes proved to be a great resource for Yarrell, from which he quoted liberally on both fishes and birds.

Yarrell asked Lord Derby for help in establishing the status of the 'Polish' swan with its white cygnets because he needed this information for his *A History of British Birds.* This was provoked because of the controversy surrounding the Mute Swan occasionally producing white, instead of the usual grey, cygnets. In January 1838 there was an unusual display of this feature when several flocks of these so-called 'Polish swans' flew south along the north-east coast from Scotland to the Thames. Yarrell exhibited a specimen sent to him by the Rev. L. B. Larking of the Ryarsh Vicarage near Maidstone at a Zoological Society meeting. Lord Derby had purchased a pair of Polish swans in London and sent them to Knowsley. Yarrell decided, with other evidence from correspondents, that the Polish swan was a different species and named it *Cygnus immutabilis,* though this opinion proved incorrect and the Polish swan is now classified as a Mute Swan *Cygnus olor.* After his death in 1851, Lord Derby's pair of

Polish swans was purchased by Abraham Dee Bartlett for the (London) Ornithological Society and placed on the lake in St James's Park, where they produced a brood of seven cygnets in the summer of 1854 and another of six in 1856, all white from the egg.

In 1841 the 2nd edition of Yarrell's *A History of British Fishes* was published. It had some updates and some additions of fishes recently decided to be British. It also contained a reference to a Mr Newton who has remained elusive. Yarrell wrote. 'Since the publication of the first edition of this work, I have obtained another specimen from the Thames of what I believe to be the true *Cyprinus carassius*.' (*A History of British Fishes* 1841, 1: 355). Previously, when writing the first edition, Yarrell had told Jardine that he had got a Crucian Carp from the Thames of which Newton was making a drawing and he offered carp drawings to him. Yarrell then reported to Jardine that Newton had succeeded in making a very correct drawing from it.[8] This Newton was probably the same one as employed by Gould.

Prince sent some 29 drawings by Mrs Gould and Mr Newton to Lord Derby in 1843, which he had found in a portfolio that had not been opened for years and which Gould thought might be of interest to him, and a few days after explained: 'the more finished of the Ornithological drawings last sent are by Mrs Gould and the more slightly executed ones (the Toucans for instance) are by a Mr Newton, an artist who prior to the publication of the Monograph of the Ramphastidae, was employed by Mr Gould to make drawings of all the species he could obtain.'[9] This was W. J. Newton, who had painted watercolours of 50–60 birds, some dated 1832, in John Gould's collection of watercolour drawings sold to Lord Derby c.1843, one of which was signed WJN. In 1840 Prince had written to Gould, who was in Australia, that 'Newton has behaved like a scamp, he has left the Sat. Mag. Office and never shews his face since he got Pt 1 Trogons to shew a Gent who he thought would subscribe.'[10] 'Mr' Newton (they never knew a Christian name) was now down-graded to 'Newton' in disgrace. These drawings were deposited in the Natural History Museum, London, in 2018, from the collection of the current Earl of Derby.

In 1842, Sir William Jardine visited London and stayed with Yarrell, whom he found to be 'extremely kind and treats like a prince'. Jardine walked round London with Yarrell, where they visited the Zoological Gardens, the Royal Academy on 3 June for the annual exhibition of watercolours, the theatre at

b

a

a. Barn Owl
b. Eagle Owl
c. Peregrine Falcon
d. Falconer with cadge
e. Kestrel

d

c

e

PLATE 6 BIRDS OF PREY

the Haymarket, Linnean Society soirées and the Royal Society. Jardine thought the Zoological Gardens had 'fallen much off' since his previous visit because of 'the Feline smell', but he found the four camel-leopards or giraffes to be impressive.[11] Yarrell also found them fascinating and had a drawing of giraffes placed in a glazed, gilt frame displayed in his house.

Darwin decided to move from London and in 1842 took a house at Downe in west Kent, a village five and a half miles from Bromley. By 1846 Darwin had completed the several works on the geological and zoological discoveries while on the *Beagle* voyage. He maintained contact with Yarrell, who followed his career with interest and urged Darwin to keep pigeons, both as a hobby and to study the effects of artificial breeding. Darwin thoroughly enjoyed this new aspect of his work.[12]

In 1842 Gould went to Jardine Hall to stay with Sir William and went off to fish by himself. A water bailiff caught him and issued a summons against him for killing 'fowle or black fishe'[13] Back home, Gould wrote to Sir William in April: 'I now wish to ask when we shall have the pleasure of seeing you in London. Mr Yarrell and myself both wish to know this ... You did not mention anything respecting the summons against me for killing "fowle or black fishe" or what you have paid for me. By express desire I have given this important document to my friend Yarrell who intends binding it up with the Act of Parliament. My brother in law who is a Scotchman and brought up to the bar in your country states that it is one of none effect in consequence of an erasure which you will probably recollect was the case a wrong date having been inserted and afterwards altered. This however is of little moment to me.' Gould was to be summoned to answer the charges and expected to pay a fine. The fine was 'a penalty not exceeding Five pounds and five shillings'. The original document with the summons for the infringement by 'John Gould Esquire on the twelfth day of March' is now held in the Firestone Library, Princeton University, among other Yarrell papers. Jardine generously paid Gould's fine.

As late as 1836 Selby could write to Jardine 'My acquaintance with the London Naturalists is but limited, and with the exception of Yarrell I scarcely know the address of any of them.'[14] Six years later that had changed and Selby stayed in London with Yarrell. 'On first going up, I only spent 3 days at Acton, during which I contrived to get to Town and saw Yarrell, Van Voorst, and a few other acquaintances ... On the Monday following, I took up my abode with Yarrell, who most kindly profered (*sic*) me a bed and where I remained till the Saturday during which time I contrived to see the Brit. Museum, Zool. Gardens &c, dined with the Linn: Club and attended a meeting of that Soc. as well as one of the Entomological; on the days when we had no engagements abroad, Mr Yarrell had friends to dinner and I assure you he treated us in the most sumptuous and hospitable manner.' Selby probably would have wished to consult Van Voorst, who was to publish his *British Forest Trees* in 1842, in a similar format to Yarrell's two books.

Selby had an enjoyable day at the zoo. 'Yarrell accompanied me to the Zool. Gardens where we spent the day. I was much gratified with the living Giraffe, the young one appears quite healthy, and amused with the tricks of the ourang which continues in good health, but the Chimpanzee (since dead) was at the time in a deep decline. Some of the hybrid waterfowl are curious and they are making many interesting experiments on this subject. From Yarrells I went down to Jenyns in Cambs.'[15]

In 1843 Yarrell completed his *A History of British Birds*, and with it nine years' working to a bi-monthly schedule of publishing parts since he began in 1834 issuing his *A History of British Fishes*. There would have to be supplements, but he could now do those at his leisure. At last, he was free to pursue other interests. He procured many more books outside fish and bird subjects, though he kept pace with the market in these. His natural history interests expanded into insects and botany in particular, with zoophytes an unexpected addition. He had always bought biographical works and now added the correspondence of Ray and a life of John Constable. He had more time to enjoy his coin collection and add to his books about them. His tastes in architecture were unusual, with a mixture of baptismal fonts, gothic architecture, window tracery and Roman villas. He must have welcomed the combination of two of his favourite subjects when Newell's *Zoology of the English Poets* came out in 1845.

A new periodical, the *Zoologist*, was founded by Edward Newman of the Entomological Society in 1843, and Yarrell supported it with two articles that year. The first was about a petrel new to Britain, and the second of birds lately ascertained to be British as well as rare English fishes. He was coming to the end of writing articles by this time and only two more appeared, the last in the year he died.

W. S. MacLeay had emigrated to Elizabeth Bay, Sydney, New South Wales and in 1843 purchased the natural history books he needed from Yarrell. Writing from Bury Street, St James's, the address of his bookshop rather than his personal address in Ryder Street, Yarrell acknowledged receipt of payment of a bill for £43.0.10d dated 30 September 1841 for an earlier order for books and itemised a further consignment of books and the *Zoological Proceedings and Linnean Transactions,* as well as the last two parts of his own book on British birds. MacLeay had to wait months for delivery of an order and Yarrell further months for payment to arrive.

MacLeay had asked to be remembered and sent good wishes to the 'old members of the Linnean Club – Forster, Taylor, Bell, Bennet &c.' He then mentioned a discussion he had had with Yarrell about publishing books in Britain about foreign fishes. Yarrell replied, 'In reference to the drawings &c of Dr Stewart's Fishes and a hint about a desire to publish – I may tell you that the first part of Mr Lowe's work on the Fishes of Madeira is out and Dr Richardson has brought out the first part of a work on new species of Fishes, both with coloured plates; but the sale of them, as far as I can learn, is so limited that I much doubt whether the sale here of any work on exotic Fishes will be sufficient to pay the expences.'[16] Sound advice, if not palatable.

In April 1843 Yarrell was doing some private business for Lord Derby about purchasing a hybrid between a Capercaillie and a Black Grouse, costing £15, that had been sent by a young Swede, and four female Capercaillies for £10. Yarrell thought he could get the lot for £20 if Lord Derby wanted them. Pink-footed Geese had already gone to Knowsley. This prompted a discussion over Yarrell's classification of geese, of which there were eight in his *A History of British Birds.*[17] Lord Derby sent a different kind of request when he asked Yarrell to send him the English/Latin/French/German names of fishes – Pike/Perch, Mirror Carp/Burbot – with no explanation as to why he wanted them.[18]

Some idea of the friendship, affection even, between Jardine, Yarrell and Gould may be witnessed by a charming tradition established in London when one of Jardine's children was married in Scotland. Gould's interest in Jardine's 'little flock' as he once called them was always kindly. On 14 March 1844 he told Jardine 'Mr Yarrell is engaged to dine with me on the 21st when we shall do all honour to Mr and Mrs Maxwell.'[19] This was Jane, Sir William's eldest daughter (1821–94), who married Wellwood Herries Maxwell of Munches, Kirkcudbright, on 21 March 1844. Yarrell assisted the couple to obtain their passports for a honeymoon in Paris (he knew someone in the passport office) and invited them to call on him on their way to or from the Continent.

Catherine Dorcas Maule Jardine, Sir William's second daughter, married Hugh Strickland on 23 July 1845. Gould informed Jardine on that occasion: 'Kitty's marriage will be duly celebrated or honoured by the usual dinner of the friends of herself and husband in a few days, our worthy friend Yarrell having already issued the invitations although the day is not fixed, the next event of the kind falls on me and I care not how soon.'[20]

Sporadically, Yarrell received news from Edward Lear, now abroad, often via Gould who Lear used to maintain contact with his old friends in London. Lear invariably asked for his 'best remembrances to be given to Mr Yarrell'.[21] Lear wrote from Rome to Gould with reference to Yarrell's advice to him about wood engraving. 'And now I must beg you to thank Mr Yarrell very kindly from me for a letter I received from him yesterday: will you tell him it gives me just the information I wanted (just like Mr Y – all clinchers – not a word too much or too little:-) & has quite set me at ease about woodcutting, which I am convinced could not be done here.'[22] Lear was anxious to keep in touch with the naturalists back in England and Scotland, being mindful of their early support when he was writing his parrot book. Lear was particularly indebted to Yarrell for his practical help at the beginning of his career while producing his *Illustrations of the Family of Psittacidae or Parrots* (1830–32). Lear had declared to Charles Empson in October 1831 that except for Mr Yarrell, 'to whom I go to study bones and muscles',[23] he did not know a single person in London to visit intimately.

Yarrell's tutoring of Lear about muscles and bones had a most important effect, not just on Lear's paintings, but for natural history illustrations after Lear. Yarrell must have spotted Lear drawing in the parrot house in the Zoological Society Gardens and in the society's museum in Bruton Street, and would have noted the deficiencies in the drawings. His kindly interest in Lear took the practical form of teaching him about a basic principle now accepted widely, but then unrecognised: that to paint the outside of a bird satisfactorily, you must know the inside structure of the bird. The lie of the feathers should follow the contours of muscles beneath the skin. Lear's paintings of parrots improved as the work on his book progressed to such a degree that he is now regarded among the top rank of bird painters. Lear provided a drawing for Yarrell to use as a vignette for the Thick-lipped Grey Mullet in *A History of*

*The 'Thick-lipped Grey Mullet' for which the river Arun was celebrated. Edward Lear made a drawing of the river near its mouth with Arundel Castle on the right.* A History of British Fishes, 1841, 1: 241 and 244.

*British Fishes.* Lear had stayed with his sister Sarah and her husband in their house on the quay at Arundel, so knew this river and its topography intimately.

When Lear was in England for his summer visit in 1847 he stayed at 27 Duke Street, conveniently close (a three-minute walk) to Little Ryder Street for a call and chat with Yarrell.

Thomas Allis of York corresponded with Yarrell from 1837 to 1844, first commenting on Yarrell's *A History of British Birds.* He and Eyton met up at the 1837 Liverpool meeting of the British Association for the Advancement of Science (which Eyton described as being 'merry') and Allis confided having a live jerfalcon (Gyrfalcon). In 1844 he used 'his influence in reference to the appointment of Mr Charlesworth', for which Yarrell thanked him. Edward Charlesworth had begun work in the British Museum in 1836 and took over the *Magazine of Natural History,* often referred to as *Charlesworth's Magazine.* Allis went to Yorkshire in 1844 to be second Keeper of the Yorkshire Museum until 1858. A collection of Allis's letters, including correspondence with Yarrell, is in the York Library.

It was not only friends and naturalists who appreciated and used Yarrell's two books. Fishermen found *A History of British Fishes* invaluable as the best illustrated fish book of its time and ichthyologists admired the wood engravings and found the descriptions in the text excellent for identification purposes, but there was an admirer with a quite different background. The Prime Minister, Sir Robert Peel, at a soirée given in honour of Frederick Augustus, the King of Saxony, in 1844, was 'marked in his attention to Yarrell, seeking out the little man among the crowd, shaking hands with him, and telling him what pleasure his books had given him. These doings were the more notable as the minister did not talk to everybody.'[24] Robert Peel had a keen interest in science and appreciated Yarrell's clear descriptions and, at that time, near comprehensive inclusion of British species of fishes and birds. Yarrell once 'received a large Salmo Eriox from the late Sir Robert Peel, taken in the Tame'.[25]

Charles Darwin, full of questions, wrote to Yarrell asking about bird species from South America as given by Leonard Jenyns, among them those from Galapagos.[26] Louis Agassiz was in London in September 1846 and wrote, in French, to thank Yarrell for an invitation to visit him.[27] Jardine gossiped to Yarrell, 'Gould has lately been seized with a mania for Humming Birds' and Gould was then in Europe 'visiting all the large cities to buy up all the novelties'.[28] Amidst all these external distractions, Yarrell issued his first supplement to the second edition of *A History of British Birds.*

One of Yarrell's most prolific and productive correspondents was Jonathan Couch of Polperro in Cornwall. Couch was a doctor in the village for 60 years and knew the local fishermen, who were encouraged to alert him to anything strange in their nets. Yarrell supplied Couch with copies of the *Linnean Transactions* when issued and copies of his own books and supplements. But Couch's greatest asset for Yarrell was his intimate knowledge of marine fishes. He owned a copy of Yarrell's first edition of *A History of British Fishes* interleaved with blank pages before binding. Couch made additions for the text on nearly every page, clippings from newspapers, line drawings in ink and sometimes signed them J.C. There is also a small envelope addressed to him to which Couch added a note: 'Mr Yarrell's handwriting'. There are some letters from Yarrell in this book which include a revealing comment about Yarrell's finances. 'My thanks, my dear Sir for your kind present and communication: never think of the price of conveyance, anything from you is too interesting to be counterbalanced by money, and I am besides, thank God, too well off to

a. Bittern
b. Bearded Tit
c. Bearded Tit juvenile
d. Water Rail

PLATE 7 MARSH BIRDS

make it a matter of one moment's consideration.'[29] Couch's contribution to Yarrell's books was warmly received and graciously acknowledged. His visits to Yarrell in London were remembered with pleasure, especially when they 'dined on eels at 10d the pound'. Couch lent Yarrell his drawings of fishes that were delicately coloured. These were to become the foundation of Couch's own publication in 1860–65 of four volumes, with coloured illustrations, of *A History of the Fishes of the British Islands.*

There was an unwelcome, sharp reminder that many of the 19th century amateur naturalists, who gave so much of their time and energies to science, had to earn their livings. The possibility of them falling into difficulties was ever present and a gnawing anxiety. Yarrell communicated some disturbing news he had received from Jenyns, in 1847, about Dr George Johnston and got the reply. 'Dr Johnston of Berwick had met some reverses which compelled him to devote more of his time now to his medical profession, & less to science. I hope he had not sustained any very serious loss.'[30]

On a happier note, there was success for Yarrell's friend Professor Henslow, who was instrumental in creating a museum of natural history in Ipswich, Suffolk. Yarrell was present at the public opening of the museum on 18 December 1847 and at the dinner he replied to a toast by the Chairman to the prosperity of the Zoological Society of London.

In the *Proceedings of the Zoological Society* (1847, Part 15: 51–55), Yarrell gave a 'Description of the eggs of some of the birds of Chile.' They had been obtained by Mr Bridges and exhibited in London by Mr Cuming. Yarrell described 29 of them and gave their measurements in a paper he read on 27 April 1847. Another honour was bestowed on Yarrell – though as usual it involved more work - when his friend Robert Brown, then President, nominated him to be a Vice-President of the Linnean Society and he was also elected Treasurer in 1849.

In the same periodical (*PZS* 1847, part 15: 45) Jules Bourcier, a French naturalist, who was a hummingbird expert, named a species after Yarrell. When John Gould published his *Monograph of the Trochilidae, or family of hummingbirds* (5 vols 1849–61), he included a plate with three examples of *Calothorax yarrellii*, Yarrell's Woodstar, on plate 152, of which he said 'several undescribed species of Humming-Birds in the collection of the late Mr Loddiges, at Hackney, having been submitted to M. Bourcier during one of his recent visits to this country, that gentleman took the opportunity of complimenting several naturalists by giving their names to some of these new species: one of the most interesting of them he called *Yarrellii,* in honour of William Yarrell, Esq., so well known as one of the truest friends of natural history, and so celebrated for his valuable works on British Fishes, British Birds, &c. That the compliment in this instance, at least, is a just and well-deserved one, will be admitted by all who "take an interest in natural science", but especially by those who, like myself, are honoured by his friendship; a happiness I have now enjoyed for upwards of twenty years; it affords me therefore peculiar pleasure to perpetuate it in the present work.'

Yarrell's name was now well known by Continental naturalists, and several of them had been to visit him at his house to view his own collections of birds, fishes and other species. In 1849 the Prince of Canino, Charles Lucien Bonaparte, the naturalist who was a keen correspondent of Jardine, was in town and about to leave London, but before he went David Mitchell sent an invitation to Gould. 'Dear Gould Will you meet the Prince of Canino, Prof. Owen, J E Gray, & Mr Yarrell at 1/4 before 8 tomorrow at dinner?'[31] An invitation to dinner the next evening could be sent by post with the well-founded hope that both it, and the guests, would arrive next day.

An invitation to dine with Yarrell at 6 Little Ryder Street offered a splendid evening for all concerned. Yarrell was a cultured man with eclectic taste who spent a good deal on books, prints, drawings, engravings of portraits, scenery, sporting pictures and natural history specimens. Among the 30 glazed and framed pictures on his walls, several portraits would be of people known to visitors. Most of his pictures were in gilt frames, but special ones were in maple frames. These included Linnaeus in Lapland dress and a portrait of the late Lord Derby; 'Uncle Toby and The Widow Wadman' from Laurence Sterne's *Tristram Shandy;* a lithograph scene after the artist Frith from *Vicar of Wakefield;* an engraving after Landseer of Bolton Abbey and a painting after Callcott's *Raffaelle* and the *Fornarina.*

Yarrell kept a high standard of food and wine, and his table would be graced with silver plate and cutlery, while there was a china dessert service painted with birds. A 'three-tier mahogany dinner wagon, on turnd legs and castors', as itemized in the 1856 sales catalogue of his effects, would cut down intrusion from servants and servers. The conversation would be lively for their genial host had such a wide circle of friends and compass of interests. Politics may not have been one of them for there is not a single hint in his letters about affairs of the day, despite his handling and distributing newspapers daily in his business of newsagent. He kept that side of his life separate and there is nothing in his correspondence to indicate that he was either a Whig or a Tory.

Friends fortunate enough to stay with Yarrell for several days would have further opportunities to browse among his hundreds of prints in portfolios of engravings of illustrations and proofs. Specialists would want to see his hundreds of bottles of preserved fishes or the extensive collection of mounted birds in glass cases, many of these latter supplied by John Gould. They would be surrounded by mahogany bookshelves and cabinets with his collections of birds' eggs and shells, medals and coins.

In 1849 a second edition of the delightful small *The Sea-Side Book* by William Henry Harvey was published. Yarrell contributed Chapter VIII about fishing (see p.136). From 1849 to 1851 he had a new line of investigation when he made daily records on small cards of the weather and temperature: 'Tables of Meteorological Observations kept at Ryder Street, St James's, London by William Yarrell, Author of *British Birds and Fishes*, 1849–1851.'[32] This new interest in meteorology had been inspired by Jenyns, who made similar records for many more years. Yarrell bought three new books on climate and meteorology.

The 1840s decade had seen the completion of Yarrell's two standard works on birds and fishes, while he undertook numerous tasks for the societies to which he belonged. In addition, Yarrell had had ten periodical articles published that covered the subjects of insects injurious to turnips; eggs of birds of Chile; a new species of swan; a note about herring; trachea of Spur-winged Goose; and mucor in the air-cells of birds. The most important was one about some species of *Syngnathus*, the pipefishes and sea horses. Yarrell had discovered that it was the males who carried the young in their pouches. In the early part of the decade, he was at the height of his creative activity. By the end of the decade, when he was aged 65, he was still healthy and ready to take an interest in other natural history subjects and species, without the inexorable pressure of publishing. He bought over 200 books in this decade, pursuing his interests in architecture, travel, literature, history and coins (*see* Chapter 7). Yarrell's intellectual curiosity led him to explore across a wide field. Throughout the decade, Yarrell had attended the meetings of the Zoological and Linnean Societies, among others, and served on their committees. In his correspondence with his friends there is evidence of great activity both with them and on their behalf in the gathering of evidence about all wildlife. However, in the sources available for discovering his activities, there is hardly a whisper about his bookselling and newsagency business that must have been thriving and was sustaining his natural history pursuits. Of the three main parts of Yarrell's life – his natural history writings; his service to the major natural history societies in London; and his business – we know least about his involvement in his successful trade, either in earlier decades or in the 1840s. We are about to find out more in the last years of his life in the 1850s.

*The skeleton of a Green Woodpecker in* A History of British Birds, 1843, 2: 135. *Yarrell stated, 'The descending position of the bones of the tail indicate the mode by which the stiff points of the tail-feathers are brought into contact with the surface of the bark of the tree to form an accessory prop.'*

Chapter 6

# THE 1850s: WINDING DOWN

On 13 January 1850, Yarrell began the year by chairing a meeting of the Zoological Society, a duty he now frequently performed for Lord Derby, who by then was frail, rarely attended London meetings, and died in 1851. The Prince Consort was the succeeding President.

Fewer letters from the 1850s have survived, but on Christmas Eve 1850 Yarrell wrote a succinct letter to David W. Mitchell, about an animal for the Zoological Society Gardens, that has a sharper tone than usual. 'Dear Sir, I am sorry to differ in opinion with you - but I think - under all the circumstances - the price high - the animal useless - the purchase almost unjustifiable - every argument I can think of is against it. Yours sincerely, Wm Yarrell.[1] There was a black outline round this letter indicative of a death. His partner and cousin Edward Jones had died on 18 November 1850, leaving him in sole charge of the business at a time when he least desired such a burden. Edward Jones left a will in which he appointed Yarrell one of the joint trustees, with his wife Grace and Edward Bird, of his estates in Birchanger, Essex, and three villages north of Lymington in Hampshire. There was no mention of the business or his partnership with Yarrell.

The death of Edward Jones was devastating for Yarrell. Edward, in his will, called him 'my friend', but their relationship was much more than that. They were cousins, had been brought up together, sent to school together and then for 47 years were partners and managers in the Jones and Yarrell business. There was a wealth of sadness behind the single remark Yarrell made to his close friend Jenyns 'my partner has died and I am left in sole charge of the business.'[2] He was aged 66 and the last thing he wanted was to be sole owner with responsibility for a large business with the daily demands on a newsagent. An obituary in the *Cambridge General Advertiser* of 27 November 1850 stated that Edward had been a Justice of the Peace for Cambridgeshire for many years.

Yarrell was left with far less time to enjoy his natural history pursuits. Since the 1820s he had divided his time three ways: on the business; on his natural history interests; and on his committee work while engaging with his friends who were mainly fellow committee members at this date. It is likely that Edward Jones had done much of the administrative work of the business and been the senior partner. Now, suddenly, all the work entailed in running the bookselling business and newsagency fell to Yarrell. He had to be present all the year round, not just on alternate months, except for holidays when he left the shop to his clerks to manage. They were Frederick May of Bury Street (he had signed Edward Jones' will as a witness) and another man named Williams.

There are indications that Yarrell was one of those persons who could compartmentalise his life and give his undivided attention to whatever he was engaged in at any one time. This is partly confirmed by Edward Newman (editor of the *Zoologist*, who wrote an obituary of Yarrell). He said that Yarrell was always ready to 'afford information'. Newman had applied to him on numerous occasions and found 'Yarrell's whole attention was absorbed by it; books, specimens, memory, every auxiliary was at his finger-ends; and no sacrifice of time or trouble was ever too great for him to make, neither was the subject ever left undecided while diligence or a disposition to teach could throw on it a single ray of light. No other subject seemed to occur to him during the investigation; he had no other occupation; that one inquiry was, for the time, the object of his life. His power of concentrating his attention on a single subject was most extraordinary, and more extraordinary still was the facility with which that concentration was turned to *any* subject; he used it after the fashion of a burning glass, casting the focus wherever he pleased. This faculty was at the service of all ... given to every truth-seeking inquirer.'[3]

Another writer, in the *Athenaeum*, commented that Yarrell 'never sacrificed the duties of his business to his favourite pursuits'.[3] Since several witnesses testify to this, there would seem little doubt that his integrity was secure on this point.

In the 1851 census the entry for 6 Little Ryder Street, showed 'William Yarrell, head, unmarried, aged 66, newsagent, born St James, Westminster' and two servants, Mary Wilson unmarried 54 and Catherine Goodchild housemaid aged 42 unmarried.[4] In the London Street Directory for the same year, Yarrell was listed under 'Booksellers: Jones & Yarrell of 34 Bury Street'.

Any leisure was spent developing his interest in wood engravings and in buying books (some 83 in the first 6 years of the 1850s) that now included more obscure fauna, such as Cirripedia, stalk-eyed crustacea, lichens and marine algae. A book on Lepidoptera was a first for the library. Birds were still favourite subjects. Other than natural history (about 50 items) his choice of subjects was the same as in earlier years with travel of the greatest interest, and literature, but now with an increase in medical books and human anatomy (10; he even had 19 volumes of the *Lancet*). A small but recurring item in his book list had been books on heraldry and the peerage. The latter would be useful for the titled gentlemen with whom he more frequently came into contact.

On 12 July 1851 Yarrell wrote to William Richard Fisher, the artist for the Reverend F. O. Morris' nature books, saying he wanted to talk to Fisher on the subject of eggs. 'You are welcome to lend Mr Morris any or all drawings of eggs obtained through me as from yourself alone. The only restriction I would impose would be that my name should not be mentioned or referred to, and my reason for this I will tell you when we meet.'[5] The reason remains unknown. Between 1852 and 1863 F. O. Morris issued *A Natural History of the Nests and Eggs of British Birds* in monthly parts with four plates priced at one shilling. 'The drawings of the eggs were done, in the main, by William Richard Fisher, who had lived at Great Yarmouth until 1853 when he moved to London. Yarrell had visited Yarmouth for several years when searching fish catches that might produce some rarity. Fisher was a personal friend of his and had the use of Yarrell's cabinets containing the eggs of British birds. The 320 drawings (318 watercolours, 2 uncoloured) drawn in 1847 and interleaved with Fisher's notes and descriptions are now in the McGill University Library, Montreal.'[6] The notes were arranged after, and refer to, the 2nd edition of Yarrell's *A History of British Birds*, where it was stated that the figures of the rarer eggs were chiefly done from the specimens owned by Yarrell.

The happy relations between Jardine and Yarrell continued beyond the urgent need of both authors for specimens or loan of books. Now they were sending birds for dinner parties. Late in 1852 Yarrell dispatched 'two Canvass Backed Ducks of America' by train to Jardine hoping 'they will be on your table at Dinner', adding 'The Queen has had some and the birds are sent up with Lemon for a squeeze only over the cut slice on the plate and currant jelly as a liquid sauce sent up very hot and kept hot at table by a spirit lamp.'[7] How did Yarrell know this? A daily visit to Buckingham Palace with the newspapers was made by the staff of the firm Jones and Yarrell, and contact with the staff at the palace probably led to an exchange of news and gossip, perhaps also a chat with the chef since we know Yarrell was interested in good cookery. On 8 December Yarrell had received a gift from Jardine, whom he thanked 'for box of game - 3 Black Grouse and a Pheasant, for which I am sincerely obliged; and accident has doubled the value of your generous intention, for I have a party on Saturday next, and Edwin Landseer comes to dine with me for the first time.'[8] Yarrell also mentioned a mutual friend, 'Mr Selby came here about 10 days ago looking very well.' On the 29 December it was fish that arrived from Scotland – a box of vendace in perfect condition.[9] As a change from fishes and birds, Yarrell had been to the London Great Cattle Show that morning and wrote of cattle, pigs and sheep. He also offered to order a book for Jardine.

By 1853 the correspondence had slackened considerably, but Yarrell was still anxious to oblige anyone writing to him. Replying to George Newport (1803–54) he said, 'Accept my best thanks for your kindness in supplying me with a copy of your valuable paper on the "direct Agency of the Spermatozoon". I have read it with great interest and pleasure, and congratulate you sincerely on the elucidation of so intricate a phisiological fact. I regret that I have nothing of value to offer you in return, but if you have any ornithological friends, and you would descend to take quantity for quality - half a dozen copies of my paper on the Great Bustard in the last part of the Linnean Transactions are at your service.'[10]

Yarrell's first serious illness struck this year. Richardson, who was in close contact with him and about to take on the onerous task of extending his work on his *A History of British Fishes*, wrote, 'By the methodical distribution of his time Mr. Yarrell was enabled, without neglecting his business concerns, to assist in the management of the scientific societies of which he was a member, and to carry on his zoological enquiries and publications. His enjoyment of

*The Great Bustard,* A History of British Birds, 1843, 2: 362, *was once hunted by greyhounds on Newmarket Heath and around Salisbury. It was on the point of extinction in Britain when Yarrell was writing.*

social life was combined with temperance and being blessed with a sound constitution he possessed continuous good health up to the year 1853, when some premonitory symptoms of indisposition began to appear without, however affecting the activity of his intellect or the cheerfulness of his manner.'[11] The symptoms were a severe attack of fever which was his first real illness. On 30 November 1853 Yarrell wrote his will.

Jenyns was more conversant with what had happened. Writing to Selby in the following February he said, 'You have heard, perhaps, of Mr Yarrell's late severe illness, from which however he is now recovering; - but he describes himself as having been worse than he ever was before – confined to his bed for several weeks before & after Xmas and, I imagine, for some time, rather in danger. I had thought him rather ailing for some time previous, but trust he is now rallying fast and will shortly be himself again.'[12] Yarrell recovered but was not quite his old usual self.

By now, Yarrell wanted to be rid of the business and he retired in favour of his cousins Messrs Joseph and Charles Clifford in 1853. For the first time in his adult life he was free of it. He was still busy attending Linnean Club meetings and acting as chairman at Zoological Society meetings, but all was not well with the business part of his life. As detailed in Chapter 2, Frederick May, who had given his employment as 'bookseller's clerk' with Jones ad Yarrell in the census of 1851, decided to set up in an independent business with another employee by the name of Williams. It was unfortunate that they chose to set up in direct competition only four doors away at 42 Bury Street. They took a great deal of business with them. The Jones and Yarrell 34 Bury Street shop had been given up by 1853. Now that it was a smaller business, Yarrell had to allow the Cliffords to use his ground floor as the newsagent shop at 6 Ryder Street. It was a tragic end to Yarrell's business life.

Yarrell attended the 1854 meeting of the British Association for the Advancement of Science in Liverpool and there are five specimens of fishes in the Natural History Museum fish collections in London, sourced to Liverpool and dated 1854. In September 1854 Yarrell had reassurance that his books were still being both used and useful. The Reverend J. A Barron had been in Switzerland visiting a mutual friend, Schönbein, and observed a large fish there. 'He seemed to be a stupid heavy fish not resisting being turned on his back. Looked up in Hist Brit Fish and under Sturgeon stated that the fish is said to feed on small fish; this was confirmed by the fisherman who was shewing it.'[13]

Two years before his death, Yarrell wrote in the album of his relatives, the Misses Pallett, the lines:

'First and last,
The earliest summoned and the longest spared,
Are here deposited.'

*'The Common British Sturgeon' of* A History of British Fishes, *1843, 2: 475. After it was exclusively reserved for Henry 1 (reigned 1100–1135), any Sturgeon caught in British waters were supposed to be sent to the King. Over succeeding centuries, this went more in the breach than the observance.*

All the recent events and the feeling of being left alone were weighing on Yarrell. He still had cousins and other more distant relatives, but no close family left.

In 1855 Dr George Johnston died. He had been an enthusiastic fisherman in the Tweed and sent many notices of fishes to Yarrell. Theirs had been a long and productive collaboration.

The queries received by Yarrell did not stop. He identified a curious looking swan for George Frederick, 'I have pleasure in stating that your bird is a very fine and adult specimen of the Polish or Changeless Swan, Cygnus immutabilis of the British Birds. We are indebted to the late severe weather for many rare Northern visitors.'[14]

For several years Yarrell had encouraged the natural history pursuits of a young boy who had been born at Colnbrooks, South Buckinghamshire, the son of a Hanoverian father. William Bernhardt Tegetmeier was trained by his father, who was a surgeon, and in 1841, when a qualified surgeon himself, aged 25, he lived in a house in Bury Street owned by Yarrell. They had a mutual interest in fancy pigeons and exotic poultry, and when the Philoperisteron (meaning 'pigeon lover') Society was established in 1849 they attended the annual exhibitions held in the great hall of the Freemason's Tavern in Great Queen Street. Yarrell took Charles Darwin to the 1855 exhibition, where he introduced him to Tegetmeier. Yarrell had been urging Darwin to study the varieties of pigeons, having no doubt that they were all descended from the original wild pigeon *Columba livia* through selective breeding. Tegetmeier became an enthusiastic correspondent and supplier of information for Darwin, who joined the Philoperisteron Society in November 1856 and erected two pigeon houses at Down House. Darwin had asked Yarrell where to purchase some of the fancy pigeons he wished to breed and Yarrell directed him to John Bailey, a London poulterer and live bird dealer. Darwin reported back to Yarrell on his purchases and said he was sending him 'the cage', evidently borrowed from Yarrell. Was this the 'parrot cage' of the December 1856 sale of Yarrell's effects (see p.133)? When Yarrell died, Darwin wrote to Tegetmeier lamenting 'our old & excellent friend'.[15] In some areas Tegetmeier took over from Yarrell by providing evidence for Darwin's subsequent publication of the *Origin of Species*.

The year 1856 did not start well for Yarrell. He wrote to Gould on 19

January 'I am so situated from medicinal interference, that I cannot leave the house either this day, or tomorrow. Pray continue to send the birds down to me to look at, I will not retain them, or the messenger, more than a few minutes.'[16] Alfred Newton had been drawn into the circle of friends and collaborators. Writing to Gould he said, 'I made some rough sketches of these and a few other birds (which Mr Yarrell now has for you) ... I should like to hear from you when you have got the drawings from Mr Yarrell.'[17]

In January Yarrell's short notice of a Great Bustard with a broken leg, caught in Berkshire about a mile from Hungerford, that had been taken to Leadbeaters to be preserved, appeared in the *Proceedings of the Zoological Society*. People were still notifying him of such rare occurrences, but it was the last note he published of a rarity. His final article appeared in the *Journal of the Linnean Society*, 'On the influence of the sexual organ in modifying external character', 1856, volume 1, p. 76.

On 3 August 1856 as he was returning from St James's Church, which for some years he had constantly attended, a slight giddiness seized him, his steps became uncertain and he felt for a moment unable to proceed. After a short rest he reached home without assistance. This attack proved to be a slight paralysis. Yarrell said at that time that he felt a 'wooliness' in his brain and was on a diet.

On the last day of August 1856, Yarrell suggested to his executor and publisher Van Voorst that Sir John Richardson should finish the work on the 3rd edition of *A History of British Fishes*, which would be published in 1859 with Van Voorst's biography of Yarrell. Yarrell then kindly accompanied an invalid friend on a voyage by sea to Yarmouth. He enjoyed his dinner at the Royal Hotel, then he went to bed but felt a difficulty in breathing so, fearful he might die and no one know it, he got up, unlocked the door and rang the bell. Medical assistance was procured without delay, but he expired calmly at 12.30 on 1 September.

**Events post 1 September 1856**

Van Voorst went to Yarmouth and took Yarrell's body to London and then Bayford. There was no autopsy, but the cause of death was stated in the *Gentleman's Magazine* to be 'ossification of the heart'.[18] The following Monday he was buried at Bayford within the railed rectangle where his parents and siblings were already buried. His coffin was attended by the President, librarian Mr Kippist, officers and other members of the Linnean Society; his executors

*The (now rusty) railed enclosure of Yarrell graves in Bayford Churchyard. William Yarrell's grave is on the back row in the centre between Caroline and Harriot's graves.*

(his friends Edward Bird and John Van Voorst) and relatives.[19] It was a long journey to Bayford to be undertaken by so many.

The engraving on his stone reads:

Here lies the remains of William Yarrell V.P.L.S. (of St James's Westminster)

AUTHOR OF 'A HISTORY OF BRITISH FISHES' AND OF 'A HISTORY OF BRITISH BIRDS' BORN JUNE 11TH MDCCLXXX1V DIED SEPTEMBER 1ST MDCCCLV1
HE WAS THE SOLE SURVIVOR OF TWELVE BROTHERS AND SISTERS WHO WITH THEIR FATHER AND MOTHER ARE ALL PLACED CLOSE TO THIS SPOT

First and last
The earliest summoned and the longest spared
Are here deposited.
Wordsworth

The Yarrell family liked to quote poetry on their gravestones. Here are two more recorded long ago, but now illegible:

Since like the rose youth quickly flies,
Riches had wings and fled away,
Francis Yarrell d. 25 March 1794. Aged 46.

The short life dates the same;
O let this lesson make you wise
Great Auther (*sic*) of your frame
Harriet Yarrell 1796.

The St Mary's Church at Bayford in Hertfordshire that was known to Yarrell had been rebuilt in 1802 in brick. In the Lady Chapel on the south there is a memorial to him very high up near the rafters where it is unreadable. There is also a tablet in the church to William Yarrell, who left £500 to be invested and the interest to be used to keep the family grave in repair with any surplus to be distributed to the poor of the parish annually.

Some measure of Yarrell's importance as a naturalist and the high regard in which he was held is indicated by the number of obituaries that appeared in a dozen scientific journals in the months after his death. The summings up of his value and contribution as a naturalist were laced with happy personal memories of dinner with Yarrell and working with him as a colleague. It is usual to find obituaries eulogising and glossing over character flaws, but with Yarrell sincere obituaries were written, assessing his work and stressing how kindly had been the man they were all now missing. Some of his close friends who wrote obituaries were Professor Bell (President of the Linnean Society, who attended his funeral in Bayford), Dr R. G. Latham, Edward Newman, and Lovell Reeve, who referred mainly to Yarrell's scientific achievements with little of a personal nature (see Bibliography, p.202).

In no fewer than 40 newspaper obituaries in September 1856, his death was reported in terms of 'the good old sportsman', 'one of our greatest naturalists' and a reference to the 'extensive newsagency' of which he was a partner. These were the main strands of Yarrell's life that had appealed over twenty-five years to different sections of the public, but every newspaper notice agreed about him being both 'kind and good'. The newspapers were not so concerned with his sterling work for natural history societies, although they mentioned his books, but that was appreciated in the natural history publications carrying obituaries (see pp.201–202).

More personal notes occurred in two letters, both sent to Yarrell's colleague and friend, John Gould: Alfred Newton wrote 'I shall miss Mr Yarrell very greatly – he was so uniformly kind in supplying information on any point of ornithology – as far as it lay in his power.'[20] John Stevens Henslow was also sympathetic, 'You must all sadly miss poor Yarrell, whose death was so sudden but to all appearances such as one ought not to regret.'[21] Van Voorst wrote to Leonard Jenyns about the sale of Yarrell's collections and referred to the 'Death of my kind old friend William Yarrell'.[22] Jonathan Couch called him 'My excellent and amiable friend'.[23] Charles Darwin wrote to their mutual friend W. B. Tegetmeier on 18 September 1856, 'I was most sincerely sorry to hear of the death of our old and excellent friend Yarrell.'[24]

The familiar, small figure regularly walking from Piccadilly to the City each Monday or crossing Piccadilly heading to meetings in Soho and Leicester Squares, or making his way to the Zoological Gardens often with a visitor in tow, was going to be sorely missed by many Londoners. His genial presence at society meetings, with his sage advice from long experience, left gaps in the lives of many naturalists, but his name would live on in the press from one end of the country to the other, for another half century and more. Each time a query arose about a fish or bird, the editors of newspapers would quote Yarrell's two books as the authority on the subject. His enduring reputation was underlined when an American naturalist named a new genus after him some 40 years after his death (see *Yarrella,* p.118).

**Yarrell's will**

Transcript of Yarrell's will: 'Will of William Yarrell of Little Ryder Street, St James Westminster, dated 30th November 1853. Proved London 12 Sept 1856. Probate 11/2239 quire 239.' Note the 19th century legal use of the initial double 'ff' for ffifty and ffive; also the lack of punctuation.

This is the last will and testament of me William Yarrell of 6 Little Ryder Street St James in the City of Westminster Gentleman I give and bequeath the following legacies to be paid by my executors hereunto named free from legacy duty To Mrs Grace Jones widow of my late partner and now residing with her brother Mr Edward Bird I give the sum of one thousand pounds to Mary Pallett and Jane Pallett now residing together in St Martins yard I give the sum of one thousand pounds each to Caroline the wife of Mr Henry Mill? wine merchant Lucy Goldsmith Eliza Goldsmith and Sophia Goldsmith the three daughters of my old friend Mr Edward Goldsmith I give the sum of one thousand pounds each To Mrs Andrews widow of my late friend Dr...Andrews of New Bond Street Librarian I give the sum of Two hundred and ffifty pounds to Mrs Louisa Farquier widow of my late friend Louis Farquier late of New

Bond Street aforesaid I give the sum of ffifty pounds to Mr Alexander Gordon residing at Windsor I give the sum of one hundred pounds to my servant Mary Wilson I give the sum of ffifty pounds To my servant Kitty Goodchild I give the sum of twenty ffive pounds To the Reverend H L Webb Rector of Bayford in the County of Hertford and the Reverend Charles Thornton Curate of Bayford aforesaid I give the sum of one hundred pounds Consolidated Bank Annuities Upon trust out of the dividends deriving therefrom to keep or repair my family vault or burial plot in the church of Bayford aforesaid and in case the same shall in any year be more than sufficient for the purpose of doing the necessary repairs then I give the surplus of such dividends from time to time to the poor of the Parish of Bayford aforesaid And I appoint my friends Edward Bird of Clapham Park John Van Voorst of Paternoster Row executors of this my will to whom I give in equal shares and proportions the residue of my estate and effects real and personal writings In witness whereof I have hereunder set my hand this thirtieth day of November in the year of our Lord one thousand eight hundred and fifty three.

Signed by said William Yarrell as his last will and testament in the presence of us ...Fred Lucas Capron and Edward Patten Edwd Hare London solicitor

Proved at London 12 Sept 1856...to Edward Bird and John Van Voorst executors.

His property amounted to about £17,000.

His appreciation of the difficulties that widows could experience following the death of their husbands is shown in his generous provision for five widows. No member of his family by the name of Yarrell was included, just two cousins, who were daughters of his aunt Mary Blane, i.e. his mother's sister, the Misses Pallett (daughters of William Pallett and Mary Blane, born 18 November 1753, who married William Pallet on 27 June 1775 in Bayford). William's two servants were not forgotten, Mary Wilson having been with him many years.

The two executors were Van Voorst, his publisher and long-time friend, and Edward Bird, who like Yarrell was born in the parish of Westminster, went to school in Ealing at the same time and was a life-long friend of both Yarrell and another fellow pupil, Edward Jones. Edward Jones had been in the business with Yarrell from 1803–50 and when he died all his goods and extensive property were left in trust to Grace his wife (who was also Edward

Bird's sister) and his two friends William Yarrell and Edward Bird. In 1851 (the census year) Edward Bird was aged 63, a bachelor and a secretary to Royal Exchange Assurance. He had taken widowed Grace, his sister who was two years his junior, into his home, The Nest, in Atkins Road, Clapham. Van Voorst and Edward Bird not only acted as Yarrell's executors but also arranged and paid for the monument to William Yarrell to be put in St James's Church, Piccadilly.

*Wall memorial in St James's Church, Piccadilly, paid for and placed there by William's life-long friend Edward Bird and his publisher John Van Voorst, sculpted in bas relief by Neville Northey Burnard 1818–78 (see p.208).*

**Sale of Yarrell's museum and library** *See* Chapter 7 for details.

Yarrell's extensive library of natural history books was sold 13–15 November 1856 and his valuable collection of British birds and fishes with household effects were sold by auction 4-6 December 1856.

## Bird specimens – current locations

The University Museum of Zoology, Cambridge, conserves one bird and one bat specimen formerly belonging to Yarrell that were presented via Leonard Jenyns in 1869: *Vespertilio nattereri* (E.5763.B) and a sternum from a *Larus minutus* (246.b) The bird collection formerly in the Cambridge Philosophical Society Museum, that contained items given by Yarrell, was moved to the Cambridge University Museum in 1865 but no written records appear to exist either of the specimens before being transferred or after they were received.

A collection of the tracheae of water birds was presented by Yarrell to the Royal College of Surgeons in 1825.

One specimen of Yarrell's *Sylvia sylviella,* a Lesser Whitethroat, was donated by him to the British Museum on 10 March 1827 and two more in the 1830s.[25] In 1830 he also donated 'A young female *Cygnus Bewickii* shot on the English coast.'[26] Three more bird skins were presented by Yarrell before 1836: a male Common Teal *Anas crecca* and two Common Terns *Sterna hirundo* (one from Sussex and one with no locality).[27]

At the Stevens' sale of Yarrell's specimens held on 13–15 November 1856 the British Museum bought 472 bird skeletons, sterna and trachea (BM registration numbers 711–1183), including in lot 440 'A quantity of trachea, skulls of birds &c.', in lot 438 'Breast-bones of birds various'; and, from the sale on 4 December 1856, lot 856 'British birds and eggs, books etc.'. The natural history collections of the British Museum were transferred to the new British Museum (Natural History) in 1881, and since 1972 their ornithology collection has been held at the Natural History Museum at Tring, Hertfordshire.

After 1856 some of Yarrell's birds were donated to the Haileybury & Imperial Service College museum at Hertford Heath, a hamlet in S.E. Hertford. Most of this collection was destroyed by a flood in 1988, after which the remnant was donated to the North Hertfordshire Museum at Hitchin.[28]

## Eggs

In the sale catalogue eggs were sold in lots 347–407. The egg of the Great Auk was lot 399 that was sold for 20 guineas (£20 + 20 shillings = £21). Errol Fuller in his *The Great Auk* 1999, p. 275-278, reported Alfred Newton (1894) writing 'I would ask for the admission of a few lines in which to state what is known exactly of the origin of that specimen, which I well remember in the collection of the late Mr William Yarrell. He told me, as he told others of his friends, that he bought it in Paris; and to the best of my belief, not many years after the peace of 1815. In a little curiosity shop of mean appearance, he saw a number of eggs hanging on a string; he recognised one of them as...*Alca impennis*, and... was told that they were one franc apiece, except the large one, which from

*Photograph of a Great Auk's egg. Yarrell's measurements for the egg were '3 1/4" in length; 1" 11 lines in breadth at the large end', i.e. one inch and eleven twelfths wide. Courtesy of W. G. Hale. For a detailed update on the egg that was repaired by Yarrell, see Birkhead in* Archives of Natural History, *October 2020.*

its size was worth two francs. He paid the money and walked away with the egg in his hat.' The egg was sold at Stevens Rooms in 1856. At that sale it was procured by the London taxidermist James Gardiner, acting on behalf of Frederick Bond of Kingsbury, Middlesex, who paid 20 guineas for it. A much publicised and reported sale in the newspapers of 1894 resulted in the egg going for 300 guineas (i.e. £300 + 300 shillings). After several more owners,

*The painting of the egg of a Little Stint, inscribed in Yarrell's handwriting 'Little Stint. Brit Birds v.2. p. 643', with a signature 'W. Yarrell' on the reverse. This was not included in the entry for the bird in the first edition of* A History of British Birds. *Courtesy of D. Clugston.*

it was bought by Dr John Alan Gibson (1926–2013) in 1993. Following his death, his Great Auk egg has been sold twice.

Errol Fuller, the authority on the Great Auk and its preserved eggs, kindly informed me that, following the Gibson sale of the three eggs with Yarrell connections, one that was badly broken and put back together rather poorly by Yarrell is now in Sweden and owned by a Finnish gentleman, the second he may have purchased for a lady is in a private collection in London and that Errol himself now owns the third.

The set of Yarrell's British birds' eggs that was originally in the Cambridge Philosophical Society collection was moved to Cambridge University Zoological Museum in 1865.

### Mammal specimens

In 1830 Yarrell presented 'A specimen of a Blue Cat, said to be from New Holland'. In 1831 he presented to the British Museum: 'Specimens of the Hay-Stack variety of the common mouse, (*Mus musculus*) and of the Harvest Mouse (*Mus messorius*) from the vicinity of London.'[28] In 1856 'Skulls of English and Italian greyhounds' were presented to the museum by W. Yarrell, (W. Esq.), The well-known ornithologist.'[29]

### Fish specimens

In the Stevens sale of Yarrell's natural history specimens, 4-6 December 1856, groups of bottles of fishes were sold in 11 lots 442–453, at least 198 bottles in all. There was also, in lot 441, a 'large and valuable collection of fish, with a variety of manuscripts, collected with a view to publishing a work on the subject'. There were also dried fishes.

a) The fish specimens and the specimens illustrative of his papers in the *Transactions of the Linnean Society* were secured by the Trustees of the British Museum when sold in 1856. Their fish collection is now in the Natural History Museum, London. The full collection inferred by this may have been transferred to the museum, with individual specimens noted in an Accessions register. A few are traceable to Yarrell, including five specimens of *Leuciscus* (dace and roach) sourced to Liverpool, dated 10 September 1854, registered 2005.7.28.1.
b) In 1830 Yarrell had donated: 'Some specimens of various ages of *Gasterosterus trachurus, G. semiarmatus* and *G. leiurus,* a large lobster, and two Chars. Two

a. Wheatear
b. Wryneck
c. Kingfisher
d. Snow Bunting
e. Stonechat

PLATE 8 PERCHING BIRDS

specimens of the *Salmo alpinus.'* [30] In 1831 Yarrell donated: 'Two specimens of the Char (*Salmo savelinus?*) from Wales: A specimen of *Solea pegusa,* from Brighton; a specimen of the Alise of Pennant (*Clupea alosa,* Cuv...); and a middle sized specimen of the common Sturgeon (*Accipenser sturio*), from the English coast.'[30]

c) Albert Gunther's *Catalogue of Fishes in the British Museum* recorded a lot of small coastal fishes including blennies, gobies, etc, received from Yarrell mostly as dried skins. A mounted specimen of a *Clupea* on a wooden block signed William Yarrell on the base has been re-registered 2005.7.28.18.

d) G.A. Boulenger's chapter on 'Fishes' in the *History of the Collections contained in the Natural History Departments of the British Museum* (vol. 2, 1906) notes under the date 1856 (p. 536) that 'The collection of British Fishes made by Mr Yarrell, containing types of the species described by him, was acquired.' and further notes under the entry for Yarrell (p. 550) that 'The collection of British Fishes made by Mr Yarrell, forming the basis of his book, 'British Fishes', published in 1835-1836, was received in 1856.'

### Manuscripts and drawings

The Marine Biological Association, Plymouth. Watercolours and engravings of fishes are conserved in the library in two collections: a) (PYA1) 31 watercolours and drawings annotated William Yarrell and two sheets of newspaper cuttings dated 1864-65; b) (PRN1) fish illustrations arranged systematically and an album with mounted and unmounted illustrations (originals and plates) used by Richardson in preparing the 3rd edition of Yarrell's *A History of British Fishes,* with annotations. The collection also includes a letter from Yarrell to John Richardson in 1833 discussing fishes.

Firestone Library, Princeton University, Library, New Jersey. Fish drawings, papers, and 13 letters received by Yarrell.

Society of Antiquaries, London. Manuscripts: 'Notes and other material used by William Yarrell for the chapter on the Mute Swan in his British birds.'

Wellcome Historical Medical Library. Letter by WY answering question on perpetual motion (see A. T. Gage, 1938 *A history of the Linnean Society.* London, Taylor & Francis).

### The Linnean Society Archives' items relating to Yarrell:

a) Miscellaneous manuscripts include a letter to John Curtis about a Java

Thrush, 1832; four reports on colleagues' papers for the Linnean Society; publications by Jonathan Couch on the genus *Hemiramphus,* 1843; Thomas Forster on the migration of the Swallow, 1846; R. Knox on the food of gregarious fishes, 1854, and one by Edward Newman in 1856.

b) In Yarrell's correspondence with Jenyns, M. E. Bloch's *Ichthyologie,* published in Berlin in 1796, is referred to on several occasions. Yarrell owned the 5th and 6th parts and plates 1–216 that are annotated by Yarrell, with notes by Jonathan Couch, and a letter from H. W. Wheelwright to Couch.

c) A collection of 7 Manuscript articles by WY for Journal of the Linn. Soc. Two manuscript articles written by WY with report on it by Thomas Bell. Three manuscript articles by other authors (Jonathan Couch; Thomas Forster and Edward Newman) with written report by WY. With this collection is a watercolour of a fish received by WY from W. Thompson.

d) Copies of the minutes of the Zoological Club of the Linnean Society are preserved in the Linnean Society and manuscript extracts from those minutes, made by Yarrell, are in the possession of the Zoological Society.

## Species named after Yarrell

Birds

Two of Yarrell's close friends, Gould and Bennett, honoured him by naming two new species after him. In addition, his American friend, Audubon, named a South American bird after him, as did Bourcier.

*Motacilla yarrellii* Gould,1837. *Mag. Nat. Hist.* new series 1, p. 460. Gt Britain.

This British resident, the Pied Wagtail, now considered a subspecies *Motacilla alba yarrellii,* was named by Gould in 1837, the same year that Yarrell's first volume of *A History of British Birds* was published. Gould established the British race and named it in his honour, saying 'I have named it after my friend W. Yarrell, Esq as a just tribute to his valued acquirements as a naturalist.' (*A History of British Birds* 1: 363)

Yarrell informed Sir William Jardine in January 1838 'It is our common black and white Wagtail to which Mr Gould has attached the name of Yarrellii, believing it to be distinct from the continental Pied wagtail.'[31]

*Carduelis yarrellii* Audubon, 1839. *Syn. Birds N. Amer.* p.117. 'Upper California' [error]. Now known as *Spinus yarrelli* (Audubon, 1839), the Yellow-faced Siskin's type locality was designated by Todd (1926. *Ann. Carnegie Mus.,*

17, p.32) as Bahia, Brazil. Range encompasses two disjunct areas in north-east Brazil and the Carabobo region of north Venezuela.

*Crax yarrellii* Bennett, 1835. *The Gardens and Menagerie of the Zoological Society* delineated. Vol. 2: Birds, pp 227–230. Red-knobbed Curassow. Described from a specimen living in the Zoological Society Gardens. Jardine & Selby (*Illustrations of ornithology*. 1836, vol IV, Plate 6) contains a plate of this species (artist: signed Edward Lear del 1836, Lizars sc.). Jardine sent Lizars the manuscript, etching and drawing for this on 9 October 1836.

The bird died soon after and Yarrell dissected its trachea to find that it differed from all those *Crax* species previously known. *Crax yarrellii* is now subsumed within *Crax globulosa* Spix, 1825, the Wattled Curassow.

*Pied Wagtail* Motacilla alba yarrellii, *named after Yarrell by John Gould.* A History of British Birds, 1843, 1: 362.

*Trochilus yarrellii* Bourcier, 1847. *Proceedings of the Zoological Society of London*, pt 15, p. 45 Coast of northern Chile. Now known as *Eulidia yarrellii*, the Chilean Woodstar, it is a globally endangered species present only in a few desert valleys in northern Chile and southern Peru.

Crax yarrellii. *Illustration by Edward Lear from Jardine & Selby (*Illustrations of ornithology. 1836, vol IV, Plate 6*).*

Eulidia yarrellii *Chilean Woodstar, plate 152 of John Gould's* Monograph of the Trochilidae, or family of Humming-birds.

Fishes

Genus *Yarrella* Goode and Bean *Oceanic Ichthyology, a treatise on the deep sea and pelagic fishes of the world, based chiefly on the collections made by the steamers Blake, Albatross and Fish Hawk in the North Atlantic.* 417 figures. Special Bulletin no 2 of the U.S. National Museum, 1895. 'It is named in honour of William Yarrell, F. L. S. (1784-1856), the English ichthyologist.' *Yarrella* is a genus of lightfish.

Yarrell's Blenny. Valenciennes sent a drawing to Yarrell and 'M. Valenciennes has done me the honour to propose that in future it should be called Blennius Yarrellii.' (Cuvier and Valenciennes *Histoire Naturelle des Poissons* t. xi, p. 218 see 1841, 1: 263). This is still known as Yarrell's Blenny, with the scientific name *Chirolophis ascanii.*

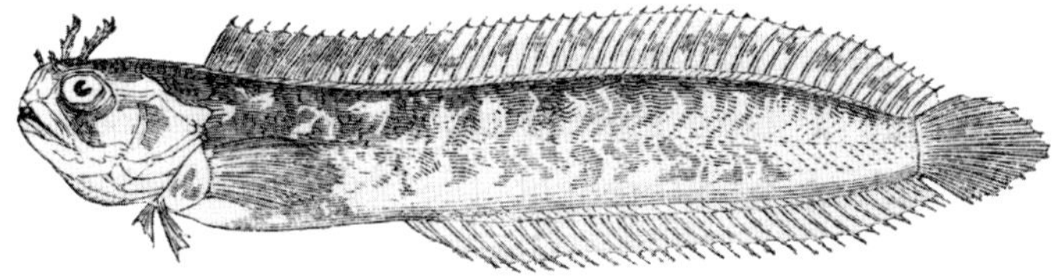

*Yarrell's Blenny. 'At the superior anterior margin of the eye on each side is a small fimbriated [i.e. fringed] appendage, which is connected with that on the opposite side of the head by a fold of skin forming a transverse union' – Yarrell's precise description.* A History of British Fishes, 1841, 1: 263.

*Laemonema yarrellii* (R.T. Lowe, 1838)

A codling in the family Moridae of deep-sea cods, codlings and hakelings, from Madeira and the Great Meteor Bank.

*Bagarius yarrelli* (Sykes, 1839)

William H. Sykes, Fishes of the Deccan, 1839: 163. A very large species of catfish, known as the Giant Devil Catfish, found in the rivers of South Asia.

Insects

*Stigmodera yarrellii*, one of the Jewel Beetles of Australia in the family Buprestridae. This was originally described by the Reverend Frederick W. Hope on p. 3 of a paper of 1836 entitled 'Buprestidae' that was not formally published. It was subsequently redescribed by E. Saunders in a paper read 4 November 1867 and published in *Transactions of the Entomological Society of London* 1868, pp 32–33, plate II, figure 18.

## A summing up

Professor Bell, who knew Yarrell well, tried to sum up his character and commenced by writing, 'In speaking of Mr Yarrell's intellectual and social qualities, it is difficult to do them justice without danger of appearing hyperbolical. His truthfulness and simple heartedness were even child-like, his temper gentle.' There is no doubt that Yarrell was a paragon of virtue, but not a prig. He was liked, not because he was upright at a period when that was much appreciated, but because he was kind with a sense of humour and fun. His boundless curiosity had led him to investigate mammals, birds and fishes beyond the contemporary way of endlessly listing and categorising, to look below the surface to see what made these creatures function. His interest in people allowed him to enjoy endless committees and dinners and meetings of fellow members of natural history societies, where something new might be revealed at any time. His tireless work for those societies was much appreciated because of the manner in which he undertook his duties. He was greatly missed at the time of his death when he was still serving as Treasurer and Vice-President of the Linnean Society. Members of the Linnean Society subscribed for a portrait in oils that remains in the Linnean Society in Piccadilly (see p.77).[32]

*Yarrell's curious choice of tail-piece for his own Blenny.* A History of British Fishes, 1841, 1: 268

## Chapter 7

# YARRELL'S LIFESTYLE AND INTERESTS

The sale of a deceased person's effects can reveal much about his lifestyle and interests. Yarrell's collections covered a wide range of subjects indicative of his intellectual curiosity and spending power. In each category he bought the best quality and work of first-class manufacturers. The number of items was so extensive that it took two sales, each lasting three days. The first sale occurred in November, two months after his death, and comprised his extensive library. The second sale in December included items that tell us much about Yarrell's lifestyle and tastes.

### The sale of Yarrell's library

*A Catalogue of the Valuable & Interesting Library of the late Wm. Yarrell, Esq., V.P.L.S, F.Z.S &c, &c, including In the various Branches of Natural History, the Works of Gould, Hewitson, Gray, Cuvier, Selby, Owen, Yarrell, Bewick, Bell, Agassiz, Daniel, Richardson, Walton and Cotton, Block [sic = Bloch] Jardine, Forbes, Pennant, Shaw, Smith, and a great many other esteemed authors. Rare Editions of Walton and Cotton's Angler and other works on angling and rural sports; Transactions and Proceedings of Scientific Societies and numerous standard works, with additional illustrations and notes, also three mahogany bookcases, sets of bookshelves Etc which will be sold by auction by Mr J. C. Stevens at his great room, 38 King Street, Covent Garden on Thursday, the 13th of November, 1856, and two following days, at one o'Clock precisely.*

32 pages.

The books were sold for £1,100.

The 764 lots were grouped by size of the books: Octavo lots 1–200 and 520–671; Quarto lots 201–503 and 672–738; and Folio lots 504–519 and 739–764. There was no attempt to arrange the lots by subject matter or alphabetization. Within a single lot there were disconcerting groups of disparate subjects, with sometimes two or three additional book titles within a lot, amounting to approximately 881 extra books. Many of these additional items within a lot were not dated, and some had no author cited. As well as these additional titles, there were dozens of lots with the phrase 'and x others' – sometimes up to 'and 20 others', but with no clue as to whether the additional items were by the same author or on the same subject. These 'and others' have been counted separately and amount to over 474. Add 474 and 881 to the numbered 764 lots (Lot 765 was bookcases) and there were over 2,000 titles. However, there were duplicates because Yarrell bought new editions of some favourite titles, e.g. Walton and Cotton's *Compleat Angler*; White's *Selborne*, and Bewick's *British Birds*. These were among his favourite authors, others being Davy, Charles Dibdin and J. Akerman on coins, with several books about Shakespeare and Dr Johnson.

What he inherited as a family library would lie within the publication period from 1700 to 1794, acquired by his grandfather Francis Yerrall (died 1786, when only a handful of books may have been present) and his father Francis Yerrall/Yarrell (died 1794, who owned some 50 titles). Another 30 titles were added before 1812 while his mother was alive. It would appear that a love of books and reading had been inculcated from an early age, with book-buying a regular family habit. William continued to acquire books, and this increased over the following years to the end of his life.

The pattern of his buying varied over the decades. Just counting the numbered lots, the purchases increased from approximately five in 1800–09; 40 in 1810–19; 80 in 1820–29; 160 in the 1830s; 210 in the 1840s and 100 in the last six years of his life in the 1850s. In the 1830s he was buying books required for his *A History of British Fishes* and *A History of British Birds*, as well as keeping up with the new flood of natural history books in that decade. Up to the middle of the 1840s, when he was finishing his two books and issuing supplements, he was still purchasing bird and fish books, but in the late 1840s this relaxed and he took a greater interest in other disciplines in natural history including some of the less well studied phyla and quite obscure species. He was also collecting plates and wood engravings (see the sale of December 1856 for these) both separately and in books.

For the first half of the 19th century this was a substantial library involving potentially considerable outlay. However, Yarrell was a bookseller and would obtain many items at trade prices and exchange his own works with other natural history authors. Yarrell may have regretted his lack of a university education, but his self-education by means of acquiring books was evident. The range of subjects is equally impressive, revealing a cultured, intelligent man with an enquiring mind anxious to broaden his knowledge over a wide field.

In 1812, when his mother died, Yarrell was aged 34 and had earned an income of his own from 1803. His books acquired from this time onwards indicate a consistent interest throughout life in biographies; languages (supported by German, Italian, Gaelic, Swedish, Danish, pronouncing and etymology dictionaries); and literature. Books on various sports had been acquired, including horse riding and falconry, a surprising number on sporting tours and sportsmen, and seven books on gunpowder with eight on shooting. This is not to mention the large number of books on angling (31) – a favourite sport with Yarrell. Natural history books covering a wide field were present from his father's day, but he added only a few between 1800 and 1819. It was in the 1820s that purchases of over 20 natural history categories increased per decade from c. 40 in the 1820s, 100+ in the 1830s, over 200 in the 1840s and some 90 between 1850 and 1856.

To subjects that had interested his grandfather and father – coins, travel and voyages worldwide, antiquities and history – Yarrell added art and architecture that was represented by classical Greek and Roman as well as English buildings, especially cathedrals. They were all three buying literature, but were not as interested in fiction as in plays and poetry, with poetry the favourite. There were only nine novels in the whole library by 1856: *Rasselas* by Dr Johnson, titles by Smollet, Sterne and Swift, Goldsmith's *Vicar of Wakefield* (probably bought for the illustrations by Mulready) and *Don Quixote.* There was not one title by Charles Dickens, a great favourite of his close friend Sir William Jardine.

Yarrell's leisure activities were revealed in this library catalogue. We know he had two pianos and music featured in his life, from classical to popular ballads and songs of the day, sung on stage at the theatres he so enjoyed. There was also an indication of his playing games, with a book on chess and two histories of playing cards. The 23 books on coins and medals in his library dated from 1664 through to 1850, biased towards Greek and Roman coins. The wide spread of the dates when the coin and medal books were published suggests a long-sustained interest in his family's coin collection.

There were scores of general natural history books, but Yarrell's greatest interest was naturally in birds and their eggs (approximately 100 titles) and fishes with fishing (c. 80). A surprising number of books on botany (over 50), mammals and molluscs from the 1810s were joined in the late 1840s and 1850s by books on obscure crustaceans and insects, algae, fossils and corals. With Yarrell's habit of dissecting everything to discover how it functioned, it is not surprising to find he had over 30 books on anatomy and physiology, including human anatomy as well as that of vertebrate and invertebrate animals. An increased interest in medicine occurred from the 1820s: however, the cataloguer gave short shrift to medicine and religion, frequently lumping together a large number of books on these subjects in one lot. The phrase 'and other medical' books occurred in half of the dozen medicine lots. Religion suffered a similar fate with the extraordinary case of 'Harmony of the Gospels and 17 various'.

In addition to all the books, there were hundreds of volumes of the 23 periodicals to which he subscribed. Perhaps his mother had subscribed to *British Critic*, because the run extends from 1793, when it was founded as a monthly publication. It was a conservative journal and after 1811 High Church, but in 1804 Mrs Yarrell cancelled their subscription so that in Yarrell's library there were just 22 volumes with an index. This may be the sole indication in all of the material on the Yarrell family of any political leaning – and it was before William took charge of the library.

It is probable that most of the foreign natural history books were obtained through Baillière in Paternoster Row, although being a bookseller himself Yarrell had no difficulty in obtaining foreign titles that he needed in the 1830s and 1840s from Albany and New York in America, Lund in Sweden, Frankfurt and Leipzig in Germany, Zurich in Switzerland, from Paris and from Italy. In Yarrell's *A History of British Birds* there is a surprising amount of information relating to the distribution of British birds in other countries, some of it extracted from the literature about explorers and overseas travellers, of which he owned many volumes. Books on travels abroad indicated an early interest carried throughout his life.

The huge increase in his purchase of books in the 1830s and 1840s was during the period when Yarrell was writing his books on fishes and then birds. Some retrospective buying of earlier published works was necessary, which is when he would have acquired Ray & Willughby of 1678 and Sibbald of 1684. It is likely that retrospective purchases from the 1700s include these two authors again, also Linnaeus, Latham, Pennant (Arctic zoology, Quadrupeds, British zoology), John Walcot and Bewick (British birds). The huge number of books published in the 1840s and present in the library (some 250), probably bought by him, is not so easily explained unless he was using them to prepare a history of woodcuts and engravings, as mentioned in an entry to a lot in the December sale of his effects. He completed work on the first editions of *A History of British Fishes* in 1836 and *A History of British Birds* in 1843. He subsequently issued several supplements and interim sheets, so up-to-date works were still needed. During the last six years of his life, Yarrell obtained over 100 books (12 within the last eight months January to August 1856). His interest and purchasing never decreased right up to the time of his death.

There are two sources commenting on the sale and prices of individual copies:

1. *Hampshire Chronicle,* Sat Nov 22 1856, p. 8: 'The late Mr Yarrell's books, dispersed by Mr J C Stevens have realized £1100. Gould's *Birds of Europe, Birds of Australia* £79, *Humming Birds* £23. The first edition of Bewick's *British Birds,* were sold for £5.15s, Gray's *Genera of Birds* £16.5s, Walton and Cotton's *Complete Angler* with many additional illustrations inserted by Mr Yarrell, £9, Forbes and Haney's *History of British Mollusca and their Shells,* £12, Audubon's *Birds of America* £36 and his *Ornithological Biographies,* £10.10s, the *Zoology of the Beagle* £7.10s, Smith's *Illustrations of the Zoology of South Africa,* £13.10s, Prof. Owen's *Odontography* £9.15s. Copies of Mr Yarrell's own works also sold for good prices.'

Whoever attended the sale for this paper was evidently more interested in the bird books, but gave a useful view of the most memorable sales and prices.

2. A letter dated 25 November 1856 from Van Voorst to Leonard Jenyns (in the BRLSI) said he had bought 'a few of the books, one of them the only

coloured copy of the *History of British Fishes*'. Van Voorst also said 'I enclose an invoice of the books bought for you, the others went at too high a price. More than I could sell you new copies for – Johnston's Intro. to Conchology a guinea Volume sold for 20/- and Leach's Moll. fetched 14/- the selling price being only 15/-. The parcel is tied up and waits your instructions as to its disposal.' The two books were: Dr George Johnston's *An Introduction to Conchology: or, elements of the natural history of molluscous animals,* 1850, and William Elford Leach (1790–1836) MD FRS, entomologist and marine biologist, author of *Synopsis of the Mollusca of Great Britain,* 1852.

**Second sale 4–6 December 1856**

The bulk of the sale lots in the second catalogue was concerned with Yarrell's bird collections – the first 428 items being ornithological. Nevertheless, the rest of the sale catalogue of Yarrell's possessions tells us much about his cultural as well as other interests. While naturalists nowadays know about his two books on birds and fishes, they are not aware of his activities in other fields. J. C. Stevens, the auctioneer, divided the 522 lots into several categories to be sold over three days, 4–6 December 1856, that were itemized on the front cover:

*1856 4 December A Catalogue of the interesting collections of objects of NATURAL HISTORY, &c of the late Wm Yarrell, Esq V.P.L.S., F.L.S., including specimens of stuffed British Birds and fishes (many of which are the types of his great Works); Comparative Anatomy, Birds' Eggs, amongst them the GREAT AUK and other rarities; preparations in spirits, remaining Books and Books of Prints, several collections illustrative of the progress of wood engraving, and progress of the gun lock; pictures, framed prints and original water-colour drawings, Cabinet of Coins & Medals, about 150 ounces of useful plate, mahogany cabinets, double gun by John Manton &c &c which will be sold by Mr J. C. Stevens at his Great Room, 38 King Street, Covent Garden on Thursday, the 4th of December, 1856 at one o'clock precisely.* 19 pages.

The categories as they appeared in the sale catalogue are followed here. The specimen component sold for £719.

**Books, books of prints &c pp. 1–8, lots 1–114**

Five mahogany bookcases, some with glass fronts, were itemized among the miscellaneous objects. All the sale objects in wood were made of mahogany, a quality wood of the period. However, the books in this catalogue have the

a. Meadow Pipit
b. Missel Thrush
c. Skylark
d. Willow Warbler
e. Redwing
f. Wren

PLATE 9 SONG BIRDS

distinct feeling of 'leftovers' from the Library sale held a few weeks earlier in November. Indeed, there were more than 100 of the same titles as in the Library sale.

Yarrell had obtained proofs or engraved illustrations for scores of books – on landscape, poetry, fables, religious emblems – probably from all the publishers he knew from his business contacts and Van Voorst. Many of the books listed in this sale catalogue were itemized for their plates only, for example the illustrations from Bloch's *Icones Systematica* that had coloured plates, similarly the egg plates from Hewitson's *Oology*, but that was a rare collector's item being a presentation set. Another special collection of illustrations from Northcote's *Fables* was one of only 25 published. Similarly, he only bothered with the coloured plates to H. L. Meyer's 2 volumes of *British Land and Water Birds*. There was just one photograph itemized, 'of Game'. Photography was first employed to depict animals in the Zoological Gardens in 1852, but there is no evidence of any of these in Yarrell's possession. The only item clearly indicating photographs occurred in the Library sale, which had included 'Photographic portraits 1856', probably the Ipswich Museum book of photographs. His own illustrations that appeared in periodicals included anatomical drawings he had collected together, e.g. organs of the voice in birds, trachea and sternum, with coloured drawings of hermaphrodites, British and foreign birds' eggs, with a MS list of them.

Yarrell owned a microscope (Lot 148 A microscope by Carpenter, with objects, in mahogany case), an expensive piece of equipment but vital for his anatomical work and to enable him to make detailed drawings from his dissections, some of which appeared as vignettes in his two books.[1] He had a book to guide him with his microscope, 'Pritchard *A Microscopic cabinet*, 1832'. Two other books in his library were about 'animalcules', a term for microscopic organisms that cannot be seen by the naked eye.

Yarrell attended his local parish church of St James's where he, his brothers and sisters had been baptized, and in his collection of books had several volumes of sermons and two pictures, 'The Last Supper' and the 'Finding of Moses', among other scriptural items. A bible was not listed separately but he had some illustrations from one.

The number of books represented by the illustrations taken from them is remarkable, but reflects his main interest in other people's books – the engravings. Whether he read the text of the Waverley novels, or *The Vicar of Wakefield*, is open to surmise, but the last one was very special: '32 of Mulready's Illustrations of *The Vicar of Wakefield*, on India paper, 6 only printed'. Sir Walter Scott's Waverley novels that were published 1814, 1819 and 1824 were among the few novels in the library.

There were very few etchings in Yarrell's collection, though three by Rembrandt shows he knew their historical importance. Among natural history books and illustrations gathered for reference were items covering botany, mammals and reptiles. These were useful when dealing with queries from other naturalists.

**Framed and glazed prints & drawings, paintings &c pp. 7–8, lots 115–147**
For visitors to his home these were probably the points of interest most accessible, hanging on the walls of the dining and sitting rooms. There were 33 lots, but many of them contained several paintings. They would be interested in the portraits of fellow naturalists. Named in the catalogue were Professor Edward Forbes (1815–54, eminent naturalist in several fields), Sir Charles Lyell (1797–1875, Scottish geologist, author of *Principles of Geology*, 1830–33), Peter Mark Roget,[2] Sir Stamford Raffles, W. Whewell, Richard Owen, Captain Ross, H. Strickland, J. Hunter, General Hardwicke, J. G. Children, Georges Cuvier, W. Clift, H. Cuming, J. Brookes and his publisher John Van Voorst.

Yarrell also had a framed portrait of Dr Johnson of dictionary fame, who had sold Goldsmith's minor classic (and a favourite book with Yarrell) *The Vicar of Wakefield* for £60 on Oliver Goldsmith's behalf to save him from bankruptcy. There were also three theatrical prints. He owned a set of the 'Ipswich Gallery of Scientific Men of the present day' in a portfolio that included one of himself. The framed portraits were in gilt frames. His other framed pictures were in maple frames (see p.94) and perhaps his favourites, though it is a mixed collection with no discernible connections one to another. The six maple-framed pictures comprised: a Landseer engraving; a lithograph scene by William Powell Frith (1819–1909) from *The Vicar of Wakefield*; a portrait of the late 13th Earl of Derby; a painting after Sir Augustus Wall Callcott (1779–1844) of *Raffaelle and the Fornarina*, by L. Stocks; an engraving from Laurence Sterne's *Tristram Shandy*; and a portrait of Linnaeus in his Lapland dress after Hoffman by Kingsbury.

**Silver plate, p.9, lots 150–162**

Yarrell was fond of entertaining and had silverware for his table. The weight of the silver pieces in ounces, plus the dwts (= troy weight, a system of weights for metals), was noted for each lot. Several of the pieces would have been carefully stored in an iron-bound plate chest, with two lifting trays, lined with velvet. Tea, dessert and table spoons came by the dozen, with 18 forks. The Georgians devised special cutlery for serving fish – a slice, tongs for asparagus, a marrow spoon, nutcrackers, muffineers[3], sugar tongs and soup ladles. Silver coffee pots and teapots were accompanied by cream ewers. Salts had their usual blue glass linings. Some of this might well have come from his family, who were relatively well off.

Opera glasses are an odd inclusion in this group. Yarrell no doubt took them on his frequent visits to the theatre and perhaps in the field, for this was some years before binoculars had been invented. They became used for bird watching from the 1860s, too late for Yarrell's use.

Yarrell's other articles for entertaining appeared in Lots 500–510 under Miscellaneous (see below).

**Coins, medals, etc pp. 9–10, lots 163–203**

In all the correspondence read for this book, there is not one hint of Yarrell's interest in coins and medals, and the 1,000 plus items in the 40 lots are indeed just the kind of surprise that rewards the reading of a sale catalogue of a deceased person.

The medals occupy three lots, each with a variety of medals, e.g. one for the 1851 Exhibition, the 'fine medal of Rubens by Hart, others of Louis Philippe, Captain Cook and Shakespeare'. Yarrell owned Pinkerton's book on medals and Walsh on early coins that would have given him a working knowledge of medals to assist him in cataloguing his own collection.[4]

Of gold coins there were various Continental small coins, but an interesting 'gold nugget' with no specified weight. Silver coins made up the bulk of the coinage sale, with ancient coins of Greek and Roman origin and his contemporary coins from Switzerland, Spain, Austria, France, the Netherlands, Prussia and Russia. Among the English silver coins were those of the reigns of George IV, William IV and some issued in the early years of Victoria's reign. There were far fewer lots of copper coins that included copper tokens, jettons (stamped metal used as counters in card playing, casting accounts) and foreign coppers of Russia and northern Europe, France and Germany and various English. The brass coins were Roman. A quality 'mahogany medal cabinet of 56 drawers and one deep drawer', with '8 mahogany priced trays for coins in deal trays and wainscot box', had housed this large and varied collection.

The books on the subject of coins included a *Thesaurus Gemmarum et Numismatum Graecorum,* with plates, of 1696 and *Regum at Imperatorium Romanorum Numismata,* with plates, 1654. Yarrell was conversant with Latin after his schooling. In total, there were 23 books on coins and medals in his library.

**Birds, in cases pp. 11–14, lots 204–338**

Yarrell valued his bird skins, dissected and set up by himself, as some of his most treasured possessions. They were what his naturalist visitors particularly wanted to see. He owned as complete a set of British birds as possible, with duplicates of most. They were mounted and placed in glass cases, or under shades, many having been arranged, under instructions from Yarrell about the size of the cases, by John Gould. That is how bird specimens were kept at this period. Later, from the 1840s, skins were more likely to be placed in envelopes or kept in drawers.

The 75 glass cases represent far more than 75 species because more than one species was often cased with another, e.g. 'Kestrel Hawk and a Merlin Hawk; Redwing and pair of Twites; Kingfisher, rock Pipit and Wagtail', etc. There were 106 species, plus some in different plumage and other duplicates. Cases were more efficient at deterring destructive insects than later glass shades placed over the mounted bird.

**Bird skins p. 14, lots 339–346**

Unmounted bird skins in the collection were far more numerous than the lot numbers suggest. Each lot had a few of the more rare species named and were followed by 'various', meaning others: consequently it is not possible to know how many unmounted skins were in the collection other than the 26 named.

**Birds' eggs pp 14–15, lots 347–407 (408 was left blank)**

These were another source of great pride in Yarrell's collection. He had as complete a set of British birds' eggs as possible, with duplicates of most. Again, the lots occasionally had groups of different birds' eggs. A 'Grey phalarope' had

Yarrell's comment 'the best authenticated egg known' (fetched £1.10s). Lots 400–407 were trays of eggs or a 'Box with 3 lifting trays of American eggs' and a 'Tray of small birds' eggs, from America'. The famous egg of the Great Auk warranted capital letters opposite Lot Number '399 GREAT AUK' (The egg sold for 20 guineas or £21). There were three mahogany cabinets, one of them with 12 drawers adapted for eggs, shells, minerals, etc.

**Comparative anatomy pp. 16–17, lots 409–441**

One of the strengths of Yarrell's bird and fish books was his careful anatomical notes, and drawings that were engraved for the text. The dissections also formed the basis for many of his discoveries explained in articles in journals. This section of the catalogue contains 21 such items as skeletons, breast bones, trachea, two drawers of skulls of birds. There were skulls of mammals – leopard, lion, human, tiger, bear, monkeys, small mammals and others, plus stuffed mice and a bat and rat. Just two lots were stuffed fishes – perch, trout – but the last lot in this section was 'A large and valuable collection of fish, with a variety of manuscripts, collected with a view to publishing a work on the subject', probably the research material for his *A History of British Fishes.*

**Preparations in spirits etc. pp. 17–18, lots 442–484**

This section is where the fish preparations, mostly contained in bottles, are listed. The auctioneer almost gave up in despair at this section, resorting to 'Twenty-two bottles containing reptiles, Crustacea, shells &c.', 'Thirty-seven small bottles, containing fish, some of them named', and so many small bottles were sold in one lot that it is impossible to assess the extent of Yarrell's fish collection. Butterflies and other insects, centipedes, a mole, shells, Crustacea, mouse, young turtle – the lots fetched between 8/- and 13/-, being the only ones in the Royal College of Surgeons' copy of the catalogue to have a pencilled price opposite them. Seven lots were minerals, and a few botanical specimens of mosses, ferns and corked box of insects, with shells and finally the 'grinder of an Elephant & parcel of tusks, teeth &c'. A large parcel of dried fishes and more skeletons of birds concluded the anatomical preparations.

**Miscellaneous articles pp. 18–19, lots 485–522**

This final sales section comprising Miscellaneous Articles provides further clues to Yarrell's interests beyond natural history. The first item is a plaster bust of the late Wm Yarrell, an item unsuspected for no later reference as to its whereabouts has been found. The presence of 'A ditto bust of the French Empress, under glass shade, on a stand' is equally inexplicable, but most of us would prefer the bust of Yarrell to be found.

His interest in the weather, prompted by Jenyns, might have been the reason for Yarrell's owning an aneroid barometer, another barometer, three boxwood thermometers, a wheel barometer by Potts and another barometer by Watkins & Hill. The last was a firm, Francis Watkins and William Hill, trading 1810–1847 at 5 Charing Cross, London, in quality optical instruments including very good barometers.

Yarrell was a keen sportsman. When he died, obituaries in newspapers across the country referred to him as a 'good old English sportsman', owing to his fishing abilities but above all to his exploits with his Manton gun winning shooting competitions around London. His fishing tackle appeared in Lot 495 'Fishing rod, winches and a quantity of tackle.' '18 Watercolour drawings of freshwater fishes...drawn for Major's edition of *Walton's Angler* in 6 frames, glazed.' Major's edition of Izaak Walton's *The Compleat Angler* of 1653 was issued in 1824. A watercolour of the freshwater fishes of England by one of the best fish artists, Henry Leonides Rolfe, in a handsome gilt frame; a drawing in colours entitled 'Spear Fishing by Moonlight', in a gilt frame.

Lot 149 was the double-barrelled gun, by John Manton, in a case, with apparatus. This was his famous gun with which he won shooting matches and was a treasured possession to the end of his life. Manton was a personal friend, and if Yarrell saw Manton in his shop in Bond Street as he walked past he would raise his walking stick to his shoulder in gun position to remind him of their competitive shooting days. A related interest was in a volume containing plates of 'Military Exercise at the time the Match Lock was in use, 1603' that also had 'an immense number of prints, drawings, manuscripts &c, apparently preparations for a History of the Gun Lock from the earliest time.' He had sporting books, e.g. Thornton's *Sporting Tour in France,* 2 volumes, published in 1806. This might well have been an early purchase while he was very active as a sportsman himself as a young man, when Colonel Thomas Thornton (1757–1823) spent his time and fortune hunting, shooting, angling and hawking and was a sporting hero of the day.

Yarrell's other sporting interests were represented by paintings: Spaniels and Ducks, and Dog and Pheasants in colours, gilt frame; The Stag and Hounds;

Coursing; Pheasant shooting; Spaniel and Pheasant, all coloured paintings in gilt frames.

Yarrell had owned two pianos – a '6½ octave cottage piano by Matthews in a mahogany case, silk front, on turned legs', and a 'Six-octave square piano, by Tomkison, on turned legs.'[5] We know Yarrell loved singing and went to the theatre to hear popular songs of the day, so he may have enjoyed playing the piano too, but his sister Caroline lived with him for a number of years and one of the pianos may have been hers. There was another lot, a 'Mahogany Canterbury (a stand with divisions for holding music) and rising music stool.' The 'rising' stool would have been useful to a man of short stature, and the seat may have contained sheet music, which is not otherwise represented in the sale catalogue, though the Canterbury infers it once contained their music.

Another recreation may have been enjoyed by Caroline and William: a set of chessmen and board were present. There was a book by Sarratt, *Chess,* published in 1804, in his library.

Also offered was a 'parrot cage along with two travelling bags, portmanteau and mahogany box'. There is no other intimation of a parrot having been in the house; however, there might well have been a further use for the parrot cage. Was it this cage that Charles Darwin borrowed when he went to John Bailey the poulterer and live bird dealer's shop to collect some pigeons in 1855 (see p.103)?

Yarrell's love of entertaining is further demonstrated in lots 500–510, where tableware included very many wine glasses – '7 quart, two pair of pint and claret decanters, and wine coolers.' There was a 'Handsome China dessert service, beautifully painted in birds, consisting of 3 dishes, 2 centres and 9 plates.', but the dejeuné set was painted in flowers. Several china ornaments included rabbit, fish, bird, heads of dogs and a hare.

Minerals, crystals, meteorites, native gold, dendrites, marbles and other polished specimens, fossils, shells, etc., show Yarrell's wider, if less intense, interest in natural history objects, but a rather more extensive collection of insects were correctly housed in corked boxes, including two for butterflies.

The reason for Yarrell's interest in wood-engraved illustrations is immediately obvious from his own use of them in his *A History of British Fishes* and *A History of British Birds,* but another motive becomes obvious when reading items regarding woodcuts and wood engravings in the sale catalogue. Lot 56 gives the reason for several lots of both: 'A guard book, containing proofs and other impressions of WOOD CUTS by Albert Durer and other early and late artists. A collection formed with a view to a History of Engraving on Wood.' There was another portfolio of woodcuts and plates: *Mario Cento Favoli Morali woodcuts; woodcuts and Verses,* printed at the Lee Priory Press, 1820. More proofs of woodcuts were in another volume with many MS names of the artists; also a similar one of the Northern School and the London School, with proofs of Bewick's landscapes, again with MS names of the artists. The standard work of the time, by John Jackson, *Treatise on Wood Engraving, Historical and Practical,* with upwards of 300 illustrations, issued in 1839, was in Yarrell's library.

Wood engraving inevitably meant a deep interest in the work of Thomas Bewick. Yarrell had collected *Bewickiana* containing portraits, proof illustrations of wood engravings, and the original prospectus of his various works, with many 'MS Notes and Letters from T. Bewick and Atkinson's *Sketch and Life of T. Bewick.*' A rare volume of Scripture illustrations, by Bewick and others, illustrated with wood engravings, was another lot. He also had a supplement to '*Bewick's Birds; the figures of Bewick's quadrupeds,* 2nd ed 1824; a set of three volumes, one with numerous cuttings from rare works previous to 1740, two mostly by Bewick, and collections of proofs by the best engravers of the present day; a portfolio containing 'History of Engravers, loose prints, maps Etc.' Yarrell did not get around to writing a history of woodcuts and wood engravings, which is to be regretted.

There was a newspaper that commented on this second sale:

**Morning Post, London, 8 December 1856, p. 2.**

Mr Yarrell's Sale 'At the sale on Saturday week of the late Mr Yarrell's specimens of natural history, the most remarkable purchase was that of an egg for £21, the egg of the Great Auk, a bird of the diver tribe...The egg of the broad-billed Sandpiper fetched £1.9s, A Broad-billed Sandpiper egg was noted as having been supplied by Mr Dann [See Richard Dann p.212] an egg of the Grey Phalarope £1.10s and one of the Golden eagle £2.10 A specimen of the Buff breasted Sandpiper £5.5s and one of the Spotted Sandpiper £1.13s.

Among miscellaneous objects a large drawing in watercolour – View on the Thames by Aaron Penley – selected, we believe, by Mr Yarrell for an 80 guinea prize in the Art Union, sold for £27.6.

Bewickiana, a valuable miscellaneous collection of proof wood engravings £9.15; and a miscellaneous lot of woodcuts by Durer £5.10s.'

Reading through the sales threw up constant surprises. Expected items appeared in such quantities as to give one pause for reflection both on the great expenditure on, and quality of, the items. Hitherto unsuspected interests entertained by Yarrell were accompanied by a reflection on the breadth and depth of those interests, not only in the objects themselves but his literature about them. Indeed, his library reflected his intellectual curiosity about a huge range of subjects. His friends benefited from their association with such an intelligent and knowledgeable person, and this explains why so many delighted in his company.

*One of the best depictions of the plumage of the Starling in any bird book. Signed THOMPSON DEL ET SC (delineat et sculpsit, drawn and engraved).* A History of British Birds 2: 44

Chapter 8

# YARRELL'S PUBLICATIONS

Yarrell published two major book titles, *A History of British Fishes* and *A History of British Birds,* as well as a small booklet, *On the growth of the Salmon in fresh water,* a chapter on marine fishes in William Henry Harvey's *The Sea-Side Book,* 3rd ed, pp. 237–269, and 80+ periodical articles, all within the period 1825–56.

Yarrell lived at a time when interest in natural history grew phenomenally and was fed by an increasing number of periodical titles and books on all aspects of the subject, from the 1830s on through the 19th century. Yarrell's reasons for writing his own two books can be summarised as:

1. To establish which species are found within the British Isles.
2. To determine how long they had been considered British and when they were first recorded as such.
3. To establish the distribution of each species from reported locations in the British Isles.
4. To provide a definitive description of both external and anatomical features for each species.
5. To record the habitats as well as habits of the species. For fishes, their salt or fresh water environment and depth at which the species could be found; for birds, their habitats and life styles within those habitats.

6. To record food eaten from analysis of stomach contents.
7. To record methods of capture, transport and marketing.
8. For some species, to cook them and ascertain how edible they might be.
9. To provide an accurate, wood-engraved portrait of each species.

His two major books on birds and fishes filled the gaps in literature when he was writing and fulfilled a need for up-to-date data both on the less popular subject of fishes and the public's favourite subject, birds. He wrote the fish book first (1834–36), then the bird book (1837–43), in a uniform format similar to that adopted by Thomas Bewick. Each book was an instant success, becoming standard, indispensible treatises that remained pertinent to the end of the century. There were several editions of each and supplements in between editions. They were reputed by Van Voorst, his publisher, to have netted Yarrell £4000.[1]

What use are they today? They formed an accurate basis on which to build modern scientific taxonomic advances and distribution records. Anyone interested in fishing methods and fishing boats, the development of fish markets and transport, will find historical notes of importance. This does not apply to methods of catching birds, but before powerful binoculars there was only one way to accurately describe a bird and that was from one in the hand. Examples of captured birds provided the means of writing and depicting accurate portraits for the wood engravings in *A History of British Birds.*

After 1900, authors accepted that his statements of earliest records and later history, as well as old taxonomy, had been well established and need not be repeated. The emphasis shifted to recording new arrivals and distribution, and adopting new methods of illustrating the species.

**Yarrell's publishing strategy**

The first task for an author of a non-fiction book is to establish what is already in the public domain, either in the form of a book or a document. In London, Yarrell had access to the libraries at the British Museum and the Linnean Society. He listed some of the books he had consulted under each fish and bird species. This was particularly apposite for a scientific text where the synonymy needed to be recorded. His own library and those of friends and colleagues in colleges and other private libraries were mentioned in the text. Help came from the generous sharing of notebooks and catalogues of species by correspondents.

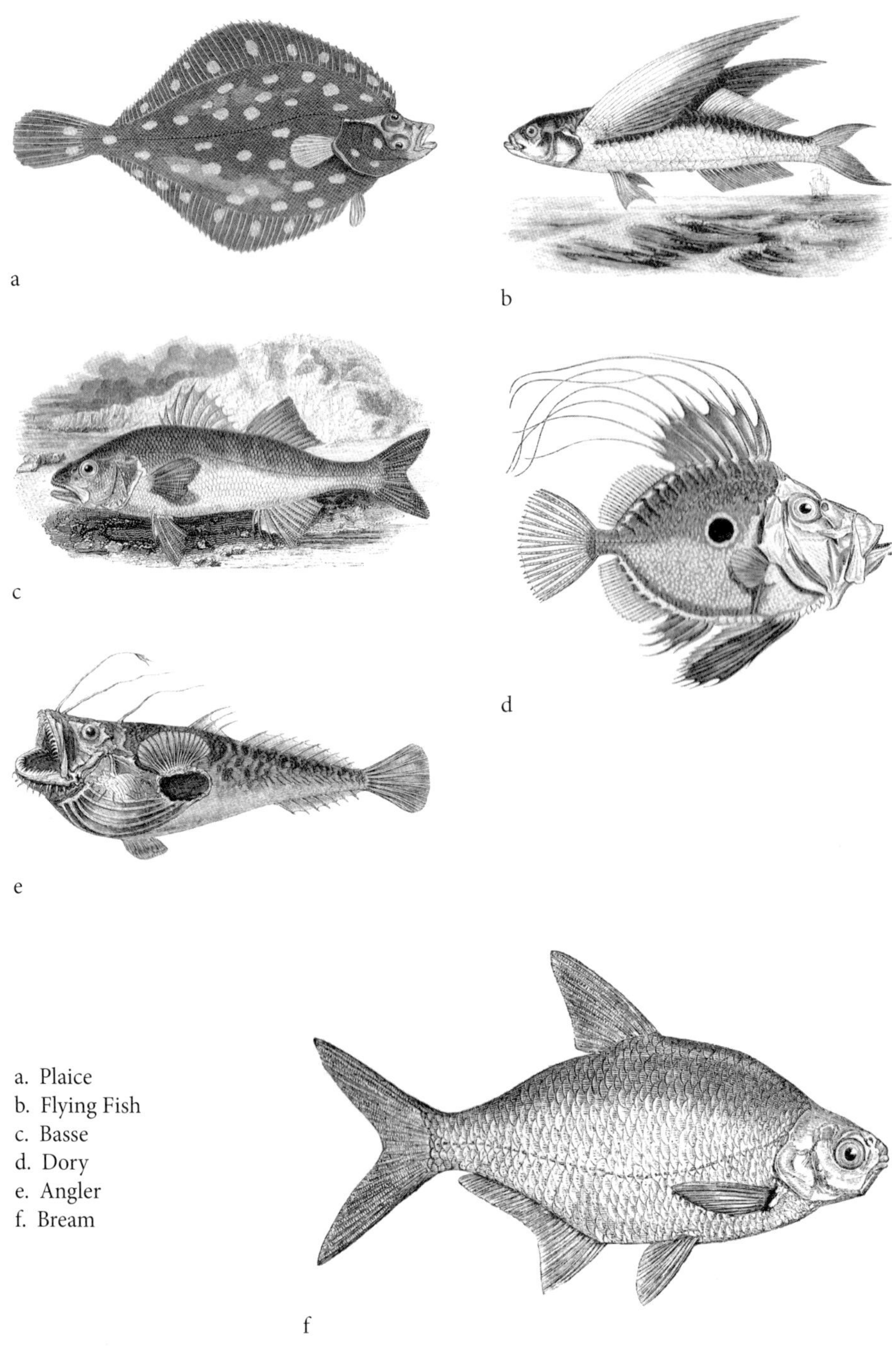


a. Plaice
b. Flying Fish
c. Basse
d. Dory
e. Angler
f. Bream

PLATE 10 MARINE FISHES

The second task was to discover hidden, not usually accessible, material and gain access to it. A wide circle of acquaintances was helpful here. However, Yarrell had a specific additional requirement of his own at the time of writing. He not only needed any specimens of species that were unknown, but he required data such as distribution, habitat, food, etc., for each one. In his text in *A History of British Fishes* and *A History of British Birds* he expresses gratitude for notes from a wide circle of people not only known to him, but also from complete strangers. What might have been a dangerous undertaking for an author, by embarking on a book with only partial knowledge and limited resources, was mitigated by publishing the book in parts. Word spread that he needed more information and specimens. Both were sent to him in increasing numbers throughout the months it took to complete his book. There were c. 80 contributors to *A History of British Fishes* and c. 130 to *A History of British Birds*, though only c. 20 contributed to both titles. An incentive to assist him was provided by his scrupulous acknowledgement of the help he had received from people by naming them in the text. That his work in progress was noted in the British press, nationwide, provided additional interest and response to his need for local information.

The part of each book for which Yarrell took most credit was on geographical distribution; for birds he noted that 'he smuggled in a certain amount of geography in the garb of ornithology'.[2] From the Orkneys in the north down the east coast, including Edinburgh, Northumberland, Lincolnshire, Norfolk and Suffolk and Kent, and along the south coast all the way to Cornwall, there were contributors for marine species. Inland, there were rather fewer for fishes but a greater number for birds.

It was a brave attempt to furnish distribution records for all species, not attempted before Yarrell published. He was supported by a large group of excellent correspondents and of particular note were some dozen reverend gentlemen naturalists in the tradition of Gilbert White. Foremost among these were the Reverend Leonard Jenyns, Vicar of Swaffham Bulbeck, Cambridgeshire, and the Reverend Robert Lubbock of Norfolk. Among other notable professional colleagues were Sir William Jardine and two medical doctors, George Johnston of Berwick-upon-Tweed and Jonathan Couch, for 60 years a doctor in Polperro, Cornwall. They all ably supported Yarrell in providing information on both fishes and birds.

## PUBLICATIONS

The publisher of Yarrell's books was John Van Voorst (1804–98, retired in 1886), who was born into a family of Dutch descent. He worked at first for Longman, Green, Orme, before setting up his own business in 1833 in Paternoster Row. He began to specialise in natural history books and was appointed bookseller to the Zoological Society in 1837. Van Voorst (he always used double capital V letters) and Yarrell were first brought together by a mutual friend, Mr Martin, the librarian of the Duke of Bedford. Van Voorst not only published William Yarrell's two books, but they became close associates. Van Voorst was frequently at Yarrell's house, joined in excursions to shoot and fish around London and was there, at the end of Yarrell's life, to take his body from Great Yarmouth to Bayford to his grave and erect the memorial to him in St James's Piccadilly. He may also have erected William's tombstone in Bayford Churchyard, perhaps as designed by Yarrell. Van Voorst kept Yarrell's books up to date after his death with later editions of both titles (see p.141 for fishes and p.157 for birds). He also attended the sale of Yarrell's library in December 1856 and bought several books for himself and for Leonard Jenyns (see p.124).

Van Voorst took James Edmund Harting to visit the Yarrell graves in Bayford Churchyard, telling Harting much about Yarrell whom he had known for many years. Harting published an account of the visit, but says disappointingly little about the grave, churchyard, or Yarrell.

Van Voorst published six other natural history titles in the same uniform size and format as those by Yarrell: two by Bell on quadrupeds and reptiles; one by Forbes on British starfishes; *A General Outline of the Organisation of the Animal Kingdom* by Professor Rymer Jones; Selby's *British Forest Trees*; and Newman's *History of British Ferns*. Unfortunately, any archives for the firms in Paternoster Row went up in flames in the Second World War, along with six million books.

### *A HISTORY OF BRITISH FISHES*

*A History of British Fishes*, 1835–36 2 volumes. Published in parts, finished in 1836. Vol.1. 408pp., vol. 2 472pp. 226 species described and figured + 140 vignettes. 19 parts, 2/6d each with the index in the last part.

Supplement, March 1839 (vol.1, pp 48, vol. 2, pp 78, containing 27 new species).

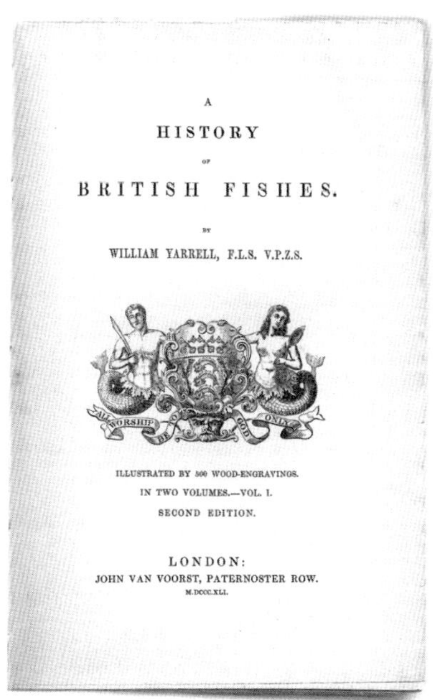

A
HISTORY
OF
BRITISH FISHES.
BY
WILLIAM YARRELL, F.L.S. V.P.Z.S.

ILLUSTRATED BY 500 WOOD-ENGRAVINGS.
IN TWO VOLUMES.—VOL. I.
SECOND EDITION.

LONDON:
JOHN VAN VOORST, PATERNOSTER ROW.
M.DCCC.XLI.

2nd supplement to 1st edition of *A History of British Fishes,* edited by Sir John Richardson MDCCC.LX. Being also a first supplement to the second edition. Includes a Memoir of William Yarrell pp. v–xviii, and a List of Mr Yarrell's writings pp xix–xxiii (periodical articles as well as books).

2nd ed. 1841 2 vols (vol. 1, pp 464; vol. 2 pp 628, containing 263 species and 500 figures.

Supplement to 2nd ed. October 1845.

3rd edition 1859, 2 vols; edited by Sir John Richardson, with a memoir of Yarrell by Van Voorst.

*On the growth of the Salmon in fresh water...with six coloured illustrations of the fish of the natural size, exhibiting its character and exact appearance at various stages during the first two years.* London, 1839, oblong folio (height 30.5 x width 44 cm), 3pp with drawings in the text and 3 plates with 6 illustrations drawn by C. Curtis, engraved by R. Sands, printed by Samuel Bentley, Bangor House, Shoe Lane, London.

'On marine fishes', chapter VIII in William Henry Harvey *The Sea-Side book; an introduction to the natural history of the British coasts,* 3rd ed, pp. 237–269, 1854.

Yarrell did not acquire expertise in systematic zoology until after becoming a member of the Linnean Society in 1825 and of the Zoological Society in 1826.

His contacts with other members led to his more scientific studies of natural history objects. When he found new species or made original observations, he reported them to the *Zoological Journal* and the *Linnean Transactions.* His first dozen notices were mainly about birds, but in 1828, in the *Zoological Journal* (iv: 137), his earliest publication on the subject of fishes appeared in print: 'On the supposed identity of Whitebait and Shad', disproving that whitebait could be shad. The more substantial contribution 'Remarks on some English Fishes, with Notices of three Species new to the British Fauna' followed in 1828/9 (*Zool. Journal.* iv: 465), but his most notable early contribution to the

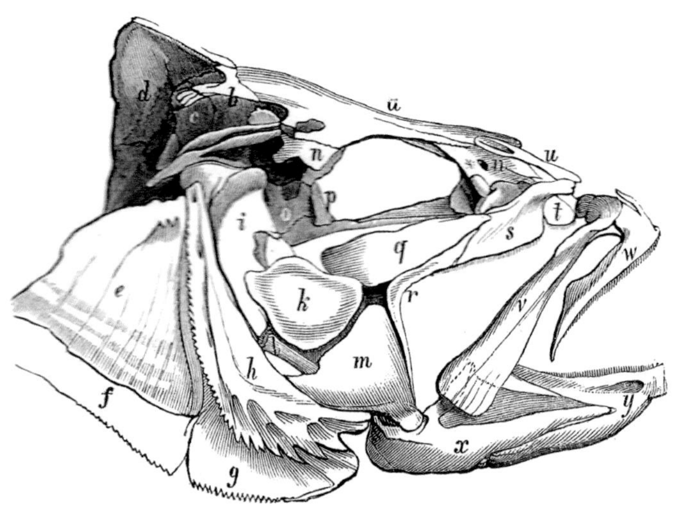


a. Principal frontal bone
b. parietal.
c. Inter occipital.
d. Inter parietal.
e. Operculum.
f. Suboperculum.
g. Interoperculum.
h. Preoperculum.
i. Temporal.
k. Tympanal.
l. Sympletic.
m. Jugal.
n. Posterior frontal.
n*. Anterior frontal.
o. Great ala.
p. Sphenoid.
q. Internal pterygoid.
r. Transverse.
s. Palatal bone.
t. Vomer.
u. Nasal.
v. Superior maxillary.
w. Inter maxillary.
x. Articular portion, and
y. Dental portion of the lower jaw, or inferior maxillary bone.

*Head of Perch,* A History of British Fishes, 1841, 1: 7. *Sensibly placed at the beginning of the book on British fishes with the bones named.*

study of fishes was revealed to the British Association for the Advancement of Science meeting in 1833, when he first unequivocally established that the Eel was oviparous (egg-laying).[3]

By August 1834 Yarrell was ready to embark on a full-scale account of British fishes. Although three years earlier he had 'from some authority or other a coloured figure of many of the British species – fishes', he informed Jenyns that he had begun to work on a book of British fishes, basing it on Bewick's book format and using wood engravings for illustrations. He added that he already had engravers at work. He proposed to produce three sheets with publication of a part every three months. He said the publishers wanted him to work faster 'but with superintending all the wood cuttings and twice reading three sheets of proofs every three months will bring me as much additional labour as I dare promise to encounter, and will consume probably the whole of my leisure'. It has to be remembered that Yarrell had a full-time job with his business as well as writing the book. He had also written a prospectus advertising his British Fishes to be inserted in other books, as and when they were published in parts.

There were few books that Yarrell could consult for his *A History of British Fishes*. There was only one book entirely devoted to British fishes published in the previous 30 years: Edward Donovan's *The Natural History of British Fishes*, published 1802–08 with 120 coloured plates. Several zoologies of British fauna had sections on fishes and those Yarrell included in his synonyms were: John Fleming's *A History of British Animals* 1828, which listed 170 fish species; and, going back in time, Thomas Pennant's *British Zoology* 4th edition 1812, 4 volumes (volume 3 was fishes); and Thomas Bewick's *A Natural History of British Quadrupeds...Fishes...*1809, with very few images of the fishes. Leonard Jenyns had had Yarrell's cooperation for many years while preparing his fish section for *A Manual of British Vertebrate Animals*, published in 1835, that listed 264 fish species, so that Yarrell already knew the contents of Jenyns' book. Looking at the list of sources in his synonyms, a large proportion of them are simply 'Penn. Flem. Jenyns', followed by any appropriate foreign books.

Again, Yarrell found few available foreign books on fishes. His main sources were Baron Georges Cuvier et A. Valenciennes' *Histoire Naturelle des Poissons* that was in progress from 1828 and Marcus Elieser Bloch's encyclopaedic *Allgemeine Naturgeschichte der Fische*, a 12-volume folio work published in Berlin 1785 that was in Yarrell's library and which had some beautiful coloured illustrations. There was a French version with the same title as that of Cuvier, issued in 1801, and Yarrell also checked the British Museum copy of this. Occasionally he made reference to the more obscure Antoine Risso's *Histoire Naturelle de l'Europe Méridionale,* 1826, that included fishes of Nice, where Risso lived, with Yarrell remarking that it contained most of the Mediterranean fishes.

It was Cuvier and Valenciennes who provided order with groupings of similar species. Yarrell owned a copy Cuvier's prospectus of his intended work on fishes, in which on page 20 he mentioned how many species and specimens he had. There were then 6,000 specimens in Paris in the King's collection from which he was doing his research, and he expected more by the time he published. Yarrell admitted to Jenyns in August 1833, 'I have reason to believe some of my synonyms are not correct – my catalogue was written before Cuvier published his Histoire and his views and names I suppose must be the law in future.'[4] Yarrell decided to follow Cuvier's arrangement of fishes on the recommendation of Bicheno, so 'My next job which I have begun upon, is to arrange all the genera and species systematically according to Cuvier's Histoire des Poissons.'[4] Obscure articles in periodicals had to supplement these resources and Yarrell was to add much to the knowledge of fish species, including a number of new species. The synonymy quoted early classical authors, standard current English authors and European authors. He was also aware of other authors of Chinese and Japanese drawings of fishes (*A History of British Fishes* 1841, 1: 197).

*Coalfish,* A History of British Fishes, 1841, 2: 251, *reputedly the British fish with the most local vernacular names. Now commonly known as the Saithe.*

Common or local names followed the synonyms. Yarrell stated that the Coalfish had more provincial names than any other species, some of which only refer to the species when of a particular size.

## The format of *A History of British Fishes*

Yarrell followed Bewick in the way he arranged the information under the species' scientific and English names, following a wood engraving of the fish. A synonymy and text followed, introduced by 'Generic characteristics describing the physical characteristics of each fish; when it was first noted as a British species; anatomical features of interest; habits including shoaling and depth at which the individuals were found; locations on the coast where the fishes were seen or taken.'

It was not just the species' name that Yarrell was trying to establish; as there was no recognised sequence for arranging the species, he followed Cuvier and Valenciennes' *Histoire des Poissons* in preference, but there his aids ended. He had no guidance for the sequence of the families and orders of his fishes. He told Leonard Jenyns, 'The guidance for establishing the Characters for genera of fishes are taken from form of body, size, number and situation of fins and also the characters of the fin rays, spinous or soft – character and disposition of teeth – some being places on both maxillary bones, palatine bones, vomer [see 't' in diagram of the Perch head on p.142] and occasionally in the throat. Specific characters from colour, and number of the various fin rays – teeth, known habits and habitats also assist.'[5]

Yarrell had any fishes he thought likely to be palatable cooked for him and pronounced on their flavour and texture, for example: 'The Atherine is a well-flavoured fish; but in our opinion, not so good as the Smelt: it is more dry; but when in season, and fried without being embowelled, the liver and roe make it a delicious fish.' (*A History of British Fishes*, 1841, 1: 230)

There was also a thread running through the book of Yarrell's comments on the historical differences in fishing and getting fishes to market, e.g. 'A large portion of the Dorees [i.e. John Dory] supplied to the London fish-market are brought by land-carriage from Plymouth, and some other parts of the Devonshire coast .... Fish for the supply of London market was not brought by land-carriage until 1761.' The improvement in roads was followed by the introduction of steam-boats which Yarrell thought likely to effect another change. In the summer of 1834, a cargo of Salmon from Scotland was deposited in the London market within 40 hours of catching. (*A History of British Fishes* 1841, 1: 189). He was interested in the different fishing vessels around the coast and included vignette wood engravings of 16 different boats.

Where a contributor had sent a specimen of significance, Yarrell

*Vignettes of boats: Coracle.* A History of British Fishes, 1841,2: 62.

*Vignettes of boats: Thames Peter-boat used by fishermen about Greenwich and down the river.* A History of British Fishes, 1841 2: 317.

acknowledged his contribution. Yarrell said he could not find any written accounts of methods of preserving fish specimens, so he gave advice about preservation in alcohol that he used for specimens in his own museum.

Finally, for some sections there was a 'tail-piece', as Bewick had called them, or 'vignette' as Yarrell called them, and he provided a 'Classed Index' of these under separate headings: anatomy, boats, bones of the head, fishers and fishing, heads, invertebrate animals, localities, nets, scales and teeth. There was also a 'General Index' of the English and the scientific names of the fishes.

**Contributors to** *A History of British Fishes*

Yarrell had to rely on his correspondents for records of the distribution of each species. Apart from the contributions from fellow fish enthusiasts, Yarrell's input was derived from his own expert fishing expeditions while on visits to seaports, particularly those most accessible to him along the south coast, e.g. Brighton, Hastings and Weymouth. He inspected fish stalls wherever he went but, most importantly, those of the fishmongers in London's Leadenhall Market. Another very important source were the specimens held in the British and other museums. Yarrell's own museum expanded to contain numerous fish specimens, sufficiently important for them to be purchased for the British Museum after his death and they are now in the Natural History Museum.

He had been gathering information from before 1823/4 and contributed nearly 20 articles on fishes to periodicals from the late 1820s to 1845. What is never referred to, but must have assisted in his research, was his wide acquaintance among the customers of his newsagent business. Probably, several of them would have been amateur fishermen. Following his attendance at the societies' meetings in London (Linnean, Entomological and Zoological, and especially the Walton and Cotton Club established 1817) from the 1820s onwards, fellow members doubtless took along examples of fishes to meetings for him.

In the preface to the first edition, Yarrell thanked the men whose contributions had helped him to lay down the basis of his knowledge of the fishes of Britain and Ireland. He named eight fishermen naturalists with extensive knowledge of the subject, some of whom would continue to support his efforts after the first edition was published. They were Jonathan Couch (1789–1870) of Polperro; W. J. Broderip; the deceased John Walcott (flourishing1788–92), whose son forwarded John's notes with a collection of more than 100 drawings of British fishes executed while he lived at Teignmouth; the much-admired Sir William Jardine of Dumfriesshire, who, besides sending various species, also provided notes on the genus *Salmo* 'from which materials were drawn for the elucidation of this difficult but important genus'; Dr George Johnston of Berwick-upon-Tweed; Dr Edward Moore of Plymouth, who provided local names for the fishes taken in his neighbourhood; W. Thompson, Vice-President of the Natural History Society of his home town Belfast and a person whom Yarrell called his 'friend'; and Edward Turner Bennett (1797–1836), then Secretary of the embryonic Zoological Society, which he helped to firmly establish before his death in the year that Yarrell completed his first edition of *A History of British Fishes.* The names of Broderip, Moore and Bennett do not recur in the text very often, while the other contributors' names occur frequently.

A major issue when Yarrell was compiling his book was the question of the development of the Salmon from fry to breeding adults. In the second volume, the first 68 pages were necessary to deal with the conflicting evidence then available concerning the Salmonidae. Much of the evidence depended on slight variations in form caused by local conditions and is now discounted as warranting separate scientific name identification. There was also confusion over the different forms of young Salmon – parr, smolt, etc. Yarrell solved the problem to his own satisfaction. On pages 18–19 in the text on Salmon, he explained how he had kept some parr in a pond from July to the following April and watched their development. In May he caught some with a casting-net and 'satisfied every individual present that they had assumed the usual appearance of what are called *Salmon smolts* or *fry*'. So his long-held view that parr were young Salmon had been vindicated. Despite this, he gave the parr specific status, commencing his account in the 1835 first edition of *A History of British Fishes*: 'This little fish, one of the smallest of the British *Salmonidae*, has given rise to more discussion than any other species of the genus.' There had been just too many ichthyologists not agreeing with him that the parr preceded the smolt in the development of the Salmon. He corrected this error in 1839 in his *On the growth of the Salmon in fresh water* (see p.155). However, despite his conviction that parr were young smolts and Salmon, he continued to give it a separate entry in his 1841 second edition of *A History of British Fishes*, but also said that many were convinced that the parr 'as a distinct species, does not exist', and that further experiments were in progress.

His report on the 1835 salmon season in a letter to Jardine would make any of today's fishermen envious. 'The Salmon season has been a good one as regards the London supply and particularly remarkable for more large sized fish than I ever saw before in one season. I saw 12 or 14 fish that exceeded

40lbs in weight and one fish weighed 55lb – the largest I have recorded was in the year or season 1821. This salmon, a female, weighed 83lbs and was as short, as deep and as thick as a large fat hog.'[6]

Yarrell wrote in his preface to the first edition, 'To Mr Couch of Polperro, the indefatigable ichthyologist of Cornwall, the author is indebted for several examples of the most rare species found on the Cornish coast, for the use of a large and valuable collection of characteristic drawings, and the whole of his manuscript notes.'[7] Couch contributed by far the largest number of species and notes on British fishes. Couch had trained a considerable number of local fishermen to supply him with specimens and information and he continued to send information, drawings and specimens to Yarrell, and then to Sir John Richardson when he was preparing a further edition of Yarrell's book after Yarrell's death.

*Vignette of a fisherman with his back to his creel and fishes lying on the ground being pilfered by a cat. A* History of British Fishes, 1841, 1: 422.

Dr George Johnston of Berwick-upon-Tweed was a friend of Yarrell, Jardine and Selby and an enthusiastic fisherman who sent Yarrell fresh specimens from the Tweed and north-east coast. Other contributors were mentioned in the text and the list grew over all the years that Yarrell continued to monitor the fishes of Britain and Ireland, i.e. until his death in 1856.

Of Heysham's association with Yarrell, Jenyns wrote: 'Mr Heysham, of Carlisle, a well-known naturalist there, was a great friend of Yarrell's and his name must be familiar to those who have read Yarrell's works, as that of a frequent contributor of notes on the British birds and fishes .... Heysham was well acquainted with the fishes of the Solway.'[8]

## Yarrell's own sources of specimens

As early as 1831 Yarrell had 220 species of fish in his own catalogue.[9] Living in London, Yarrell's initial main source of specimens came from the London Fish Market (Leadenhall), but he was a keen fisherman and obtained many of his own specimens that he preserved and placed in his museum. He caught the common Grey Mullet, and various other fry, when fishing with a small but very useful net between Brownsea Island and South Haven, at the mouth of Poole Harbour, Dorset. He went to many coastal towns and persuaded the commercial fishermen to keep an eye open for unusual specimens to send to him in London. In March 1838, while writing to William Swainson he explained: 'You will find many species of interest and beauty on the coast of Cornwall', adding three other best places on the south coast to see a variety of species –'Hastings where there are about 80 registered boats constantly in use – next best is Weymouth – particularly in August and September – the ground worked for fish being the eastern part of West Bay – & the next is Devonport where you would find a great show daily in the morning market, between the high street and the ferry over to Lord Mount Edgecombe's estates.'[10] On 21 March he wrote again to say he had forgotten 'to mention Brixham in Devonshire as one of the most considerable fishing stations on the south coast'.[11] and then added on 28 March 'Fish caught by the Brixham men sent by boats to Devonport market – so go there (not to Brixham).'[12] He made the valuable acquaintance at Brixham of the vicar, Reverend Richard Holdsworth, who sent him many notices and specimens.

From Yarrell's correspondence it is evident that he was familiar with fishing villages and towns along a stretch of the south coast, including Hastings, Eastbourne, Brighton, Portsmouth, Bournemouth, Poole and Brownsea Island, Weymouth, Brixham and Devonport. It was not necessary for him to go beyond Devon because Jonathan Couch kept him adequately informed of Cornish catches. He knew the fish markets and fishmongers as well as the fishermen, who he sometimes joined in their boats on fishing trips at sea. He also visited Yarmouth (now Great Yarmouth), then the chief port for the Herring fishing industry on the Norfolk coast and home to his friend William Richard Fisher, and Aldeburgh on the Suffolk coast.

Yarrell also engaged the services of amateur fishermen, including several more reverend fishing enthusiasts (W. F. Cornish of Totnes; F. W. Hope; Robert Lubbock of Norfolk; and T. Salwey of Tenby). Ichthyologists in museums, fellow naturalists and authors were contacted or, once the parts of the book were being issued, contacted him. All of these were eager to forward his great work that they found so useful. If their support might have been expected, there was one delightfully unexpected contributor. The reason for the common name 'Miller's thumb' being used for the River Bullhead was communicated to Yarrell by the Suffolk artist John Constable, whose father owned the mill at Flatford. Constable said his father maintained the reason for the name arose from the movement of the miller's thumb in spreading a sample of the flour over his fingers (the thumb being a gauge of the quality and thus value of the flour.) 'By this incessant action of the miller's thumb, a peculiarity in its form is produced which is said to resemble exactly the shape of the head of the fish constantly found in the mill–stream, and has obtained for it the name of miller's thumb.' (*A History of British Fishes,* 1841, 1: 73–4, Bullhead, *Cottus gobio*). Even better, John Constable lent Yarrell his drawing of a view of the undershot water-mill at Gillingham, Dorset, which Yarrell used as a vignette.

*Sketch of a watermill from* A History of British Fishes 1841, 1: 74, *used as a vignette. John Constable 'also very kindly sent me a view of an undershot water-mill at Gillingham worked by a branch of the stream from Stourhead'.*

For any ichthyologist, the greatest gratification was to have a species named after him. To then be able to explain and detail this process in his own book was even more special. Writing about 'Yarrell's Blenny', he said 'M. Valenciennes has done me the honour to propose that in future it should be called *Blennius Yarrellii.*' (*A History of British Fishes,* 1841, 1: 263). The English name remains as a tribute to Yarrell.

It was not unknown for men to arrive on Yarrell's doorstep in Ryder Street bearing a gift. His friend Thomas Bell caused great excitement when he turned up in Ryder Street with a fish that Yarrell had not seen before. Not many people would be excited over a visitor holding a Gattoruginous Blenny from Poole Harbour.[13] Yarrell was even better pleased when another blenny was sent to him in a bottle of spirits by Dr George Johnston from Berwick-upon-Tweed which was 'the only specimen of this fish I have ever seen'.[14] It was his own blenny *Blennius yarrellii.*

When Yarrell received specimens, he needed to act quickly to preserve them. Writing to William Swainson, Yarrell said that he 'did not remember seeing anything in print beyond a recommendation to use spirit of wine, which will bear to have one third of water added; if the specimens are of small size. I find that fish come very well from Iceland and Scotland in whiskey and the Zool. Soc. have received a considerable collection from Cuba that came in very good condition in rum. Gin sold at retail in England will not preserve any fish long, and on the coast as well as at home for my own collection, I have always resorted to spirit of wine. It is scarcely possible to have the spirit sufficiently strong to preserve the soft parts effectually without destroying part of the colours, some of which as the green and the blue in the Labridae are taken up and held in solution. The quantity of animal matter soon reduces the strength of the spirit. It is important that each specimen is wrapped in cloth and tied up for packing for transport, so that the scales will not be rubbed off. If a layer of loose tow be interposed between each layer of fish for a voyage, so that the contents keep to their position in the jar or barrel, & fresh spirit be added, as much as the vessel will hold, when thus packed, they will be likely to come to hand in the best condition.'[15] Placing his own experience on record like this was invaluable for all collectors wishing to preserve their specimens.

## Yarrell's wood-engraved blocks

Yarrell had 'from some authority or another a coloured figure of every British species or very nearly' but chose to use wood-engraved illustrations. William Swainson wanted Yarrell to let him have separate proofs of the illustrations in *A History of British Fishes* and suggested that these, coloured, would be a profitable extra source of income. Yarrell's reply to this was 'The proof sheets of the text are pulled and corrected before the blocks are set, I have therefore no proof sheets with fish. I am aware of the desirability of wood blocks but my object in strictly limiting the number of loose proofs was to prevent the representations being seen except in the work itself. Bewick, however, I have reason to believe helped to wear out his blocks, ... [top of sheet very thin and faded so cannot read it] ... as they were by having numerous copies taken off of the Birds and Vignettes only. Nothing of this sort is done with the series now bringing out - the blocks are never worked except when guarded and saved by the surrounding surface of type in the printer's form.' He suggested to Swainson that he contact the distributor, Longman's, to let them know what he wanted and 'they would immediately send you down a copy which you could cut up and arrange as you please. You will find many species of interest and beauty on the coast of Cornwall and I should think coloured plates of fishes would sell.'[15]

*Vignette of Folkstone fisherman selling his fish by auction on the beach after landing. 'This is done, according to the Dutch fashion, by lowering the price demanded for the lot till a bid is made, when the bargain is struck by dropping the shingle, which is held, as represented, between the fore-finger and thumbs.'* A History of British Fishes, 1841, 2: 314.

### Friends' comments on *A History of British Fishes* in letters

On 16 March 1835 Selby wrote to Jardine, 'have you got Yarrell's 1st No. of fishes? Mine arrived on Saturday and I am much pleased with it. The Cuts are beautifully executed, and the letterpress very good, it will when finished be a valuable addition to our British works on Nat. Hist.'[16] Yarrell was not so pleased with the wood engravings. He wrote to Thomas Allis, 'The woodcuts in the British Fishes are not so uniform in execution as I could have wished to have seen them – owing to the necessity of employing ten or twelve different artists in order to keep pace with a monthly publication.'[17]

When *A History of British Fishes* was completed in 1836 and Selby received his copy, at the first glance he concluded that it was a 'very beautiful work'. He informed Jardine, 'Upon looking over Yarrell I find very little to sound out upon, and I must say I was more gratified on looking it over as a whole, than when I saw it disjointed and in numbers. I wish few of the figures might have been better, as the Swordfish, Mullet, Wolf fish, &c.'[18] Selby also commented on the first part of *A History of British Fishes* in a letter to George T. Fox of Durham, 'Yarrell's work will indeed be a valuable accession to Naturalists as well as to the general reader, the Cuts are beautifully executed and the letter press clear & well expressed.'[19]

Jardine reviewed *A History of British Fishes* enthusiastically in the journal he edited, *Magazine of Botany and Zoology*, for which Yarrell thanked him for the 'liberal notice'. Selby also approved: 'Your review of Yarrell I like much.'[20]

In correspondence with William Swainson, Yarrell said 'The work has been very favourably received and had an extensive sale. Some effect of the publication has been to put observers at work around the coast and I receive various communications which will enable me to give additional interest to the 2nd edition. I shall publish a supplement to the first edition at the same time, to make the first edition, with that, as good as the second as a tribute due to the purchasers of the first.'[21] On 13 July 1838 Yarrell confirmed that he was proposing '2nd HBFishes'.[22]

Dr George Johnston, a frequent contributor to Yarrell's *A History of British Fishes*, wrote to say 'On the conclusion of your work, I must again renew my thanks for the handsome present of it.' He then added a revealing comment of a source for Yarrell's illustrations, 'As you will not have any further use of Mrs Johnston's drawings of Berwickshire fish, I will be obliged by having them returned, at your convenience.'[23] Yarrell was meticulous in acknowledging help but did not give credit to Mrs Johnston, so whether he used her illustrations is a moot point. Perhaps the lady did not wish to see her name in print.

Having completed the fish book, Yarrell barely paused for breath. He told Thomas Allis of York Library that he had 'No intention of publishing a supplement to the British Fishes until I am called upon to produce a new edition', but he had eight or ten new fishes to put in. He was 'Now writing the history of British Birds. I hope it will be admitted that wood engraving as an art has not stood still during the 40 years that have transpired since Bewick published his original work on British birds in 1797.'[24] The wood engravings of both fishes and birds were delightful, Bewick would have been proud of them.

Having taken a risk by embarking on publication in parts, Yarrell had not only escaped a possible failure but bravely achieved a remarkable success. New information kept coming in the form of original records of species to be added to the British list. This necessitated supplements and further editions which were issued by Yarrell up to 1845 then Dr John Richardson undertook this task, completing the 3rd edition published in 1859 with Van Voorst's biography of Yarrell.

In 1839 Yarrell published *On the growth of the Salmon in fresh water...with six coloured illustrations of the fish of the natural size, exhibiting its character and exact appearance at various stages during the first two years,* correcting an error he had made in *A History of British Fishes,* where he had given separate species status to the parr, against his own better judgment. This was based upon the experiments of John Shaw in Drumlanrig, Dumfriesshire, where he had developed the tiny parr in three ponds near Nith from ova to seven months, when they assumed a silver colour. The next stage had been taken by Thomas Upton of Ingmire Hall (between Selkirk ad Kendal), who put Salmon parr from the river Lune in three ponds and watched them grow into smolt and go down to the sea in May of their second year. These proved that the parr were the fry of the Salmon. Drawings on three plates drawn by C. Curtis and engraved by R. Sands in1839 followed their progress, proving the facts gathered by Shaw and Upton and what Yarrell had known all along.

Yarrell, William, On marine fishes, chapter VIII in William Henry Harvey *Sea Side Book; an introduction to the natural history of the British coasts,* 3rd ed, pp. 237–269, 1854, John Van Voorst.

Yarrell used the first pages of his chapter, from 237 to 259, to write about the different nets used to catch fishes, and the rod and line. He discussed the various methods of catching Mackerel, Herrings and Pilchards, but by far the most interesting portion of the chapter lay in the last few pages where he evaluated the value of fish as food, the catching of it as an industry, and the men who provided fish as important national assets. His summing up is worth quoting as an exposition of the economy of fishing rarely met with elsewhere. 'Value of fish and an article of food – the supply immense, the source inexhaustible, its positive worth, an amount of human food equal to little less than a million of money drawn forth annually from the water, obtained at moderate cost, giving employment to thousands of adventurous, hard-working, honest men, who are most serviceable members of the community either in peace or war; hence an obvious advantage as islanders in promoting that occupation which is the nursery of seamen, in willing, able and powerful agents of our commerce and our defence.'

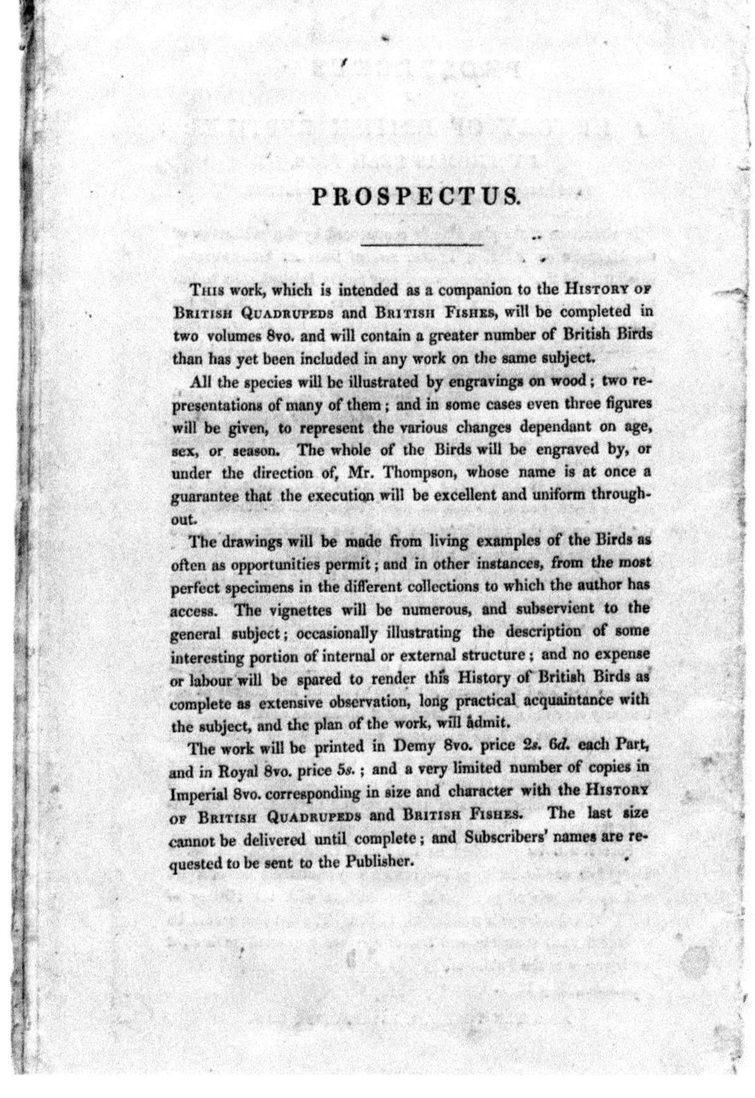

PROSPECTUS.

THIS work, which is intended as a companion to the HISTORY OF BRITISH QUADRUPEDS and BRITISH FISHES, will be completed in two volumes 8vo. and will contain a greater number of British Birds than has yet been included in any work on the same subject.

All the species will be illustrated by engravings on wood; two representations of many of them; and in some cases even three figures will be given, to represent the various changes dependant on age, sex, or season. The whole of the Birds will be engraved by, or under the direction of, Mr. Thompson, whose name is at once a guarantee that the execution will be excellent and uniform throughout.

The drawings will be made from living examples of the Birds as often as opportunities permit; and in other instances, from the most perfect specimens in the different collections to which the author has access. The vignettes will be numerous, and subservient to the general subject; occasionally illustrating the description of some interesting portion of internal or external structure; and no expense or labour will be spared to render this History of British Birds as complete as extensive observation, long practical acquaintance with the subject, and the plan of the work, will admit.

The work will be printed in Demy 8vo. price 2*s.* 6*d.* each Part, and in Royal 8vo. price 5*s.*; and a very limited number of copies in Imperial 8vo. corresponding in size and character with the HISTORY OF BRITISH QUADRUPEDS and BRITISH FISHES. The last size cannot be delivered until complete; and Subscribers' names are requested to be sent to the Publisher.

*Prospectus for* A History of British Birds. *As many as 700 copies of a prospectus were printed for insertion between pages of other authors' parts of a book they were publishing and in periodicals, etc.*

*A HISTORY OF BRITISH BIRDS*

Published by John Van Voorst, Paternoster Row, London.

*A History of British Birds,* 1837–43 3 vols (published in parts at intervals of two months, the first one in July 1837 and the last one in May 1843).

vol.1. July 1837–March 1839 Parts I–XI pp. 525

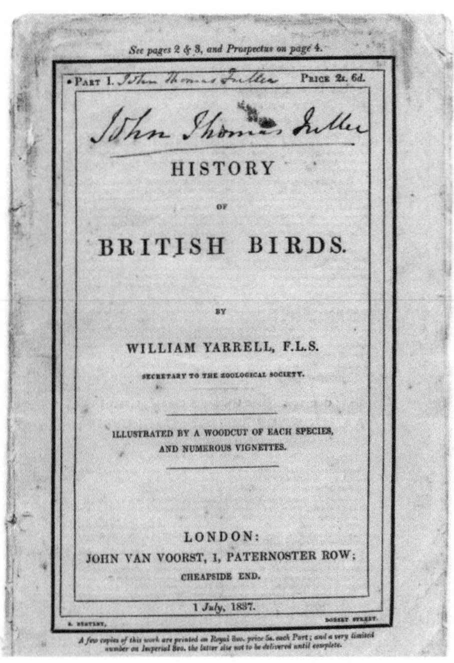

*See pages 2 & 3, and Prospectus on page 4.*

PART I. PRICE 2s. 6d.

HISTORY

OF

BRITISH BIRDS.

BY

WILLIAM YARRELL, F.L.S.

SECRETARY TO THE ZOOLOGICAL SOCIETY.

ILLUSTRATED BY A WOODCUT OF EACH SPECIES, AND NUMEROUS VIGNETTES.

LONDON:

JOHN VAN VOORST, 1, PATERNOSTER ROW;

CHEAPSIDE END.

1 *July*, 1837.

R. BENTLEY, DORSET STREET.

*A few copies of this work are printed on Royal 8vo. price 5s. each Part; and a very limited number on Imperial 8vo. the latter size not to be delivered until complete.*

vol.2. May 1839–July 1841 Parts XII–XXV pp. 669

vol.3. Sep 1841–May 1843 Parts XXVI–XXXVI pp. 528

Preface, v: 'New subjects have been engraved on single leaves, so paged, that the bookbinder may insert the separate leaves among the birds of the genus to which each respectively belongs.' There were 27 with text for them on pp. v–xii.

Supplement 1843 14 figures

1845 Supplement to the *A History of British Birds.* London October 1845. This supplement was intended to bring the 1st edn of 1837–43 up to the date of the 2nd edition. The number of species in the first edition and supplement was 354.

2nd ed. 1845 3 vols 535 figures.

Supplement 1856 18 figures.

3rd ed. 1856 3 vols 634 (212, 197, 225) figures.

1856 Second supplement, by Sir John Richardson, to *A History of British Birds*; being also a first supplement to the second edition.
4th ed., revised and enlarged by Alfred Newton (vols. 1–2) and Howard Saunders (vols 3–4) 4 vols 1871–1885, 741 figures (186, 127, 255, 173). Van Voorst, 1871–85. Alfred Newton revised the first two volumes of the 4th edition of Yarrell's *A History of British Birds* in 1871 and 1882, then handed over to Howard Saunders, but not before making sure at the end of volume 2 to state that 'I am not responsible for anything that may follow by another editor.' The final edition, in four volumes, was finished in 1885. This had figures delineated by Thompson, A. Fussell, R. C. West, E. Neale, J. G. Keulemans, Chas Whymper. Engraved by Thompson, R. C. West, Pearson, Charles Whymper.
Howard Saunders condensed the whole book into a single volume, illustrated with the original figures, entitled *An illustrated Manual of British Birds* (1st ed., 1889; 2nd ed. 1899).

Number of engravings – Anker, Casey Wood, Nissen, etc., disagree over the number in each of the editions. The number of wood engravings was stated on the title pages of each edition (see title pages on pp.141 and 157) so why there is this disagreement is unaccountable.

Extensive notes on *Yarrell, William* (1784–1856) *A History of British Birds,* by Richard Soffer, are conserved in the Soffer Ornithology Collection Notes, Amherst College.

Yarrell wrote the 19th-century's standard work on British birds, following the great Ray & Willughby in the 17th century and Pennant in the 18th. Bewick's delightful work had been published 1797–1804, and Yarrell followed Bewick's pattern of a short text with a wood engraving of the bird and some tail pieces, but whereas Bewick's tail pieces had been diverse in subject, all of Yarrell's wood engravings were bird related. Unlike the earlier authors, Yarrell added a record of the earliest appearance and acceptance of the species as British, as recorded in natural history books and periodicals.

By deciding to include this record, Yarrell added greatly to his task. He also found that researching the geographical range of each species proved more difficult than anticipated. He explained to Sir William Jardine that his knowledge (or lack of it) of British birds in Scotland worried him. 'One of the perplexing difficulties I have to encounter in putting together this *A History of British Birds,* in order to include that extent of geographical range which I have felt desirous should be recorded, is that I have to turn to the account of

a

b

c

a. Ruff
b. Turnstone
c. Greenshank

PLATE 11 SHORE BIRDS

each of the species in 50 or 60 different volumes by which I am surrounded by works of reference. Among these are Sibbald Scotia illustrated, Dr Fleming, Mr Mudie, Mr Rennie, MacGillivray, Low, Dun, &c.'[25] Jardine immediately replied, with typical generosity, by sending him his own list of birds and where seen in Scotland.

On at least two occasions, Yarrell found himself recording not the first appearance of a species but rather trying to ascertain the last appearance. It was

*The Great Auk,* A History of British Birds, 1843, 3: 369. *'The Great Auk is a very rare British Bird, and but few instances are recorded of its capture.'*

thought that the Great Bustard may recently have become extinct in Britain and the Great Auk had been seen within living memory. The odd inclusion of the Passenger Pigeon followed the intervention of his friend, J. J. Audubon, who brought from America 70 live birds and sent 40 to the Earl of Derby who let them fly free at Knowsley. They did not thrive, rendering this species a kind of 'temporary British bird' (admittedly, not a scientific category).

On 31 January 1837 Dr George Johnston, friend of Yarrell, Selby and Jardine, wrote to Selby that he was glad Yarrell was writing a history of British birds because 'no one cd do it better'.[26] The first part appeared in July 1837. Yarrell had made sure that as many friends and earlier contributors from his fish book as possible had been made aware of his intention to write a companion volume on birds by means of a prospectus.

### The wood engravings

Illustrators: Alexander Fussell c. 1814 Birmingham – 1909.

Preface to 1st ed., 3 vols with 520 wood engravings: 'To Mr Alexander Fussell, for the ability, invention and good taste which have enabled him to give truth of character, variety, and effect to nearly 500 of the drawings on wood here employed, my best acknowledgements are due; and more particularly so to Mr John Thompson and his sons, for the skill, the zeal, the success, and I may add the pleasure, with which they have laboured throughout this very long series of engravings.' Alexander Fussell's drawings of the birds, though closely imitating Bewick's style and composition, were stiffer and less life-like. The rural background scenes, however, had just as much charm and authenticity at those of the old master. Though this indicated a clear division between the work of Fussell and the Thompsons, some of the wood engravings, e.g. Lesser Redpoll and Mountain Linnet or Twite, were signed T DEL ET SC, [T = Thompson, delineat et sculpsit] and the Mealy Redpoll, Goldfinch and Siskin, were signed THOMPSON DEL ET SC, indicating each time that one of the Thompsons was both artist as well as engraver.

The wood engraver John Thompson (1785–1866) was a former pupil of Allen Robert Branston, who was a Bewick associate. John Thompson was one of the most distinguished wood engravers of his time and in 1855 won a *médaille d'honneur* at the Paris exhibition. John's second son, Richard Anthony, also worked on Yarrell's engravings but abandoned the craft on his appointment to a post at the South Kensington Museum (now the Victoria and Albert Museum). Charles

*Vignette of rabbits and puffins disputing ownership of a burrow.* A History of British Birds, 1843, 3: 365.

Thurston Thompson, his elder son, was also a very good wood engraver. He later became more interested in photography and in 1857 was appointed as the official photographer to the South Kensington Museum. Few of the engravings were signed individually, e.g 'JT del et sc'; 'J. Thompson del et sc'; or 'J. Thompson sc', or just 'Thompson', so we cannot tell which one was responsible for each engraving. All of the Thompsons' engravings were delicate and charming, as well as accurate representations of the birds. They also engraved the tail pieces of birds, anatomical details, nests and eggs or young chicks.

Fussell was about 23 when he began to draw for Yarrell. He was the son of Joseph Fussell, an artist who taught oil painting to students in Birmingham before he moved to London in 1821 and started exhibiting his landscape and religious paintings in London exhibitions. Alexander made his debut as an artist when he exhibited his first picture at the British Institution in 1838, followed by another at the Royal Academy a year later. The Fussell family would have been well known in London's art circles in the 1830s and 1840s. Alexander worked on the first three editions of *A History of British Birds* from 1836 or earlier to 1856.

Wood engravers Dalziel Bros 2nd & 3rd ed. *HBB*

Wood engraver R C West, Ch Whymper sculp 4th ed.

The Casey Wood copy has extra illustrations by William Richard Fisher.

E. M. Nicholson expressed the general opinion: '*A History of British Birds* became, through its dependability, convenient classification, and attractive engravings (then, though not now perhaps, for they often portray methods of persecuting birds and beasts) the standard book on British ornithology for half a century.'[27] A review in *British Birds* (II, 1908–09) appreciated the book's accuracy from an accomplished ornithologist who knew exactly what the general public wanted in a popular text-book, and moreover possessed the skill of presenting his knowledge in a concise and agreeable manner.

**Yarrell's comments on *A History of British Birds* in letters**

Yarrell informed Thomas Allis on 5 June 1837, 'Now writing the History of British Birds...I hope it will be admitted that wood engraving as an art has not stood still during the 40 years that have transpired since Bewick published his original work on British Birds in 1797.' In August Yarrell thanked Allis for comments on the first part and explained: 'I began with two artists making the drawings on the wood and soon found that one of them was inferior to the other and I was obliged to give him up – there are three drawings of his in the 2nd No and two in the third No which will contain the owls – but none afterwards – all the others you will observe as they come out have more freedom, spirit and taste. I shall feel disappointed if one or two in the 2nd No to be published on the first of September do not please.'[28]

Two months later, with another part issued, Yarrell again communicated with Thomas Allis, 'The woodcuts in the British Fishes are not so uniform in execution as I could have wished to have seen them – owing to the necessity of employing ten or twelve different artists in order to keep pace with a monthly publication. Uniformity will now be obtained by Mr Thompson and his three sons engraving all the Birds, which they could not produce monthly – I think Part 3 of the Birds will be considered even superior to either of the others.'[29] The parts of *HBB* came out bi-monthly, and so the early troubles were over.

Yarrell gave Jardine an inside tip about costing wood engravings. 'The cost of cutting on wood the 5 nests in Part 7 of Brit. Birds averaged £2–13–0 each nest, exclusive of the drawing which was 5/-s each. Three or four of them were charged £2–15–0 each – they might be done cheaper (but not by John Thompson) and therefore probably not so well cut.' If Jardine wanted any cut in London, he was to let Yarrell know and he would do the best he could.[30]

*Original design for an engraving by one of the Thompsons of a Golden Eagle for* A History of British Birds, 1843, 1: 7. *Courtesy of W. G. Hale.*

**Friends' comments on *A History of British Birds* in letters**

Leonard Jenyns wrote a review on *A History of British Birds* in the 65th number of *The London and Westminster Review*, March 1840. Selby wrote to Jardine: 'Yarrells letter press is very fair, but I dislike the figures of most of the Birds, though they be well cut, that of the young Egyptian vulture is bad, drawn from an ill stuffed specimen & the legs quite out of the centre of gravity. The

Golden & White tailed eagles are also stuck leaning and not characteristic. The Goshawk I think the best.'[31]

Two of the owls are squinting, a fault noticed by Sir William Jardine. The Eagle Owl is the best of the owls, the Tawny and Snowy being the ones with squints. All of the *History of British Birds* engravings are beautifully executed, but some of the birds, especially the owls, had glass eyes inserted in the stuffed specimens that had highlights in the wrong place. In the case of the owls, the highlights were too high and they have a look that is not entirely normal because this gives them a look of alarm, being scared even.

George Johnston thanked Yarrell for 'British Birds' and said they 'please me and mine beyond measure. The letterpress gratified me much; we have been so bothered with [books about] British birds that I was afraid of repetitions and sameness ... but you have entirely avoided and given it a novelty by your way of handling ... figures ... are beautiful and those I know very accurate.' He

*The Snowy Owl suffered from unfortunate positioning of the glass eyes.* A History of British Birds, 1843, 1: 134.

liked the 'Windhover in no. 11 best of all. The Honey Buzzards perhaps least so.'[32] Johnston was worried about the proliferation of books on birds about this period.

T.C. Eyton thanked Yarrell for his copy of *A History of British Birds* (this would have been the 1st part, published 1 July 1837), but would have preferred darker ground behind the birds to show them up better. He wanted to add vignettes of anatomical details and offered to shoot the birds and draw them for Yarrell. Eyton mentioned 'the opposition' [i.e. MacGillivray, who began to publish his *A History of British birds* also in 1837] and said MacGillivray's measurements of the intestines are useless. 'I could send him tomorrow six cock sparrows which should all measure differently according to age.' Eyton, on receiving part 2, thanked Yarrell for the present, which he likes better than no. 1. 'The Goshawk and Common Buzzard are unique as wood cuts. I have a

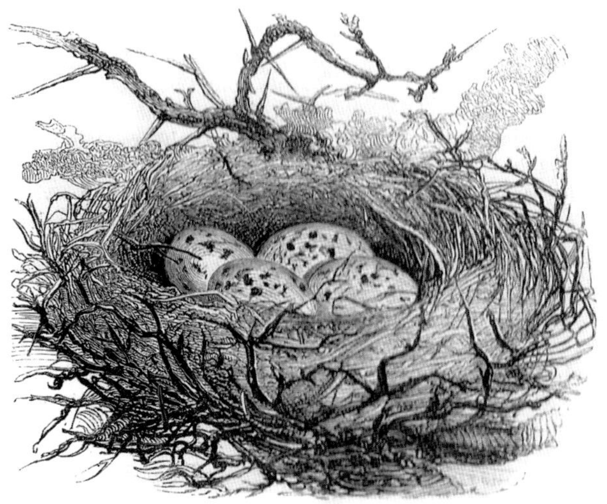

*The nest and eggs of the Hawfinch.* A History of British Birds. 1843, 1: 489.

specimen of the common buzzard stuffed in the precise attitude in which you have represented him.'[33]

A modest single sentence occurs in a letter from Yarrell to Jardine in 1838. 'It is our common black and white wagtail to which Mr Gould has attached the name of Yarrellii, believing it to be distinct from the continental Pied wagtail.'[34] It was a delightful gesture from his London colleague and close friend, John Gould, and what a thrill to have a British bird named after him.

*Large blue egg of the Guillemot,* A History of British Birds,1843, 3: 345, *on the last page in some copies only. Yarrell's measurements of the egg were: Length 3¼" breadth 1" and 11 lines at the larger end.*

In April 1831 Yarrell had written to Jenyns about the numbers of birds known to be British. 'I see some Edinburgh ornithologist ... in the last number of Jameson's Journal considers our British birds to be but 291. I think we shall be able to shew cause that they are 307 good and true.'[35] There were 324 species in *HBB* 1st edition which finished publication in 1843, but several were later to be found not to be 'good and true'.

## Eggs

Yarrell owned two nearly complete sets of British birds' eggs. These he described for each species in *A History of British Birds,* with their measurements in his text. It was asking too much of his engravers to reproduce the tiny eggs, correct in size and with all their markings, so there are very few vignettes depicting eggs. The best depictions of eggs are where they appear inside nests.

Strangely, there is a single coloured plate at the end of the third volume in some copies only, reproducing a large blue egg of the Guillemot.

Yarrell recorded the measurement of each species' egg that he had been able to handle. He used inches and fractions familiar until decimalisation: half, quarter, eighths of an inch, and then for smaller measurements below eighths he used the term 'lines'. A 'line' is a very old measure (now obsolete), the equivalent of one twelfth of an inch. This meant that Yarrell was far more accurate than had he been content with the more often used nearest eighth of an inch. He bought eggs from Leadbeater ('those of the white stork, purple heron, brown phalarope, fulmar, shearwater and stormy petrels – the smew and 2 or 3 rare ducks')[36] and collections when they came onto the market. He also paid W. R. Fisher for drawings of eggs. If he had not an example in his own collection, he endeavoured to draw one he saw elsewhere.

## YARRELL'S PERIODICAL ARTICLES

Yarrell began to publish his research in articles designed from papers that he read, mostly, to the members of the Zoological Society and Linnean Society. He illustrated the lectures with specimens, anatomical dissections and drawings made using his microscope. Having spent much of his spare time on natural history following his attendance at lectures of the Royal Institution in 1817, he had a wealth of notes of discoveries he had made about mammals, birds and fishes. He took a special interest in the tracheae of water birds, fascinated by the variations in structure related to the different sounds made by birds.

Mammals were included in lectures on Fennec, the Tapir of America, and an American flying squirrel, that were only outshone by one lecture with detailed notes on the internal appearance of 21 specimens he had collected from the Zoological Society following their demise at the Zoo.

As a direct result of his anatomical studies, he discovered: differences between Bewick's and Whooper Swans; a new species of Herring; that it was the male *Syngnathus* that carried the species' young in his pouch; distinguished the Irish Hare; and a new Smelt, among others.

A second major interest was the recording of species of birds in particular, but also fishes, that had not been noticed before in Britain. His first articles, published in 1825, listed rare British birds observed in the years 1823–25, and he continued to add to these with notices of the appearance of the more interesting species in the following years.

When Yarrell got up to speak at the Zoological and Linnean Society meetings, the anticipation of the members would be palpable. 'What has he discovered now?' would be uppermost in the minds of his audiences. This excitement may be missing today from the periodical articles that are clear, precise, reporting of facts; nevertheless these form a remarkable, even formidable, collection of records of new discoveries.

Of his articles in periodicals, Yarrell told Sir William Jardine 'I never charge for articles'.[37] Contributors of articles for periodicals published by private owners were paid. Yarrell was not paid for any of his periodical articles.

**List of periodical articles**

Abbreviations for the periodicals in which Yarrell's articles were published, arranged by date of publication.

ANH and AMNH – *Annals of Natural History* (1838–42), succeeded by *Annals and Magazine of Natural History* (1842–) printed and published by Taylor & Francis.
BAAS – *British Association for the Advancement of Science*.1833– Reports
Edin NPJ – *Edinburgh New Philosophical Journal* 1826–54
Entom. Soc. – *Entomological Magazine* (Society of Entomologists). Editor: Edward Newman. September 1832–October 1838.
LSJ – *Linnean Society Journal*
MNH – *Magazine of Natural History*, 1828–41. Proprietor and Editor: John Claudius Loudon.
PCSCZS – *Proceedings of the Committee of Science and Correspondence of the Zoological Society of London*, 1830–3. Continued as PZS 1833.
Phil. Mag. Ann. – *Philosophical Magazine and Annals*. Proprietor and Editor: Richard Taylor.
PLS – *Proceedings of the Linnean Society*
PZS – *Proceedings of the Zoological Society*
RSPT – *Royal Society Philosophical Transactions*
TLS – *Transactions of the Linnean Society*
ZJ – *Zoological Journal* 1824–35
(no abbreviation) *Zoologist*

Titles of the periodical articles as listed by John Richardson for Yarrell's British Fishes, 2nd supplement, 1860, in date order.

1825, ZJ 2: 24–7. Notices of the occurrence of some rare British Birds observed during the years 1823, '24, and '25.
1826, ZJ 2: 433–37. On the small horny appendage to the upper mandible in very young chickens. Written October 1825.
1826, ZJ 2: 492. Notice of the occurrence of a species of duck (*Anas rufina*) new to the British Fauna.
1827, RSPT 268–75. On the change of plumage of some Hen Pheasants. Written Feb. 1827, Read May 1827.

1827, TLS 15: 378–91. Observations on the trachea of birds, with descriptions and representations of several not hitherto figured. Read 6 February 1827.

1827, ZJ 3: 85–8. Notices of some rare British birds, second communication, October.

1827, ZJ 3: 181–9. Some observations on the anatomy of the British birds of prey, pl. vi . Written October 1826.

1827, ZJ 3: 401–3. Observations on the osteology of the fennec.

1827, ZJ 3: 497–9. Notices of the occurrences of some rare British birds, third communication.

1828, MNH 1: 23. Some remarks on the habits of the kingfisher. [also ZJ 3, 401].

1828, ZJ 3: 544. On the osteology of the *Chlamyphorus truncatus* of Dr Harlan.

1828, Edin NPJ 4: 290–92. Memorandum from the Right Honourable the Lord President, containing some facts relating to the natural history of the swallow and partridge.

1828, TLS 16: 109–13. Description of a species of Tringa (*T. rufescens*) killed in Cambridgeshire, new to England and Europe. Read 17 June 1828.

1829, MNH 2: 143. Descriptive and historical notice of British snipes. (Supplement to ditto Loudon's MNH 1830, 3:27)

1829, ZJ 4: 137. On the supposed identity of whitebait and shad. August 1828.

1829, ZJ 4: 210–13. Observations on the tapir of America.

1829, ZJ 4: 234. On the use of the Xiphoid bone and its muscles in the Cormorant (*Pelecanus carbo*, L.). August 1828.

1829, ZJ 4: 314–22. Notes on the internal appearance of several animals examined after death in the collection of the Zoological Society (Otter, Paradoxure, Pheasant, White Stork, Common Bittern, Crested Grebe, Red-throated Diver, Tame Swan, Wild Swan, Canada Goose, White-fronted Goose, Indian Tortoise, Active Gibbon, Diana Monkey, Weeper Monkey, Mexican Dog, Jerboa, Bobac, Malabar Squirrel, Crested Porcupine, Alpine Hare).

1829, ZJ 4: 459–65. On the structure of the beak and its muscles in the crossbill (*Loxia curvirostra*).

1829, ZJ 4: 465. Remarks on some English fishes, with notices of three species new to the British fauna (*Solea pegusa*, *Cottus bubalis*, *Anguilla*).

1829, TLS 16: 305. On the organs of voice in birds. Read June 1829.

1830, PCSCZS 1: 18. On the occurrence of the *Sylvia Tithys* of Scopoli in England.

1830, MNH 3: 81. Remarks on some species of *Syngnathus.*

1830, MNH 3: 521. Additions to the British Fauna, Classes Fishes, September 1830.

1830, ZJ 5: 277. Notice of a new species of herring. [Yarrell's *A History of British Fishes* ed.1841, 2: 193 Leach's Herring *Clupea Leachii* Yarrell pl. 12.]

1830, Phil. Mag. Ann. 7: 194. Specific characters of the *Cygnus Bewickii* and *C. ferus.* Reply to the statement respecting the Discovery of the *Cygnus Bewickii* published in the Phil. Mag. Ann. for August.

1830, TLS 16: 455–53. On a new species of Wild Swan taken in England (*Cygnus Bewickii*) and hitherto confounded with the Hooper. Read January 1830. (See also *Phil. Mag. Ann.* 1830).

1831, PCSCZS 1: 22 On the assumption of the male plumage by the female of the Common Game Fowl.

1831, PCSCZS 1: 25. On the anatomy of the *Cereosis Novae-Hollandiae,* Lath., and on the relation between the *Natatores* and *Grallatores.*

1831, PCSCZS 1: 27. On the sexual organs of a hybrid pheasant.

1831, PCSCZS 1: 27. On the specific identity of the Gardenian and Night Herons (*Ardea Gardenii* and *nycticorax*).

1831, PCSCZS 1: 31–3. On the anatomy of the chinchilla (*Chinchilla lanigera*).

1831, PCSCZS 1: 33 On the trachea of the Red-knobbed Curassow (*Crax yarrellii,* Benn.).

1831, PCSCZS 1: 34. Characters of a new species of Herring (*Clupea, L.*)

1831, PCSCZS 1: 35. On the occurrence of several North American Birds in England.

1831, PCSCZS 1: 38–9. On the anatomy of the lesser American Flying-squirrel (*Pteromys volucella* Cuv.).

1831, PCSCZS 1: 48. On the anatomy of the *Ctenodactylus Massonnii,* Gray.

1831, PCSCZS 1: 59. On the sterno-tracheal muscles of the Razor-billed Curassow (*Ourax mitu* Cuvier).

1831, PCSCZS 1: 73. On the distinctive characters of the *Tetrao medius,* Temm.

1831, PCSCZS 1: 132–3. On the two species of *Entozoa* found in the Eel.

1831, PCSCZS 1: 133–4. On the generation of Eels and Lampreys.

1831, PCSCZS 1: 151. On the Brown-headed Gull (*Larus capistratus,* Temm.).

1831, PCSZCS 1: 159. On the anatomy of the Conger Eel (*Conger vulgaris*), and on the difference between the Conger and Fresh-water Eels.

1831, MNH 4: 116–8. Additions to the catalogue of British birds, with notices of the occurrence of several rare species.

1831, MNH 4: 334. Growth of the Salmon in fresh water.

1832, PCSCZS 2: 100. On a hybrid between a Muscovy Duck (*Anas moschata*) and a Common Duck (*Anas boschas*).

1832, PCSCZS 2: 429. On two species of Mammalia new to Britain one of them (*Sorex remifer*) new to science.

1832, MNH 5: 598. Additions to the British Fauna, Class Mammalia (*Arvicola riparia, Sorex remifer*), August 1832.

1832, TLS 17: 1. Description of the organs of voice in a new species of Wild Swan (*Cygnus buccinator* of Richardson). Read 20 March 1832.

1832, TLS 17:5. Description of three British species of fresh-water fishes, belonging to the genus *Leuciscus* of Klein. Read June 1832.

1833: BAAS Report: 446. On the reproduction of the Eel. [Selby to Jardine, 'Yarrell ... read an excellent paper upon the propagation of Eels, he has now finally set the question to rest, & proved most satisfactorily that they are oviparous.' PJS to WJ 8 July 1833, Cambridge University Library.]

1833, PZS 1: 3. On the trachea of the *Penelope gouan,* Temm. and the *Anas magellanicus,* Auct.

1833, PZS 1: 9, 56. Observations on the laws which appear to influence the assumption and changes of plumage in Birds. Read February 1833.

1833, PZS 1: 24, 80. On the Woolly and Hairy Penguins (*Aptenodytes*). [also TZS 1:13].

1833, PZS 1: 24. Description, with some additional particulars, of *Apteryx australis* of Shaw. Read June 1833.

1833, TZS 1: 33. On the identity of the Woolly Penguin of Latham with the *Aptenodytes patachonica* of Gmelin.

1833, PZS 1: 88. Characters of the Irish Hare, a new species of *Lepus.*

1833, PZS 1: 113. On the deficiency of teeth in the Egyptian hairless variety of the dog.

1833, MNH 6: 230 Notice of the occurrence of *Squilla Desmarestii* on the British shores.

1834, MNH 7: 350. On *Motacilla alba,* L.

1834, PZS 2: 118–9. On the anal pouch of the male fishes in certain species of the genus *Syngnathus,* Linn.

1835, TZS 1: 13–19. Observations on the laws which appear to influence the assumption and changes of plumage in birds. Read April 1833.

1835, TZS 1: 71. Description with some additional particulars of *Apteryx australis* of Shaw. Read June 1833.

1835, PZS 3: 57. On the mode of union after fracture of the processes of the vertebrae of a Sole (*Solea vulgaris,* Cuv.)

1835, PZS 3: 183. Notes on the foetal pouch of the male Needle Pipe-fish (*Syngnathus acus,* Linn.).

1835, PZS 3: 183. On the trachea of the Stanley Crane (*Anthropoides paradiseus,* Besch.)

1835, PZS 3: 183–4. Notes on the economy of an insect destructive to turnips (*Athalia centifolia,* Leach)

1836, AMNH 9: 131. On mucor observed by Colonel Montagu in the air-cells of a bird.

1838, BAAS Report: 108. On a new species of Smelt from the Isle of Bute (*Osmerus hebridicus*).

1838, PZS 6: 19. On a new species of Swan (*Cygnus immutabilis*).

1838, PLS 1: 65. On an interwoven mass of filaments of *Conferva fluviatilis* of extraordinary size.

1838, Entom. Soc. 5, 421. On the preservation of Crustacea.

1839, ANH 3: 81. Remarks on some species of *Syngnathus.*

1841, PZS 9: 70. On the trachea of a male Spur-winged Goose (*Anser gambensis*).

1841, TZS 2: 67–70. Observations on the economy of an insect destructive to turnips (*Athalia centifolia*). Read November 1835.

1843, Zoologist 1: 79–80. Note on the occurrence of birds lately ascertained to be British.

1843, Zoologist 1: 85–86. Note on the recent occurrence of new or rare fishes in England.

1845, PZS 13: 91. Note on the herring (*Clupea harengus*).

1847, PZS 15: 51–55. Description of the eggs of some of the birds of Chile.

1853, TLS 2: 155–60. On the habits and structure of the Great Bustard. Read 18 January 1853.

1853 Zoologist 11: 3947–3950. Occurrence of a Petrel new to Britain on the west coast of Ireland. Written June,1853.

1856, JLS 1: 76–82. On the influence of the sexual organ in modifying external character.

1856, PZS 24: 1. Great Bustard *Otis tarda* taken in Berkshire.

*Lithograph of portrait by Thomas Henry Maguire in 1849 when Yarrell was Vice-President of the Ipswich Museum, for inclusion in the* Portraits of Honourable Members of the Ipswich Museum. *1852.*

## Chapter 9

# SOCIETIES

William Yarrell gave much time and energy to natural history societies based in London from 1825 until his death in 1856. He served them as Secretary, Treasurer and Vice-President, and on their councils and committees, promoting their interests and tirelessly attending meetings and dinners. He became acquainted with all the leading members of these societies from all walks of life and mixed easily with them, earning their respect and gratitude for his services. The following are the societies with which he was associated, in order of the societies' establishment.

## ROYAL SOCIETY 1660–

Following a lecture by Sir Christopher Wren, the Royal Society was founded in Gresham College, London, on 28 November 1660 with King Charles II as its patron. Their *Philosophical Transactions* began publication in 1665.

William Yarrell, though not a member, had one paper published in the *Philosophical Transactions* in 1827 (268–275 On the change in the plumage of some hen-pheasants), written in February and read in May 1827.

In *The Times* obituary for Yarrell (3 September1856), it was stated that he was recommended to the Royal Society but never elected to fellowship 'owing to the corrupt practice – which still in measure prevails – of disregarding scientific claims of gentlemen connected with trade, while individuals were gaining admission to the society on account of mere social position and connoisseurship, it was intimated to Yarrell that he had no chance of success and he withdrew his certificate.'

LINNEAN SOCIETY 1788–
William Yarrell elected a Fellow on 1 November 1825
On Council 1831–56
Treasurer 24 May 1849–1856
One of its Vice-Presidents from 1849 to 1851

Presidents while William Yarrell was a member:
Sir James Edward Smith 1788–1828; 13th Earl of Derby 1828–33; Edward St Maur, 11th Duke of Somerset 1833–36; Edward Stanley, Bishop of Norwich 1837–49; Robert Brown 1849–53; Thomas Bell 1853–61.

The Linnean Society, founded in 1788, was the first scientific society after the founding of the Royal Society. One of its founders, Sir James Smith, purchased Linnaeus' collections of plants and animals and these were bought by the Linnean Society in 1828. They met in 32 Soho Square (the home of Sir Joseph Banks 1743–1820) from 1821–57, until they moved in 1857/8 to the old Burlington House in Piccadilly. Natural history specimens were arranged in a museum from 1828 until it was sold in 1857. Linnaeus' library formed the basis of the book collection.

A Linnean Club was formed on 16 December 1811 that later became the Linnean Society Club for Fellows of the Society and the Librarian. In 1831 the regular arrangement was for them to meet every Tuesday, when an Ordinary Meeting of the Society was held, and for dinner at the Freemason's Tavern in Great Queen Street. The club also arranged excursions in the summer, e.g. to Black Notley, Saffron Walden, St Albans and Verulamium, Brentwood, etc. The Black Notley arrangements, described by Yarrell, were of a pattern that combined serious study with pleasant socialising. Some 20 Fellows took the stage or mail coach to the White Hart in Braintree, Essex, in the morning, then walked to Black Notley after lunch to visit the house and tomb of John Ray in the afternoon. They returned to Braintree for dinner and to stay overnight. The following day they returned to Black Notley to go to church.[1]

Several members who wished to 'study all areas of zoology and comparative anatomy, particularly in relation to the domestic UK and Ireland animals' formed a Zoological Club of the Linnean Society in 1824, with Edward Turner Bennett 1797–1836, a zoologist who practised as a surgeon near Portman Square, London, taking the lead. With the establishment of the Zoological Society of London, the need for this group ceased and in 1829 they disbanded. Yarrell had enjoyed the club's dinners and excursions.

Robert Brown, a Scottish botanist and friend of Yarrell, elected Fellow of the Linnean Society in 1822 and President of the Linnean Society from 1849–53, obtained the position of one of the Vice-Presidents for Yarrell, who also became treasurer of the society in 1849. He appointed his old bank Herries, Farquhar & Co as the society's bankers. The banking company was amalgamated with Lloyds in 1893. Lloyds were the Linnean Society bankers until very recently.

James Ebenezer Bicheno (1785–1851) was the secretary of the Linnean Society of London from1825–32, appointed F.R.S. in 1827. Yarrell consulted Bicheno as an authority on classification in 1831. In 1832 he left London to live at Ty Maen, Glamorgan. Yarrell told Jenyns that Bicheno wanted them to visit him in Glamorganshire together.[2] Bicheno was in partnership in a Glamorgan ironworks, and as an amateur botanist published articles in the *Transactions of the Linnean Society*. He was renowned for his girth; reputedly 'he could fit three full bags of wheat into his trousers'.

Professor Thomas Bell, writing an obituary of Yarrell in the *Proceedings of the Linnean Society* (1838, 2: 33–37) about the loss to the members of a true and faithful friend, said that he was 'A valuable adviser to the Society on account of his quiet unpretending manners, his varied information, his plain method of stating facts, and the clear precision of his inferences, the straightforward simplicity of his character, and his unvarying command of temper, rendered him on all occasions a most valuable adviser.'

## ROYAL INSTITUTION 1799–

The Institution was founded for diffusing knowledge; for facilitating the general introduction of useful mechanical inventions and improvements; and for teaching, by courses of philosophical lectures and experiments, the application of science to the common purposes of life. It met in Soho Square in the house of the President of the Royal Society, Joseph Banks, with an original

*A medallion, diameter 41.5cm, with a portrait of William Yarrell by Neville Northey Burnard (1818–1878), a Cornish sculptor, presented to the Linnean Society by his publisher, John Van Voorst, in December 1859. Courtesy of the Linnean Society.*

58 members paying 50 guineas each as founder members. William Yarrell, though not a member, attended some lectures in 1817.

**WALTON & COTTON CLUB 19 March 1817–**

William Yarrell elected a member on 8 March 1837.

Edward Jesse wrote to Yarrell telling him he had been 'elected a member of the Walton & Cotton Club by general acclamation (not as usual by ballot). It was a little compliment paid to science, good sense, and that kindness of heart for which all your friends love you, and no one more than myself.'[3]

Owing to sentiments of veneration for the memory of the honest Izaak Walton (1593–1683), author of *The Compleat Angler, or the Contemplative Man's Recreation*, 1653, coupled with high respect for the eminent fly-fisher Charles Cotton (1630–87), a poet and friend of Walton, a new society was instituted in 1817 with the title the Walton & Cotton Club. The annual subscription was 3 guineas, the members meeting to dine three times a year on the second Wednesday in April, May and June. These original rules were amended at a meeting held in 1840, attended by William Yarrell, John Gould, Edward Jesse and four other members. Gould reported to Jardine that he was elected a member in 1836.[4] A copy of the *Rules for the Walton & Cotton Club*, 1821, was in Yarrell's library.

## CAMBRIDGE PHILOSOPHICAL SOCIETY 1819–

Founded in 1819 by Adam Sedgwick (1785–1873), a massive, craggy and often temperamental Yorkshireman but witty and clever, and Professor John Stevens Henslow (1796–1861) of Cambridge University. It was a place where university graduates could meet to discuss current scientific ideas and present new research. Fortnightly meetings were set up within a year, also Cambridge's most extensive scientific library and first curated museum of natural history. The society further published Cambridge's first scientific periodical. Yarrell visited the CPS museum and knew Henslow very well.

The scientific society of Cambridge University was given the name 'Philosophical' in the medieval use, for research undertaken outside the fields of theology and medicine. Audubon visited the CPS, and Sedgwick, Woodwardian Professor of Geology, took him to dine in hall with 40 students and they then retired to his rooms. Audubon found him 'gay, full of wit and cleverness; the conversation very animated, and I enjoyed it much'.[5]

Yarrell's close friend Leonard Jenyns was a member and noted in 1828 that the museum of the Cambridge Philosophical Society had a fine collection of British birds, adding that 'Yarrell was more particularly interested in this collection because it had been purchased by subscription in 1828 from Mr Morgan, formerly a surgeon in London and an intimate friend of his. He looked out especially for the Great Auk.'[6] All of the natural history collections in the museum were incorporated in the Zoology Museum and Comparative Anatomy Museum of Cambridge University in 1865, in return for accommodation for its library.

On 26 September 1829 Leonard Jenyns sent to Cambridge two copies of the printed catalogue of Yarrell's collection of birds – with one copy for Mr Morgan – and informed Yarrell: 'I have transmitted to Camb Phil Soc the last portion of the cat. of British Birds referring to the 5 large cases now ready. You will find these birds arranged as nearly as possible to the written lists you sent up. I should be much obliged by a copy or two of this catalogue when printed and one for Mr Morgan it may help to produce desiderata.'[7]

There are no registers of any specimens in either the Cambridge Philosophical Society or the Cambridge Museum of Zoology of the contents of the CPS museum, so all records of the specimens have been lost.

## MEDICO-BOTANICAL SOCIETY 1821–49

William Yarrell Council Member 1827–

This had been founded in 1821 by J. Frost, a lecturer at St Thomas's Hospital, who was the first director of the society from 1821 to 1828. He was expelled from the society for arrogant behaviour by a new president, the Earl of Stanhope, in 1829. Yarrell had been elected to the Council of the Medico-Botanical Society in 1827. Yarrell hated controversy, and it is probably significant that in all his correspondence he rarely alludes to this society. The society did not survive long – its dissolution came in 1849.

## ZOOLOGICAL SOCIETY OF LONDON 1826–

William Yarrell: Member 1826; Secretary 1836–38; Vice-President from 1839–44 and 1845–51. He was in the chair at many meetings of the Zoological Society and on the Council almost uninterruptedly from 1831–56. He was a regular attender at the meetings; even when a quorum could not be found he was there to attend to any necessary business. The varying fortunes of the zoo were an important factor in his life.

The object of the society was to create a collection of animals for scientists to study and to form a museum and library. The museum was established in 1827, when John Gould was appointed as taxidermist and curator. It was disbanded in 1855, when many of the specimens went to the British Museum.

In 1829 a farm was established at Kingston Hill, near Richmond Park, to provide relief by removing quadrupeds and birds for breeding purposes to a quiet place; for the rearing of domesticated animals; and for conducting experiments in all matters relating to breeding. The Council appointed Yarrell to superintend Kingston Hill, fixing the annual expenditure not to exceed £1400. A query over title of the Society for the land was investigated by Mr Hardisty and Yarrell in 1836, and it was decided to sell the farm immediately. (Minutes of the Council of the Zoological Society, 1829–November 1836).

While the arrangements for the formation of the society were being made, copies of a circular outlining a prospectus of the objects of the society were circulated privately and two copies, dated February 1825, are among Yarrell's papers. These were with Yarrell's copy of the first Report of the new society's committee, presented by the Council to a General Meeting held 29 April 1829, that is in the possession of the Linnean Society with the word 'First' in his clear handwriting. Scherren (p. 25) stated 'Thanks to Yarrell's methodical habits, one of the first circulars for instructions to corresponding members has been preserved.'

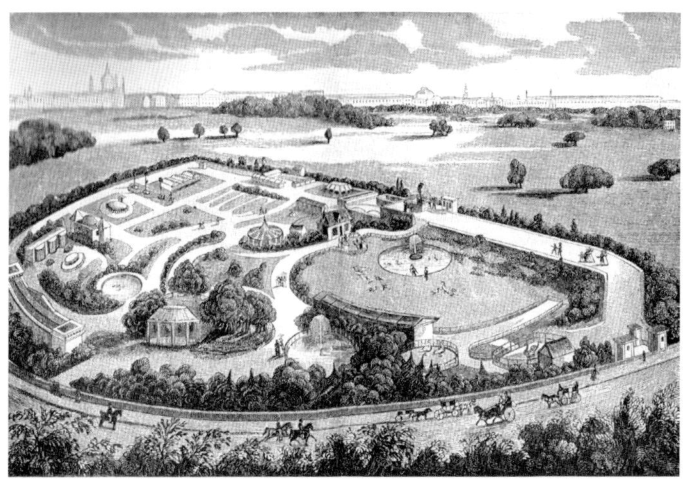

*Gardens of the Zoological Society, Regent's Park, London 1829. From the Zoological Keepsake. Reproduced in Scherren, Plate 3.*

Lord Derby was concerned with the inhabitants and potential new additions to the Zoological Gardens, exchanging queries about purchases with Yarrell. Lord Derby also found Yarrell a useful contact at a time when much information and livestock were exchanged between his menagerie at his Lancashire residence, Knowsley Hall, and the London zoo. He was also keen on news about hybrids – cross-breeding undertaken at the zoo.

For a short time, 1836–38, Yarrell acted as Secretary of the Zoological Society after his close friend of many years, Edward Turner Bennett, died in August 1836. He told Sir William Jardine, 'since the death of Mr Bennett in August last, I have had on my shoulders the onerous duties of Sec of the ZS with its 3,000 members.'[8], adding that these duties plus his own business occupied the whole of his time. Lord Derby, the President of the Zoological Society, had a stroke in 1840, which left him in a wheelchair with his left-hand side paralysed. He attended the meetings in London rarely after this, and further duties fell to Yarrell as Vice-President when he frequently chaired the meetings of the society.

While he was secretary, Yarrell had to sort out problems arising at the zoo. In January 1837, William Youatt, the veterinary surgeon to the Zoological Society, was distressed by the action of some zoo staff. 'Blackbirds and thrushes from neighbourhood seeking food and shelter in our garden. [The keepers] Rivers and White and others are shooting all that they can, Rivers has destroyed the greater part of a gross, there is cruelty, dastardly cruelty. Would not want the public to become aware of this being done in the ZS gardens. Would agree to be known as the complainant if WY takes it up with Miller.'[9] Alexander Miller was the superintendent of the Zoological Gardens from 1829 until 1852.

Youatt and Yarrell had a difference of opinion as to the occasional cases of rabies in the dogs. Writing to Youatt, Yarrell cited several instances of rabid dogs getting into the Zoological Gardens 'Until the Council enclosed not a month ago, the space to which your kennels are placed, no dog was secure in his wired den from inoculation. There is plenty of room between the wires for the introduction of the muzzle of a tolerably sized dog. Either to lick or to bite the inhabitant of the den. We have now prevented the possibility of danger.'[10] Youatt wrote a book about dogs published in 1845, of which Yarrell had a copy in his library.

David William Mitchell (1813–1859, Secretary to the Zoological Society 1847–59) graduated from Oxford University in 1836. After his marriage in 1837 he moved to Cornwall. There are numerous notes in Jonathan Couch's records of notices from Mitchell in Cornwall between 1839 and 1841. He later also had a house in London, having been appointed Secretary of the Zoological Society in 1847, and was still in post when he died in 1859. Yarrell was one of his proposers for election to the Fellowship of the Linnean Society in 1843 and he was elected Fellow of the Zoological Society in the same year. He was elected Honorary Secretary of the Zoological Gardens and Arrangements Committee and instigated new exhibits, e.g. a reptile house in 1849, a hippopotamus enclosure in 1850, an Aquatic Vivarium in 1853, and he wrote a popular guide to the gardens 1855. The growth in membership and popularity of the Zoological Gardens owed much to his enterprise.

In 1845 Yarrell was involved with a small Committee for Purchase of Animals, and kept Lord Derby informed of new arrivals. He had learned that

Whitfield, a collector overseas, 'has brought with him 2 Cheetahs, 2 Servals and 2 Jackals which your L[ordship] was not likely to desire to keep. The ZS would be glad to have the cheetahs and servals. Louis Fraser [Lord Derby's first curator at Knowsley] thinks we ought to have the Jackals as well. Thompson [Lord Derby's menagerie manager at Knowsley] left London on Friday for Paris and Hamburgh to obtain a Zebra or a Quagga and would return to Knowsley by way of Hull.' This was followed up in September, 'asking for rollers and rock thrushes for ZS. We should be ready to buy the Servals and Jackals without the Cheetahs... 2 baboons for sale but monkey house when full leads to deaths from the more rapid depreciation of the quality of the air. 3 lion cubs all died – no palatal bones or roof to the mouth so could not suck.'[11]

In the history of the Zoological Society there had been both high and low points. A surge in interest was occasioned by the arrival of giraffes in 1836 (Yarrell had a drawing of them in a gilt, glazed frame). Early 1850 was a low point, with falling numbers of visitors and therefore revenue. A spectacular new attraction was needed to revive the Society's finances. The Committee for the Purchase of Animals, comprising the Secretary David Mitchell, Professor Owen and William Yarrell, with the backing of the President, Lord Derby, made a risky decision to import a hippopotamus, an animal reputedly not seen in Britain since Roman times. In May 1850 a young male from Obaysch, an island in the Nile, Egypt, arrived alive in the ship *Ripon* and was put on a train to London and the zoo. It was placed on view on 29th May and became a huge success, with 10,000 people going to view it daily, restoring the zoo's finances. Once again, Yarrell's quiet background influence had contributed to a new opportunity for people to appreciate and enjoy a different aspect of natural history.

When Yarrell had visitors staying in his house for a few days, he almost always took them to the Zoological Gardens. This applied to Jenyns, who was also an original member, and members Jardine and Selby among others.

Yarrell's contribution to the Zoological Society was appreciated by council members following his two years in office as Secretary. In accepting his resignation 'owing to his business engagements', the 'Council spoke in high terms of his zoological attainments and the general acquaintance with business details which enabled him to fill the responsible office of Secretary in a manner equally creditable to himself and advantageous to the Society.' In reporting this, Scherren added that 'His services to the society, from its foundation till his death thirty years later, can hardy be overrated.'[12]

## BRITISH ASSOCIATION FOR THE ADVANCEMENT OF SCIENCE 1831–

A charitable and learned society whose aims were to improve the perception of science in the UK and to promote the study of science. At the first meeting in 1831 over 100 attended. The meetings were held annually, lasted for a week, and were originally with four sections: Physics, Chemistry, Geology, and Natural History.

Yarrell tried to attend the annual meetings each year. At the 1833 meeting in Cambridge he read a paper on the 'Propagation of eels', and he reported 'On a new species of Smelt from the Isle of Bute' at the Newcastle meeting in 1838. At the 1834 meeting Jenyns gave the annual 'Report on Zoology' – a formidable task about which he said, 'without Yarrell's help I never could have undertaken the task ... he not only gave me much advice in this matter, with the run of his own library; but got me access to other sources of information, and further helped me by procuring several foreign works, which it was absolutely necessary to consult, and allowing me to have them at trade price, he himself being a bookseller as well as news-vendor.'[13]

## ENTOMOLOGICAL SOCIETY 1833–

William Yarrell Founder member in 1833.

Treasurer from 1834 to 1852.

Yarrell contributed only one article to their *Entomological Magazine*, 'On the preservation of Crustacea' (1838, 5: 421). His main interest in insects was as food for fishes and birds, but he regularly attended the meetings and took along any naturalist visitors (Jardine, see p.41, and Jenyns among others) he had staying with him.

In London's Central Criminal Court on 29 January 1849 a case was tried that was a complete waste of time for everyone involved. The reporter could only make it interesting by dragging in William Yarrell's name. Some drawings, paintings and engravings of butterflies and other insects, parcelled up, had gone missing from the Entomological Society, whose premises were in Bond Street. The defendant, in whose house the police had found the parcels under a table, claimed he had them from another man and he was acquitted. The defendant's wife said they had planned to open a shop and sell the pretty pictures. There were 1,170 of them, valued at £6, and were 'the goods of William Yarrell and others'. Jonathan Obadiah Westwood, the secretary of the society when the theft occurred, had been called as a witness and declared

a

b

c

d

a. Tufted Duck
b. Pintail Duck
c. Egyptian Goose
d. Bernicle Goose

PLATE 12 Birds for St James's Park

that William Yarrell was a member of the society and when 'the rooms in Bond Street were not in use, the key is left with the treasurer, Mr William Yarrell.' Was it usual for the treasurer to have to turn up to meetings early to let in all the members and then remain until they had all departed so that he could lock up? Yarrell evidently tolerated this situation.[14] Since these large bundles of paintings and drawings were the property of the Entomological Society one would expect them to have been returned, but they were reported not to be there today.

**ST JAMES'S ORNITHOLOGICAL SOCIETY** 1836–37/Ornithological Society of London 1837–58/London Natural History Society.

*The Morning Post* reported in their paper of 22 October 1836, 'On the 20th instant the St James's Ornithological Society held their first meeting. William Yarrell Esq F. L. S. was in the chair. The subscription is £1. The object of the society is to form a complete collection of hardy aquatic birds in the garden.' A journalist for *The Naturalist* (1836, 1: 274) had got hold of a prospectus and decided that 'The names of Yarrell, Swainson, Mudie and Jesse, so well known in the scientific world, are a pledge that some useful purpose is designed by, and will be obtained for the Ornithological Society.' One of these objects turned out to be a hope that 'the lower orders of society would enjoy seeing the feathered tribe without the mischievous wish to pelt them.'

The *Literary Gazette and Journal of the Belles Lettres ...* (1837: 58) took the story on to the next stage. 'The aquatic birds turned out on the sheet of water in the New Gardens, by the St James's Ornithological Society, are in full feather and go on swimmingly. Among them we notice the Chinese, bean, white-fronted, Egyptian, and barnacle goose. Of the duck tribe are to be seen, the Sheldrake, Muscovy, hookbill, pintail, tufted and call. The list of members is rapidly on the increase.'

On the 20 December 1836 *The Morning Post* reported that 'Duke of Newcastle, Earl of Southampton, Sir Coutts Trotter and Sir Robert Peel and 10 other gentlemen have been elected members of the [St James's Ornithological] Society during the past week.' This was the beginning of a 'takeover' by upper class members of London society that continued apace in the next few months.

In 1837, a new Ornithological Society of London was formed. At a meeting on 16 May 1837 their council decided that St James's Ornithological Society was too local and confined for the society after they had just adopted it.[15]

The naturalists who were original members of the St James's Ornithological Society had been given the option of being named as original members of the Ornithological Society of London! Their patron was Prince Albert and the membership small and select – a situation ensured by the expensive subscription. The new society had not only taken over half of the name of the original society, but had taken charge of the birds paid for by the St James's Ornithological Society naturalist members. Their declared aims, to protect the birds and add to their number, were the same.

In volume 3 of *A History of British Birds*, there are nine references to birds placed in St James's Park, the first being: 'Among the many aquatic birds with which the Ornithological Society has stocked the canal and islands in St James's Park, are several Moor-hens.' Other references to birds placed on the canal included Bean goose, bernicle geese, a pink-footed goose female, a female goldeneye who associated constantly with a lonely smew, great crested grebes and a pair of Canada geese belonging to the Society, bred in 1841. Each time, the name of the society used by Yarrell is the 'Ornithological Society' but sometimes it was 'The Ornithological Society of London'.[16]

Charles Darwin took a close interest in call ducks and wrote to W. D. Fox in May 1855 to say that while he was in London he had seen Yarrell, who had told him that he had 'carefully examined all points in Call Ducks and did not feel any doubt about its being specifically identical and that it had crossed freely with common varieties in St James's Park.'[17] Call ducks were white, imported ducks from Holland, characterized by incessant noisy chattering and were often used as decoys for that reason for sporting purposes. Yarrell would have kept a close eye on what the ducks were doing in the Park long after he had been instrumental in placing so many on the lake there. He lived a very short walk from the park.

## ART UNION OF LONDON 1837–1912

Established in London in order 'to aid in extending the love of Arts of Design, and to give Encouragement to Artists beyond that afforded by the patronage of individuals'. Each member paid a subscription of one guinea a year and received a large engraving annually. Additionally, they had the chance to win a prize at a yearly draw, at first either a proof copy of that year's print, or a painting. The winners of the prize draw had a free choice of any painting, up to a given value, shown at any of the London exhibitions that year. As membership grew so the amount available to offer prizes, totalling about £9,000 annually, increased. The Art Union lasted until 1912.

In the sale catalogue of Yarrell's collections in December 1856, there were four lots of these art prints. Lot 60 Thirty illustrations of Childe Harold, for the Art Union, 1855; Lot 80 Una, Water Party, River Scene in Devonshire; Lot 102 Numbers of the Art Union, 3; Lot 118 Drawings and Water Colours, View on the Thames, between Reading and Sonning by Aaron Penley, in handsome glazed gilt frame. PRIZE, SELECTED BY MR YARRELL AT THE ART UNION. In the sale catalogue of Yarrell's goods in December 1856, this large watercolour 'View on Thames by Aaron Penley – selected we believe by Mr Yarrell for an eighty guinea prize in the Art Union – sold for £27.6.'

THE RAY SOCIETY 1844–

Named after John Ray, the 17th century naturalist, this is a scientific publishing charity mainly interested in British flora and fauna. The initial idea was that of Dr George Johnston, who enlisted the help of Sir William Jardine and his son-in-law Hugh Strickland, as well as representatives of southern naturalists, particularly James Bowerbank, and key naturalists in London, including Yarrell, Robert Brown and J. E. Gray. Yarrell's name appeared among council members in 1847.

In 1844 the formation of what was to become the Ray Society was discussed among naturalists in the north (Sir William Jardine, Dr George Johnston and P. J. Selby) and in London (Edward Forbes, William Yarrell, J. E. Gray, Robert Brown and James Bowerbank). It was realised that the society had to be based in London, with the northern naturalists to support it at a distance. Although the railways had facilitated movement between north and south, it was still thought that the northerners could not be prime movers as office holders because distance presented problems when the logistics of attending meetings and publishing the books proposed by the Ray Society had to be overcome. The sole purpose of the society was to publish books, e.g. facsimiles or historically important out-of-print books, translations of original works and monographs.

**The PHILOPERISTERON SOCIETY** 1847, altered its name in 1868 to what it remains today, **NATIONAL PERISTERONIC SOCIETY**. It claims to be the oldest continually running pigeon society in the world. The original name meant a lover of things relating to pigeons.

In 1855 Yarrell's friend William B. Tegetmeier became Secretary of the society, which then held its annual meetings in the great hall of the Freemason's Tavern in Great Queen's Street, London. At the annual show that year, Yarrell attended accompanied by Charles Darwin, who he was encouraging to take up the study of pigeons. Yarrell pointed out the remarkable variations produced through domestication and man's intervention in the breeding of pigeons over a long period of time, but all (he believed) were traceable to the original bird, the Rock Dove, *Columba livia*. At this exhibition in January 1855 Yarrell introduced Darwin to Tegetmeier, who was to become a great contributor to Darwin's study of pigeons with drawings, texts and engravings.

In the *Cottage Gardener* issue for January 1856 the exhibition at the Philoperisteron was covered by describing the pigeons on display and then continued with, 'The company was numerous, and included some of our first naturalists. Mr Yarrell whose name is a "household word" with all Zoologists, and Mr Darwin, whose "Naturalist's Voyage round the World", is known all over the world, were present and with our old correspondent Mr Tegetmeier, were examining bird after bird, with a view to ascertaining some of those differences on which the distinction between species and varieties depend.'

Tegetmeier was the writer of an article in the *Cottage Gardener* of 11 November 1856 where he stated, 'The late Mr Yarrell was a constant visitor to the Exhibition of the Philoperisteron shows long before Darwin had shown the slightest interest in the subject.' In March 1855 Darwin told a correspondent (W. D. Fox) that Yarrell had persuaded him to attempt to breed pigeons and that he was then fitting up a place and had written to Bayley about prices. Yarrell had recommended John Bailey, a poulterer and dealer in live birds, to Darwin as a source of some pigeons, and by February the following year he could write positively and delightedly to Yarrell, 'My dear Yarrell The pigeons are all quite well vigorous and in good spirits. They are really quite beautiful. I have now 15 Kinds of Pigeons. I send with this the Book and your Cage.'[18] It was after visiting the show in January 1855 that Darwin built his first pigeon house at Down and obtained some Fantails and Pouters, then added to their number and variety very quickly. By November 1855 he confessed he loved them to the extent that he could not bear to kill and skeletonise them. He found great pleasure as well as useful information from his pigeons over many years. Darwin became a member of the Philoperisteron Society in October 1856. In 1858 he began to write his manuscript for *The Origin of Species by means of natural selection* and commenced with the heading 'On the breeds of the domestic pigeon'. It owed much to his old friend and mentor William Yarrell's influence.

*Fancy pigeons by a rural cottage door.* A History of British Birds, 1843, 2: 264.

# NOTES

Abbreviations

| | |
|---|---|
| BAAS | British Association for the Advancement of Science |
| BRLSI | Bath Royal Literary and Scientific Institution |
| CD | Charles Darwin |
| CUL | Cambridge University Library |
| Edin. Univ. Liby | Edinburgh University Library |
| *HBB* | *A History of British Birds* |
| *HBF* | *A History of British Fishes* |
| JG | John Gould |
| LCL | Liverpool Central Library,13th Earl of Derby correspondence |
| LJ | Leonard Jenyns |
| Linn. Soc. Liby | Linnean Society Library |
| NHML | Natural History Museum, London, Library |
| Nat. Mus. Scot. | National Museums of Scotland |
| PJS | Prideaux John Selby |
| Sauer | Correspondence in NHML |
| Syd. Mitchell Liby | Sydney Mitchell Library |
| TCE | Thomas C. Eyton |

| | |
|---|---|
| WJ | Sir William Jardine |
| WY | William Yarrell |
| ZS | Zoological Society |

## Chapter 1 Family and Early Life

1. Richardson, 1860: vii–iii. Fuller dates for the family were given: 'Francis Yarrell 1749–94, born 10th of February 1749; married the 26th of June, 1772, died 25th of March, 1794. He was the eldest of seven brothers and sisters, the children of Francis Yerrall, born in 1727, died the 5th of January, 1786, and of Sarah his wife, born in 1719, died the 12th of December 1800.' These dates were noted by John Van Voorst, who wrote the *Memoir* in Richardson (1860, vii), presumably either in talking to William Yarrell or from the gravestones in Bayford Churchyard, which are no longer legible so that the dates cannot be checked, except in the parish registers. The date of 1719 for the baptism of Sarah has not been found and I think is doubtful, although the other dates are correct. A Sarah Hawkins baptised in the same church in 1727 who had a brother William born 1830, is more likely, but there were many 'Sarah Hawkins' in the St Mary, Hitchin parish registers. I was alerted to the baptism of William's father, Francis (1749–94) by my nephew David R. Smith, who also assisted in the search for other members of Yarrell's family.
2. Richardson, 1860, xi–xii. For fuller account, see p.3. In Bayford Churchyard the graves of William's maternal grandparents had the inscriptions 'George Blane who departed this life December 20th 1777 aged 76' and 'Hannah Blane departed this life July 15th 1804 aged 85'.
3. Bermondsey, Surrey, parish church: 'Francis Yerrall of this Parish bachelor, and Sarah Blane, of this Parish Spinster. By banns, 26 June 1772.' William Hawkins was present (see note 1).
4. No registers or archives remain from the school and what is known was gathered together by Dr Jonathan Oates, Archivist, London Borough of Ealing. (Online Teaching Ealing 2008; *Ealing A Concise History* 2014: 27. Amberley Local Books.) With thanks to Dr Oates. Neither Edward nor William went to one of the only two English universities then in existence, Cambridge and Oxford.
5. Richardson, 1860, xi. The rejection was detailed in an obituary in the *London Athenaeum,* 13 September 1856. The anonymous author of this obituary was said by Van Voorst to be Thomas Bell (1792–1880), one of WY's intimate friends (Van Voorst article published by Richardson in *HBF,* 3rd ed).
6. Jenyns said WY was 'Particular about his guns, and was intimate with George Manton, the well-known gun-maker of Bond Street'. (Jenyns *Reminiscences,* 1855: 5). George died in 1854. John 1742–1834 and brother Joseph Manton, 1766–1835, were gunmakers of 6 Dover Street. WY's double-barrelled gun was made by John.
7. *Morning Advertiser,* 10 September 1856; *The Times,* 6 September 1856: 7e.

8. Alfred Newton, *The Times,* 3 March 1894.

## Chapter 2 The Story of Jones and Yarrell

1. Robert Jones appeared on several occasions in the Minutes of the Inn's Parliament (1703–47), where his leases were recorded from 1734 to 1766.
2. Kent's *Directory of Businesses in London,* 1808. 'Jones and Yarrell, stationers and newsagents'.
3. 15 January 1840. TCE to WY, CUL. Can WY send a copy of *The Times* newspaper he missed on 4 January. Newspapers for JG, August 1839.
4. WY to LJ, 14 August. 1832 BRLSI.

## Chapter 3 The 1820s: Laying the Foundations

1. WY to WJ, 1828, Edin. Univ.
2. CD to T. C. Eyton, 9 December 1855. *Correspondence of Charles Darwin,* edited by Burkhart & Smith, vol. 5. Note 6 added the information that Darwin had earlier read the first volume of the second edition of *A History of British Birds.*
3. WJ to PJS, 22 September 1834, CUL; PJS to WJ, 29 September 1834, CUL.
4. WY to WJ, 1 December 1828, Nat. Mus. Scot.
5. Bewick wrote this to his close friend Dovaston on 1 September 1828 (Dovaston 1968: 117).
6. WY to LJ, 1835, Edin. Univ. DK/0/2.
7. Jenyns 1885: 6–7.
8. Jenyns 1885: 8–9.
9. N. A. Vigors. An address delivered at the sixth and last Anniversary Meeting of the Zoological Club of the Linnean Society of London, 29 November 1829. *Magazine of Natural History,* 1830, 3: 201–226. (pp. 208 and 213). I thank Robert Prŷs-Jones for drawing my attention to this.

## Chapter 4 The 1830s: The Decade of Achievement

1. WY to LJ, 30 August 1833, BRLSI.
2. PJS to WJ, 16 March 1835, CUL.
3. CD to Henslow, 9 September 1831, Darwin Correspondence, CUL.
4. WY to LJ, November 1831, BRLSI.
5. WY to LJ, 17 April 1832, BRLSI.
6. WY to Lord Derby, 7 and 17 June 1832, LCL.
7. WY to Lord Derby, 17 August 1833, LCL.
8. WY to LJ, 12 November 1833, BRLSI.
9. Hugh S. Gladstone, *The Life of Sir William Jardine,* 190–2, Nat. Mus. Scot.
10. WY to JG, 9 October 1831, Sauer 1: 32.

11. WY to JG, 28 November 1833, Sauer 1: 50.
12. WY to LJ, 30 August 1833, BRLSI.
13. WY to Lord Derby, 17 June 1838, LCL.
14. WY to LJ, 10 August 1834, BRLSI.
15. WY to LJ, 17 August 1835.
16. WY to LJ, 14 December 1834, BRLSI.
17. WY to WJ, 28 December 1836, Nat. Mus. Scot.
18. *Proceedings of the Committee of Science and Correspondence of the Zoological Society of London*, 1832, 2: 429.
19. *Proceedings of the Linnean Society*, London 1835; *Transactions of the Zoological Society, London*, 1841.
20. Wallace, 2005: 49 Chapters in my Life.
21. WJ to PJS, 26 December 1825, CUL.
22. WY to LJ, 11 August and 20 November 1836, BRLSI.
23. Sauer, 1: 151.
24. Sauer, 1: 168.l.
25. Sauer, 1: 176.
26. WY to LJ, 17 August 1835, BLSLI.
27. G. Johnston to WY, 5 September 1837, CUL.
28. WY to WJ, 9 September 1835, Nat. Mus. Scot.
29. WY to WJ, between 25 September and 14 October 1835, Edin. Univ. Liby. DK/0/22.
30. WJ to WY, 25 July 1836, Norfolk Record Office, John Gurney Natural History notes.
31. WY to WJ, 1835, Edin. Univ. Liby. DK/0/22.
32. Jesse to WY, 20 September 1836, CUL.
33. CD to LJ, 10 April 1837, BRLSI.
34. WY to LJ, 13 December 1837, BRLSI.
35. CD to LJ, 14 October 183? (no year given), BRSLI.
36. ibid.
37. WY to CD, 1 December 1838. Zool. Memorandum DAR 205.7; WY to CD, 14 July 1839, DAR 204: 185, CUL.
38. WY to LJ, 28 November 1836, BRLSI.
39. Sauer, 1: 108.
40. G. Johnston to WY, 31 January 1837 CUL; 23 September 1839 CUL.
41. Larking to WY, 7 July 1837, CUL.
42. Euing to WY, 25 November 1837; 22 December 1837; 15 September 1838 CUL.
43. Lubbock to WY, 7 August 1837, CUL.

44. Lubbock to WY, 11 December 1837, CUL.
45. Jenyns, *Reminiscences of William Yarrell*, 1885.
46. Ord to WY, 14 September 1837, CUL.
47. Ord to WY, 17 May 1838, CUL.
48. Audubon to Bachman, 14 August 1837, Sauer 1998, 1: 183.
49. WY to Swainson, 7 May 1838, Linn. Soc.
50. WY to LJ, 14 December 1834, BRLSI.
51. WY to LJ, October 1838, BRLSI.
52. WY to WJ, 16 March 1840, Nat. Mus. Scot.
53. *HBF*, 1841, 2: 434–5.
54. WY to LJ, 7 October 1838, BRLSI.
55. TCE to WY, 22, 24 or 27 May 1839(?), CUL; 24 February 1839, CUL; 5 April 1839, CUL.
56. Audubon to WY, 12 April 1839, CUL.
57. WY to WJ, 29 July 1838, Nat. Mus. Scot.
58. Prince to WJ, 10 August 1838, Sauer 1: 267.
59. Prince to JG, 4 February 1839, Syd. Mitchell Liby; Sauer 2: 26; 15 April 1839, Syd. Mitchell Liby; Sauer 2: 52.
60. Prince to JG, 30 September 1839, Sauer 2: 109.
61. Prince to JG, 29 June 1839, Syd. Mitchell Liby.
62. Prince to JG, 13 June 1839, Syd. Mitchell Liby.
63. Prince to JG, 30 September 1839, Sauer 2: 109.
64. Prince to JG 16 August 1839, Syd. Mitchell Liby.
65. WY to WJ, 5 August 1838, NHML.
66. WY to Lord Derby, 22 April and 27 May 1839, LCL.
67. WY to LJ, 20 January 1839, BRLSI.
68. Jenyns, *Reminiscences*, 1885.
69. WY to WJ, 5 August 1837, NHML.

## Chapter 5 The 1840s: Consolidating

1. Prince to JG, 6 April 1840, Syd. Mitchell Liby; Sauer 2: 164–5.
2. WY to Audubon, 10 March 1841, Herrick 1938, 2: 223–225. Herrick wrote the earliest, most detailed biography of Audubon, *Audubon the Naturalist: A History of His Life and Times.* 2nd ed, 2 vols, 1938.
3. Gladstone, 1842: 155–218.
4. TCE to WY, 15 January 1840, CUL.
5. WY to JG, 31 August 1841, NHM Gould correspondence.

6. Census 1841, HO 107 736 Bk 4 folio 32.
7. Lubbock to WY, 22 August and 20 November 1841, CUL.
8. WY to WJ, 25 September 1835, Edin. Univ. Liby DK/0/22.
9. Sauer 1999, 3: 215 and 216; Jackson 1999: 376.
10. Sauer 1998, 2: 154.
11. Jardine gave Selby a more detailed account of their visit to the Zoological Gardens. Jackson & Davis p. 92 and note 14 on p. 180. Gladstone, p. 159.
12. Secord 1981: 166.
13. JG to WJ, 25 April 1842, CUL.
14. PJS to WJ, 3 February 1836, CUL.
15. PJS to WJ, 14 January 1842, CUL.
16. WY to W. S. MacLeay, Elizabeth Bay, Sydney, 30 August 1843, Linn. Soc. Liby.
17. WY to Lord Derby, 10 April and 15 April 1843, LCL.
18. WY to Lord Derby, 3 June 1843, LCL.
19. JG to WY, 14 March 1844, CUL; Sauer 3: 293.
20. JG to WY, 30 July 1845, CUL; Sauer 3: 421.
21. Lear to JG, 12 August 1844, Harvard, Houghton Library.
22. Lear (in Rome) to JG, 12 August 1844, Harvard, Houghton Library.
23. Lear to Charles Empson, 10 October 1831, quoted by Sauer 1: 31.
24. David E. Allen, *The Naturalist in Britain: A Social History*, 1976: 88.
25. *Westmoreland Gazette*, 9 October 1868: 18.
26. WY to CD, 29 July 1845, DAR 183:1 CUL.
27. Agassiz to WY, 27 September 1846, CUL.
28. WY to WJ, 28 July 1846, Edin. Univ. Liby.
29. WY to Couch, 24 February 1846, Linn. Soc.
30. Yarrell got the news from Jenyns, who also told Selby on 11 November 1847, Insect Room, Museum of Zoology, Cambridge.
31. D. Mitchell to JG, 5(?) November 1849, Nat. Hist. Mus. Gould correspondence.
32. Yarrell's records on small cards are now preserved in the BRLSI.

## Chapter 6 The 1850s: Winding Down

1. WY to David Mitchell, 24 December 1850, CUL Add. 5354.
2. WY to LJ, November/December 1850, BRSLI.
3. *Zoologist*, 5258. *Athenaeum* no 1507, 13 September 1856: 1143–1145.
4. Census 1851, HO 107, 1484 folio 215. St James's parish Lt Ryder Street.
5. The letter from WY to Fisher, dated 12 July 1851, is in a private collection. There were extra

illustrations by Fisher in *HBB*, and he was the artist for *A Natural History of the Nests and Eggs of British Birds*, 3 vols, with 223 coloured wood engravings by F. O. Morris, 1852–56.

6. Jackson 1978: 114–116.
7. WY to WJ, 11 December 1852, National Register of Archives (Scotland) Jardine of Applegarth. One letter in bundle 127.
8. WY to WJ, 8 December 1852, Natural History Museum. London, 66 letters dated 1852 89q Jardine.
9. WY to WJ, 29 December 1852, Natural History Museum. London, 66 letters dated 1852 89q Jardine.
10. WY to George Newport, 16 September 1853, Linn. Soc. 236.
11. Richardson, 1860: xvi.
12. LJ to PJS, 21 February 1854, BRLSI.
13. Rev. J. A, Barron to WY, 20 September 1854, CUL.
14. WY to George Frederick, 7 March 1855, Norfolk County Library.
15. CD to Tegetmeier, 18 September 1856, Darwin Correspondence Project, letter no DCP-LETT-1955.
16. WY to JG, 19 January 1856, Nat. Hist Mus.
17. Alfred Newton to JG, 3 August 1856, Nat Hist Mus.
18. *Gentleman's Magazine.* Obituary, 1856, 2: 512–3.
19. Richardson 1860: xvi.
20. Alfred Newton to JG, 13 September 1856, Natural History Museum.
21. Henslow to JG, 20 October 1856, Natural History Museum.
22. Van Voorst to LJ, 25 November 1856, BRLSI.
23. Couch wrote this comment on the back of the title page of his copy of HBF, now in the Natural History Museum Library.
24. Darwin to W. B. Tegetmeier, 18 September 1856, Darwin Correspondence Project, series 2: 37, letter no. DCP-LETT1955.
25. One of these specimens was listed as still surviving in 1881 in *Cat. Birds. Brit. Mus.*, vol. 5, p.18.
26. The British Museum's *Annual Donations List* for 1830 notes that W. Yarrell donated a Bewick's Swan. It was also listed in *Cat. Birds Brit. Mus.*, vol. 27, p. 31, 1895, and still survives in the Natural History Museum's bird types collection.
27. The common teal was listed in *Cat. Birds Brit. Mus.,* vol. 27: 247, 1895, as 'Type of the species' and one of the common terns in *Cat. Birds. Brit. Mus.*, vol. 25, p. 58, 1896.
28. Gladwin, 2009: 204.
29. Noted by R. Lyddekker, in the chapter 'Domesticated Animals, Hybrids, and Abnormalities', in *British Museum History of the Collections*, 1906, vol. 2: 69 and list of donors, p. 78.

30. BM *Annual Donations List,* 1830: 27; BM *Annual Donations List,* 1831: 113.
31. WY to WJ, 22 January 1838, Nat. Mus. Scot.
32. Thomas Bell, President of the Linnean Society. Obituary of WY in *Proc. Linn. Soc.* 1858, 2: xxxiii–xxxviii. 'The testimony of Professor Bell, who knew him well, is as follows', and the text of the obituary is repeated in the Memoir of William Yarrell, in Sir John Richardson's vol. III supplementary to *HBF,* 1860, xv–xvi.

## Chapter 7 Yarrell's Lifestyle and Interests

1. Philip Carpenter founded the firm of lenses manufacture in spectacles, microscopes and other instruments in Birmingham in 1808, and moved to London in 1826. After his death in 1833 the firm continued under his sister Mary.
2. Peter Mark Roget, 1779–1869, was not only the author of *Roget's Thesaurus,* first published in 1852 and still in print, but also wrote *On Animal and Vegetable Physiology* in 1834 while Fullerian Professor of Physiology at the Royal Institution 1833–34.
3. Muffineers were either a dish for keeping muffins hot, or a castor for sprinkling salt or sugar on muffins that were soft, round and like bread, eaten hot, with butter.
4. *An Introduction to the Knowledge of Ancient and Modern Coins and Medals, Especially Those of Greece, Rome and Britain,* 1807, by John Pinkerton (1758–1826); *An Essay on Ancient Coins, Medals and Gems as Illustrating the Progress of Christianity in the Early Ages,* 1828, by the Rev. R. Walsh.
5. There were two pianoforte makers with the surname Matthews – Joseph, active c. 1814–52 in London, and William based in Nottingham with an outlet in London, where there was a bankruptcy case in 1845, but he survived to continue trading in Nottingham. Probably Joseph Matthews provided Yarrell's instrument. Thomas Tomkinson (sometimes Tomkison) was at 55/77 Dean Street, Soho, between 1799 and 1851, his trade card noting that he was 'Maker to His Royal Highness the Prince Regent'. There is currently an interest in square pianos, especially by Tomkinson/Tomkison, on the internet. In Jane Austen's *Emma* (published in 1816) Jane Fairfax was given a square piano by Frank Churchill.

## Chapter 8 Yarrell's Publications

1. T. R. Forbes, *Proc. Americ. Phil. Soc.* 12 December 1962, vol. 106, no 6: 514.
2. R. G. Latham, *Edinburgh New Phil. Jnl.,* 1856.
3. P. J. Selby informed Sir William Jardine on 8 July 1833, CUL, reporting on a BAAS meeting in Cambridge, 'Yarrell was there and read an excellent paper upon the propagation of Eels, he had now finally set the question at rest, & proved most satisfactorily that they are oviparous.'
4. WY to LJ, 30 August 1833, BRLSI.

5. WY to LJ, November(?) 1831, BRLSI.
6. WY to WJ. 14 October 1835, Nat. Mus. Scot.
7. Couch's *A Natural History of Cornish Fishes,* with pen-and-ink and coloured figures, 1836, is now in the Linn. Soc. Liby.
8. Wallace, 2005: 137.
9. WY to LJ, November(?) 1831, BRLSI.
10. WY to Swainson, 19 March 1838, Linn. Soc.
11. WY to Swainson, 21 March 1838, Linn. Soc.
12. WY to Swainson, 28 March 1838, Linn. Soc.
13. Gattoruginous Blenny, *HBF,* 1841, 1: 256 has now exchanged that odd name for an equally peculiar name, Tompot Blenny *Parablenius gattorugine.* A. Wheeler 1978: 286.
14. WY to LJ, no date, but 1831, BRLSI.
15. WY to Swainson, 19 March 1838, BRLSI.
16. PJS to WJ, 16 March 1835, CUL.
17. WY to Allis, 17 October 1837, York Library.
18. PJS to WJ, 18 October, then 29 October, 1836 CUL.
19. PJS to G. T. Fox, 24 March 1835, Glasgow University Library, Sp. Coll. F. 68.
20. WY to WJ, 28 December 1836, Nat. Mus. Scot; PJS to WJ, 24 November 1836, CUL.
21. WY to Swainson, 7 May 1838, Linn. Soc.
22. WY to Swainson, 13 July 1838, Linn. Soc.
23. G. Johnston to WY, 12 August 1836, CUL.
24. WY to Allis, 5 June 1837, York Library.
25. WY to WJ, 29 July 1838, Nat. Mus. Scot.
26. G. Johnston to PJS, 31 January1837, CUL.
27. E. M. Nicholson, *Birds in England.*
28. WY to Allis, 23 August 1837, York Library.
29. WY to Allis, 17 October 1837, York Library.
30. WY to WJ, 29 July 1838, Nat. Mus. Scot.
31. PJS to WJ, 13 July 1837, CUL.
32. G. Johnston to WY, 5 September 1837, CUL.
33. T. C. Eyton to WY, 27 September 1837, CUL.
34. WY to WJ, 22 January 1838, Nat. Mus. Scot.
35. WY to LJ, 17 April 1831, BRLSI.
36. WY to LJ, pre-November 1831, BRLSI.
37. WY to WJ, 25 September 1835, Edin. Univ. Liby.

## Chapter 9 Societies

1. WY to LJ, 28 June 1830, BRLSI.
2. WY to LJ, 12 November 1833, BRLSI.
3. Edward Jesse to WY, 9 March 1837, Edward Jesse Esq., W & C Club, Hampton Court, CUL.
4. Sauer 1998, 1: 146.
5. Audubon, 6 March 1828, in his journal, published M. R. Audubon 1897, reprint 1994, vol. 1: 288.
6. Wallace, 2005: 118.
7. LJ to WY, 26 September 1829, BRLSI.
8. WY to WJ, 28 December 1836, Nat. Mus. Scot.
9. William Youatt, veterinary surgeon to ZS, to WY, 2 January 1837, CUL.
10. WY to Youatt, 23 March 1838, CUL.
11. WY to Lord Derby, 24 September 1845, LCL; WY to Lord Derby, 27 September 1845, LCL.
12. Scherren, p. 53.
13. Wallace, 2005: 117.
14. Proceedings of the Old Bailey, 29 January 1849.
15. *London Courier and Evening Gazette*, 16 May 1837, p. 3.
16. *HBB*, 1843, 3: Moorhen p. 28; Bean Goose p. 3, Barnacle Goose p. 73; Canada Goose p. 94; Pink-footed Goose p. 165; Goldeneyed Duck p. 267; Smew p. 277; Great crested Grebe p. 299.
17. *HBB*, 1856, 2: 298–308. Darwin Notebook Pt IV, p. 136 of the fourth Notebook and Darwin Correspondence; edited by Burkhardt. Vol. 5, 1850–58: 326. There is no entry for Call Ducks in *HBB* so these were introduced to the park by the Ornithological Society of London post 1843. Darwin to Fox, 7 May 1855, Darwin Correspondence, vol. 5.
18. CD to W. D. Fox, 27 March; CD to WY, 6 February 1856. Darwin, Charles. *Correspondence of Charles Darwin*; edited by F. Burkhardt and S. Smith, vol. 6 (1856–57), 1991. The cage was probably a parrot cage listed in a lot in the December 1856 sale of Yarrell's effects.

# BIBLIOGRAPHY

## Biographical Sources

*Athenaeum.* 1856, 13 September, 507: 1143–1144, Obituary (by Thomas Bell)

*Athenaeum.* 1856, Our weekly gossip, 22 November 1436; 1520, 13 December 1537.

*Bayford Parish Registers,* 1770–1812, in Hertfordshire County Record Office.

Bell, Thomas, *Proceedings of the Linnean Society* 1858, 2: xxxiii–xxxviii, Obituary of William Yarrell, 2: 1 33–37.

Bennet, J. J., Secretary of Linnean Society 1858. Minutes of meetings of 4 November 1856 and 25 May 1857. Linn. Soc., London.

Boase, F. 1901. *Modern English Biography,* 3 vols, London.

*British Newspaper Archives 1750–1950.* c. 40 obituaries and sundry articles.

*Edinburgh New Philosophical Journal.* 1836, 3 (new series): 386–388, Obituary.

Edwards, J. C. 2004. William Yarrell, *Oxford Dictionary of National Biography.* Oxford.

Forbes, T. R. 1962. William Yarrell, British naturalist. *Proceedings of the American Philosophical Society,* 106: 505–515.

*Gentleman's Magazine* 1856, 2: 512–513.

Gladwin, Tom, Rev. William Yarrell (1784–1856), ichthyologist, ornithologist and friend of Charles Darwin and others. *Transactions of the Hertfordshire Natural History Society,* 2009, 41 (2): 201–209.

Jackson, C. E. 1978. *Wood Engravings of Birds.* 71–90. London.

Jackson, C. E. 1999. *A Dictionary of Bird Artists of the World.* Woodbridge.

Jackson, C. E. Correspondence of William Yarrell, abstracts and transcriptions of text, deposited in the Library of the Zoological Society.

Jenyns, L. 1885. *Reminiscences of William Yarrell.* Privately printed. Bath.

Kirk, H. *William Yarrell 1784–1856: A Bicentenary Tribute.* Privately published. Copies available in St Mary's Church, Bayford, Hertfordshire.

Latham, R. G. *Edinburgh New Philosophical Journal* 1856, 3 (new series): 386–388, Obituary.

Linnean Society. *Proceedings* 1858, 2, xxxiii–xxxviii. Obituary of Yarrell.

London Directories from 1730, in Westminster Record Office and London Guildhall Library.

*London Literary Gazette.* 6 September1856: 664, Obituary.

MacGillivray, J. 1842. Notes on the zoology of the Outer Hebrides. *Annals and Magazine of Natural History,* no 48: 7–16.

Mullens, W. H. William MacGillivray and William Yarrell. 1909, *British Birds* 2: 389–399.

Mullens, W. H. and Swann, H. Kirke. 1917. *A Bibliography of British Ornithology From the Earliest Times to the End of 1912.* London. 667–72.

Newman, E., *Zoologist* 1856. Obituary of William Yarrell.

*Oxford Dictionary of National Biography From the Earliest Times to the Year 2000.* 2004. 62 vols. Edited by H. C. G. Matthew and B. Hamson. OUP. *William Yarrell,* by J. C. Edwards, vol. 60: 730–732.

Richardson, Sir J., Memoir of William Yarrell, *see* Van Voorst.

Royal Society of London *Catalogue of Scientific Papers* (1800–1863), 1867.

Soffer, Richard. Extensive notes on Yarrell, William (1784–1856), *A History of British Birds,* are conserved in the Soffer Ornithological Notes, Amherst College.

*The Times,* Deaths. 3 September 1856, p. 7, column *e*; 9 September, p. 9, column *a.*

Van Voorst, John, Memoir of William Yarrell. 1859. *A History of British Fishes,* by William Yarrell. edited by Sir John Richardson, 3rd ed, 1: v–xxiii. London;

Van Voorst and *Second Supplement to the First Edition of A History of British Fishes,* with 'Third supplementary' by Sir John Richardson. Memoir of William Yarrell. London 1860: v–xviii.

## Bibliography

Audubon, John James Laforest. 1827–38. *The Birds of America.* 4 vols. London.

Audubon, Maria R. 1897. *Audubon and His Journals.* 2 vols, reprint 1994. New York.

Barrett, P. H. 1983. *Charles Darwin's Notebooks 1836–1844.* Cambridge.

Bewick, Thomas. 1797–1804. *History of British Birds.* 2 vols. Newcastle upon Tyne.

Birkhead, T. R. et al. Restoration of two great auk (Pinguinus impennis) eggs: Bourman Labrey's egg and the Scarborough egg. *Archives of Natural History* Vol. 47, part 2, October 2020: 393–401.

Bloch, Marcus Eliesar. 1785–97. *Ichthyologie ou Histoire Naturelle, Générale et Particulière des Poissons.*

With hand-coloured, copper-engraved illustrations often heightened with silver. Most of the last six volumes were destroyed in a fire. Paris.

Bonaparte, Charles Lucien 1803–1857. *American Ornithology*, 1825–33. Philadelphia.

Bridson, Gavin D. R. and others. 1980. *Natural History Manuscript Resources in the British Isles*, compiled by Gavin D. R. Bridson, Valerie C. Phillips and Anthony P. Harvey. London.

British Museum. *Annual Donations List, 1830, 1831.*

British Museum. 1874–98. *Catalogue of Birds in the Collection of the British Museum Natural History.* R. Bowdler Sharpe (ed), 27 vols. London.

British Museum. 1904–1912. *History of the Collections Contained in the Natural History Departments.* London.

British Museum Vellum Catalogue. 1830.

British Newspaper Archives, 1750–1999. Contains more than 7,000 'Yarrell' references (others constantly being added).

Brunnich, Morten Thane, 1764. *Ornithologia Borealis.* Hafnia and Copenhagen.

Catalogue of the valuable & interesting library of the late William Yarrell, Esq, V.P.L.S., F.Z.S ... which will be sold by auction by Mr J. C. Stevens ... on Thursday the 15th of November, 1856 and two following days.' London.

Catalogue of the interesting collection of objects of Natural History ... Books & books of Prints ... etc which will be sold by Mr J. C. Stevens ... on Thursday the 4th of December, 1856, and two following days. London.

*Cottage Gardener and Country Gentleman's Companion.* Conducted by George W. Johnson, vols 1–16, 1850–56.

Cotton, John. 1835. *The Resident Songbirds of Great Britain.* London.

Couch, Jonathan. *A History of the Fishes of the British Islands.* 252 colour plates, 1860–65, reissues up to 1877. London.

Curtis, John. 1829. *A Guide to an Arrangement of British Insects.* London.

Cuvier, Baron Georges and A. Valenciennes. 1828–49. *Histoire Naturelle des Poissons.* Paris.

Darwin, Charles. *The Correspondence of Charles Darwin.* 1991. F. Burkhardt and S. Smith (eds). Vols 1–6 (covering 1821–1857). London & Cambridge.

Darwin, Charles. *Notebooks on the Transmutation of Species.* Gavin de Beer (ed). *Bulletin of the British Museum (Natural History).* Series vol. 2, no 3: 75–118. 1960. London.

Darwin, Charles. *The Voyage of H.M.S.* Beagle *Under the Command of Captain Fitzroy, R. N. During the Years 1832 to 1836.* London.

Datta, Ann. 1997. *John Gould in Australia: Letters and Drawings.* Victoria, Australia.

Donovan, Edward. 1794–1819. *The Natural History of British Birds.* 10 vols, 244 plates. London.

Donovan, Edward, 1802–08, new edition 1845. *The Natural History of British Fishes.* 5 vols, with

120 colour plates. London.

Donovan, Edward. 1826. *The Natural History of the Nests and Eggs of the British Birds.* 17 plates, unfinished. London.

Dovaston, Gordon William. 1968. *Bewick to Dovaston Letters 1824–1828.* London.

Fitzroy, R. 1839. *Narrative of the Voyages of H.M.S. Adventure and Beagle, Between the Years 1826 and 1836.* 4 vols (vol. 3, *Journal and Remarks 1832–1836,* written by Charles Darwin). London.

Foster, Joseph. 2007. *Alumni Oxonienses: Members of the University of Oxford 1715–*1886. 4 vols. Oxford.

Fraser, Louis. *Zoologia Typica* 1846–49. London.

Gage, A. T. 1938. *History of the Linnean Society of London.* London.

Gladstone, Hugh S. *The Life of Jardine, Seventh Baronet of Applegarth.* Unpublished.

Gladwin, Tom. Rev. Yarrell's Law and Charles Darwin. *Transactions of the Natural History Society.* 2012, 44 (1): 50.

Granville-Smith, J. 1960. *Jones, Yarrell and Company Ltd. 1960. Bicentenary 1960, a History of the Firm.* London.

Hale, W. G. 2007. *The Meyers' Illustrations of British Birds.* London.

Harting, J. E. Account of his visit, with John Van Voorst, to grave of William Yarrell, MSS. Nat. Mus. Scot. *Athenaeum.* Our weekly gossip. 22 November 1436; 1520, 13 December 1537.

Hewitson, William Chapman. 1841–3. *British Oology.* London.

Hewitson, William Chapman. 1842–46. *Coloured Illustrations of the Eggs of British Birds.* London.

Jackson, Christine E. 1978. *Wood Engravings of Birds.* London.

Jackson, Christine E. and Maureen Lambourne. Bayfield – John Gould's unknown colourer. *Archives of Natural History.* 1990, 17 (2): 189–200.

Jackson, Christine E. and Peter Davis. 2001. *Sir William Jardine: a Life in Natural History.* London.

Jenyns, Rev. Leonard. 1835. *Manual of British Vertebrate Animals or Descriptions of All the Animals Belonging to the Classes Mammalia, Aves, Reptilia, Amphibia and Pisces Which have been Hitherto Observed in the British Isles. Including the Domesticated, Naturalized, and Extirpated Species, the Whole Systematically Arranged.* Cambridge.

*Kelly's Post Office London Directories.* 1835/6–continuing. London.

Kent, J. *Kent's Directories of London, 1759–1828.* London.

Lambourne, Maureen and Christine E. Jackson. Mr Prince: John Gould's invaluable secretary. *Naturae* no 4, 1993. Monash University, Clayton, Victoria, Australia.

Latham, John. 1781–85. *A General Synopsis of Birds.* 3 vols. London.

Latham, John. 1821–28. *A General History of Birds.* 10 vols. London.

Oates, Jonathan *Great Ealing School.* See online: Teaching Ealing 2008 and *Ealing A Concise History,* 2014: 27.

Pennant, Thomas. 1761–66. *The British Zoology.* 4 vols. London.

Pigot, James. 1814–39. *Directories of London*. London.

Risso, Antoine. 1826–27. *Histoire Naturelle Méridionale et Particulièrement de Celles des Environs de Nice* (including fishes). Nice.

Sauer, Gordon. 1998–2000. *John Gould the Bird Man: Correspondence With a Chronology of his Life and Works; Edited and Compiled by Gordon C Sauer*. Vols 1–3. Kansas City.

Scherren, Henry. 1905. *The Zoological Society of London: A Sketch of Its Foundation and Development and the Story of Its Farm, Museum, Gardens, Menagerie and Library*. London.

Secord, James Andrew. Nature's Fancy: Charles Darwin and the breeding of pigeons, *Isis*, 1981, 72: 162–86.

Selby, Prideaux John. 1819–34. *Illustrations of British Ornithology*. Edinburgh.

Stevens, J. C. A catalogue of the collections of objects of natural history, late Wm Yarrell, Esq, V.P.L.S., F.L.S., including specimens of stuffed British birds and fishes (many of which are the types of his great works). Comparative anatomy, birds' eggs amongst them the Great Auk and other rarities ... mahogany double cabinets, double gun, by John Manton, etc. at his Great Room, 38 King Street, Covent Garden, on Thursday, the 4th of December, 1856, and two following days. London.

Stevens, J. C. A catalogue of the valuable & interesting library of the Late Wm. Yarrell, Esq., V.P.L.S., F.L.S., in the varous branches of natural history, ... at his Great Room, 38 King Street, Covent Garden, on Thursday, the 13th of November, 1856, and two following days. London.

Swainson, William. 1838–39. *On the Natural History and Classification of Fishes, Amphibians, Reptiles or Monocardian Animals*. 2 vols. London.

Sweet, Robert. 1823–32. *The British Warblers; An Account of the Genus Sylvia*. 16 colour plates. London.

Tegetmeier, William Bernhardt. 1868. *Pigeons*. London.

Tegetmeier, William Bernhardt. 1868. *The Poultry Book*. London.

Tegetmeier, William Bernhardt. 1873. *Pheasants for Coverts and Aviaries*. London.

Temminck, Coenraad Jacob. 1815. *Manuel d'Ornithologie*. Paris.

Valenciennes, Achille and Cuvier. 1828–49. *Histoire Naturelle des Poissons*. Paris.

Venn, J. and J. A. (eds). 1922–53. *Alumni Cantabrigienses: a Biographical List of All Known Students, Graduates and Holders of Office at the University of Cambridge from 1752 to 1900*. 10 vols. Cambridge.

Wallace, Ian (ed). 2005. *Leonard Jenyns, Darwin's Lifelong Friend*. Bath.

Walton, Izaak. 1653. *The Compleat Angler, or the Contemplative Man's Recreation*. 1st ed 1653. The 5th edition in 1676 included a treatise on fly fishing by Charles Cotton. London.

Wheeler, Alwyne. 1978. *Key to the Fishes of Northern Europe: a Guide to the Identification of More Than 350 Species*. London.

White, Rev. Gilbert. 1789. *The Natural History and Antiquities of Selborne*. London.

Williams, R. B. Entry for Van Voorst (1804–98), in B. Lightman (ed), *The Dictionary of Nineteenth Century British Scientists.* 4 vols 2005, vol 4: 2063–2066. London.

Wilson, Alexander, 1766–1813. *American Ornithology*, 1808–14. Completed and edited by G. Ord. Philadelphia.

Wood, Neville. 1836. *British Song Birds*, London.

Wood, Neville. 1836. *The Ornithologists' Textbook*. London.

## Yarrell's Correspondence

The following correspondence has been transcribed or abstracted by C. E. Jackson and deposited in the Library of the Zoological Society.

Bath Royal Literary & Scientific Institution (previously in Bath Public Library), 63 Letters WY to Leonard Jenyns/Blomefield, and other authors of letters with references to WY.

CUL, Manuscripts Department. WJ/PJS letters contain references to WY.

CUL, Manuscripts Department. Alfred Newton papers (49 letters from various correspondents to WY); CUL. Darwin correspondence; four letters.

CUL. Letters to Sir Richard Owen (sic= 1 letter to D. W. Mitchell).

Edin. Univ. Liby. WY to WJ.

Edinburgh, National Museums of Scotland, Library, WJ/PJS correspondence.

Firestone Library, Princeton University, 13 letters.

Forbes, Thomas R. *Proceedings of the American Philosophical Society* 1962, 106: 505–55 has some MS letters transcribed.

Glasgow University. Autograph letter, signed from WY to William Euing, tipped into Euing's copy of *A History of British Fishes*, vol. 3, Supplementary 1860, at end of second supplement to second volume; one leaf folded. Accession no 2423. Bequeathed by William Euing in 1874.

Liverpool County Archives. WY, four letters to Lord Stanley, later 13th Earl of Derby.

Liverpool Public Library, Derby Archives. WY to Lord Derby, 13th Earl.

London, Linn. Soc. Liby. M'Leay, Alexander.

London, Linn. Soc. Liby. William Swainson, correspondence from 136 individuals, including WY.

London, Linn. Soc. Liby. George Newport correspondence, including WY.

London, Natural History Museum. Letters to WJ.

London, Natural History Museum, Gould correspondence. Eight letters WY to JG.

London, Science Museum. Sir Frederick Stovin, collection of letters, one from WY to Hugh Strickland, 1838.

Norfolk and Norwich Millennium Library. 1 letter Colman Colln 1855. WY to George Frederick.

Norwich Record Office, Central Library. Gurney, John H. Natural history notes, two letters to

WY, 1833, 1840.

Princeton University, New Jersey, Firestone Library, Department of Rare Books and Special Collections. Fish drawings, papers and 13 letters.

Private collection. WY to William Fisher. One letter dated 12 July 1851.

Science Museum Library. WY to Strickland.

Society of Antiquaries, London. Ornithological notes and papers.

York Library, North Yorkshire County Library, York & Selby Division. Thomas Allis. Volume of papers, including correspondence, six letters, 1837.

## Portraits

Portrait in oils, by Mrs Margaret-Sarah Carpenter, 1839. Paid for by a subscription among 40 Fellows of the Linnean Society. Linnean Society, Burlington House, London, see p.77

T. H. Maguire. *Portraits of the Honourable Members of the Ipswich Museum.* 1852, see p.174

*A History of British Fishes.* 3rd ed. 1859 frontis, prepared from a photograph taken in 1855.

Good likeness in chalk by unknown artist, owned by Professor Newton, now Cambridge University Zoological Museum.

Miniature in watercolour by Mrs Waterhouse Hawkins. No date, owned (?). A daughter, Leila (born 1841), of Benjamin Waterhouse Hawkins and his bigamous marriage to Louisa, wrote to the Linnean Society on 4 March 1885 enquiring about any possible interest from any naturalist in purchasing a small watercolour of William Yarrell that her mother (Louisa) had painted (Linnean Society Archives). Louisa exhibited a portrait at the Royal Academy in 1841 and portraits and scenes in 1851 and 1852.

Sale catalogue of Yarrell's effects. 4–6 December 1856. Lot 119 Portrait in crayon of the late Mr Yarrell, by Mrs Waterhouse Hawkins, in gilt frame, glazed.

Stipple and line engraving published 1859, F. A. Heath. National Portrait Gallery.

M. Gauci lithograph (after E. U. Eddis). 1855. National Portrait Gallery (frontispiece)

In St James's Church, Piccadilly, on the north aisle wall, his executors, Edward Bird and John Van Voorst, erected a marble tablet with a medallion portrait supported by two swans, executed by Neville Burnard. The swans represented Bewick's swan that Yarrell had identified as a new avifaunal and British species. The inscription under the memorial tablet reads:

'In loving memory of William Yarrell Treasurer and Vice President of the Linnean Society of London. A most estimable man, a distinguished naturalist and the author of several valuable works illustrating the natural history of the British Islands. He was born June 3rd 1784, in this parish, where throughout life he resided. He died unmarried September 1st 1856, at Yarmouth in Norfolk, and his remains are deposited in the family burying place, in the church-yard at Bayford in Hertfordshire', see p.109.

# INDEX OF PEOPLE

With some additional material not in the text, and text page references.

Entomological Society 41, 42

**Broderip,** William J. 1789–1859, of Thomas Street, London, a Police Magistrate 147, 148

**Brookes,** Joshua, had a museum and anatomy school in Great Marlborough Street. In 1832 WY was not aware of a long tooth in a female Narwhal. 'Mr Brookes had a very fine head of a male I suppose in which both teeth were developed, was considered a great curiosity and produced a high price.' WY owned a portrait of him 128

**Broome,** Christopher Edmund 1812–86, mycologist whose collection of 40, 000 specimens are now at Kew. He visited WY in 1832 when they went to Battersea fields looking for shells.

**Brown,** Robert 1773–1858, First Keeper of Botany at the British Museum and President of the Linnean Society 1849–53 93, 176, 177, 188

**Burnard,** Neville Northey 1818–1878, Cornish sculptor of several busts of eminent men of science, including Jonathan Couch and WY. He was trained in London by Sir Francis Chantry. The memorial tablet in St James's Church and the circular memorial plaque of WY were both sculpted by Burnard 109, 178

**Burton,** Decimus, 1800–81, London Zoo's first architect 1828–41.

**Bushnan,** John Stevenson, author of *The Natural History of Fishes* 1840 then 1845 and 1848, for Sir William Jardine's Naturalist's Library.

**Callcott,** Sir Augustus Wall 1779–1844, landscape painter 94, 128

**Charles II, King,** 1630–85 175

**Charles, Prince of Wales,** b. 1948 23

**Charlesworth,** Edward 1813–1893, geologist and palaeontologist. Began work in the British Museum in 1836. *The Magazine of Natural History* 4 vols 1837–40 is often referred to as 'Charlesworth's Magazine' before it merged with *Annals of Natural History* in 1840 90

**Children,** John George 1777–1852, entomologist, mineralogist and chemist. Employed to arrange the shell collection at the British Museum. In the Natural History dept from 1827 128

**Clarke,** Joseph 'my friend at Saffron Walden', Essex, lent WY several birds to illustrate, also referred to as Mr Joseph Clarke of Stoke Nayland in Suffolk 58

**Clifford,** Charles 1819–1870, son of William Clifford, partner in Jones and WY 1854–64. Died of paralysis due to softening of the brain, aged 64 22, 23, 102

**Clifford,** Joseph 1815–72, son of William Clifford; partner with Charles in Jones & Yarrell 1854–64. He had qualified as a surgeon, MRCS, before taking over from WY. Supervised by his elder brother William junior 22–3, 102

**Clifford,** William junior 1809–83, barrister, took over from his father in Inner Temple Lane and became head of Jones and Yarrell until 1870 22–3

**Clifford,** William senior 1778–1855? of Inner Temple Lane and Bell Yard c.1813, law stationer

**Daubeny,** Rev. Edward Andrew c.1784–1877, of Ampney, graduated Oxford University. Rector of Hampnett and Stowell and Vicar of Ampney Crucis and Ampney St Peter, Gloc. Mrs Jane Jenyns was his daughter 74

**Derby,** 13th Earl of, see Stanley, Edward Smith, 13th Earl of Derby

**Dibdin,** Charles 1748–1814, famous singer and writer of sea songs, composer of stage music and musical entertainments and actor 121

**Dickens,** Charles 1812–70, author read by Jardine among other naturalists, but not by WY 42, 79, 122

**Donovan,** Edward 1768–1837, zoologist, author of natural history books with highly coloured plates 64, 143

**Doubleday,** two brothers, Edward 1811–49 entomologist at BM 1839–49 Sec. of Entom. Soc. Henry 1808–75 also an entomologist 73

**Dovaston,** John Freeman Milward 1782–1854, Shropshire barrister and naturalist, friend of Bewick 193 (note 5)

**Dunn,** Robert, 1799–1859?, animal preserver at Hull, where he published his 'useful little book' in WYs library, *The Ornithologists' Guide to the Islands of Orkney and Shetland* in 1837. He visited Orkney in 1831, 1833 and 1835. He was a supplier of birds from Shetland and Orkney where Mullens and Swann said 'he contributed not a little to the decimation of the rarer birds'. 160

**Dürer,** Albrecht, 1471–1528, woodcutter, copper engraver, painter (anglicised as Albert Durer) 134, 135

**Edginton,** George William 1839 Sep. 20, surgeon writing to WY (CUL).

**Elizabeth II,** b. 1926, Queen from 1952 23

**Empson,** Charles d. 1861 friend and correspondent of Edward Lear from c.1831. He was a botanist in Colombia before settling in Newcastle and then Bath 89

**Euing,** William, 1788–1874, Glasgow insurance broker, correspondent and supplier of fishes, especially a smelt 63–4

**Evans,** Rev. James c.1782–1862, of Llandaff, Oxford University graduate. On 19 June 1840 offered WY (CUL) a 'Rose Pastor Starling specimen shot in the Parish of Penarth about 7 miles from here 2 or 3 years ago' for drawing to be made for *HBB.*

**Eyton,** Thomas Campbell 1809–80, had a wide circle of fishermen, naturalists and collectors and sent specimens of birds and fishes both to WY, Jardine and Gould. Offered his catalogue of where his birds were collected in British Isles in January 1837 to WY 18, 27, 55, 59–60, 69, 74, 81, 90, 166

**Fisher,** William Richard 1824–1888, of Great Yarmouth until 1853 when he moved to London. A personal friend of WY and used WY's cabinets of British birds' eggs when he wished to make

# SUBJECT INDEX